A JUST SOCIETY

- The World After Neoliberalism -

By

Professor Emeritus
David Dj. Dasic, Ph.D.

"Labor is prior to and independent of capital. Capital is only the fruit of labor, and could never have existed if labor had not first existed. Labor is the superior of capital, and deserves much the higher consideration. Capital has its rights, which are as worthy of protection as any other rights. Nor is it denied that there is, and probably always will be, a relation between labor and capital producing mutual benefits."

Abraham Lincoln,
U.S. President's First Annual Message, December 3, 1861

CONTENTS

FOREWORD

In every field of science and its practical application, there are topics and dilemmas that greatly relate to the approaches to problems in a Shakespeare drama. Some of these open questions are the subject of intensive scientific research, with a certain amount of optimism that the problem will be solved in the foreseeable future.

However, likewise, in all areas, from medicine to economics, there are open unsolved problems for which there is little or almost no basis for the expectation of optimistic results.

This book, authored by Prof. David Đ. Dašić, Ph.D., is dedicated to the study of the distribution of social wealth from the point of view of the element of justice, and the effects of this element on the economic status of individuals, groups, and states.

This is the first time in economic literature, not only in Serbia, but also in far wider frameworks, that we are faced with a systematized and complete analysis of the topic of the distribution of wealth from a point of view and with the goal of creating a just society without the exploitation of other people's work.

The author has succeeded in analyzing literature in this field to provide the reader with a historical account of the efforts to affirm the principles on which a just society would rest. In this area, the author should be given primacy and acknowledgement for his approach and understanding of the matter which, in a way, permanently accompanies the development of human society in various forms, from intellectual protests to uprisings and revolutions.

The central question that the author examines refers to the elimination of poverty as the hardest and biggest obstacle to the establishment of a just society, primarily from the standpoint of

11

removing huge material differences, both in relation to the position of the individual and the position of individual states.

The author has shown a high level of objectivity in the choice, analysis, and interpretation of different viewpoints regarding the solution for "economic injustices" in the relations among labor and capital, property relations, the way of taxing the rich, and the class division of society. At the same time, he introduces the reader to the difficulties facing the possible realization process of the programs of a just society. Analyzing various programs, Prof. Dašić draws attention to the United Nation's program to eliminate poverty in the world by 2030!

However, when trying to get from the field of economic theory to the study of the necessary measures of economic policy, the complexity of this matter comes to light, as does the limited possibilities of realizing the creation of a just society.

A serious obstacle to the adoption of specific measures is the fact that a number of basic factors in this field are extremely subjective. The notion of poverty itself is perceived and defined in different ways by individuals and in wider contexts. Although he rightly criticizes the negative consequences of the functioning of the market economy, the author does not deny the fact that the market economy method is more effective compared to any other form. If the underlying leverage of the mitigation policy is the transfer of wealth to a nonmarket basis, the question arises whether, for example, progressive taxation is a punishment for success. High tax rates, as a rule, discourage existing and potential investors, thereby slowing down the process of wealth creation, and therefore reducing the ability of transferring income from the production area (wealth layers) into the area of consumption (users of transfer payments). The author also shows the views of some prominent economic theorists in this book, along with the richest individuals (Bill Gates), who justifies the need for progressive taxation.

When it comes to transferring income from the rich to the poor, there are also a number of problems which are subjective in nature. In almost all cases of extreme redistribution of income, the wealthy think that too much is being taken away from them. On the other hand, the recipients of these funds believe that they do not get enough. Would it be acceptable if those who create wealth, the share of which is transferred to other countries, had the ability to control its use? At what level of involvement can this country-provider be accused of interfering in the internal affairs of the recipient country?

These and a series of similar issues rise to the surface in linear proportions, with attempts to alleviate economic injustice and to open up the process of forming a more just society. In this respect, there is no generally accepted theoretical concept, let alone a practical recipe.

The author, like many before him, does not answer all open questions of creating a just society, but that does not diminish the significance of this book as a distinctive challenge for the initial, albeit modest actions, in the search for possible alternatives to the current state of unsuitable economic and social differences between rich and the poor in the world.

Academic Prof. Dr. Ljubiša S. Adamović,
President of the Serbian Academy of Economic Sciences

NOTE

Contemporary neoliberal capitalism, which has been going for five decades, is designed to make the rich even richer and the poor even poorer. The differences between the rich and the poor are widening dramatically and deepening globally.

An enormous number of people live in extreme poverty (penury), while there is an accumulation of enormous wealth in the hands of members of the capitalist class, especially its elite, the so-called capitalist superclass, who possess factual (but not formal) power in society. This is known as a factocracy.

The inequalities between the rich and the poor are particularly drastic in the former socialist countries, including China, which officially considers itself a socialist state. Members of the newly formed class of capitalists (tycoons and controversial businessmen) in these countries have everything they need and more, and the poor barely survive in extreme scarcity, poverty, and misery.

Such a situation has become socially unacceptable, socioeconomically unbearable, and politically unsustainable. It represents one of the greatest threats to sustainable social and economic development, world peace, and security at the threshold of the third decade of the 21st century.

As a witness to the historical process of transforming socialist into capitalist relations, in this monograph composed of 49 essays, I critically appraise the social state created after the demolition of the Berlin Wall in 1989, primarily from the perspective of the theory and practice of Yugoslav socialist self-government (1950–1991), and on the basis of the experience gained in the development of contemporary neoliberal capitalism, especially on the territory of the former Yugoslavia, over the past three decades (1991–2019).

In this book, I draw attention to the acute problems and contradictions of the functioning of the capitalist economic, political, and social system. The main theme of this book is the search for a possible alternative to this system and includes suggestions for possible directions in building a more just and more humane social order than the existing one.

In any case, an open, critical debate is now needed on important topics and dilemmas concerning the future of neoliberal capitalism, such as private property monopoly or property pluralism, labor-capital relations between employers and workers, precarization (the general and permanent state of job insecurity aimed at forcing workers into subordination and accepting exploitation, mobbing, or any other form of harassment in the work sphere), slave labor and penury, social stratification of society, economic functions of the market and state, social security and uncertainty, taxation of the wealthy, guaranteed basic income, and numerous other open issues.

In dealing with the subject matter, I use available scientific papers by domestic and foreign authors published in printed (paper) and electronic form, as well as the texts of journalists, publicists, and other public servants. Also, I had conversations with my colleagues from the academic community and the foreign policy circles about possible ways of solving certain open issues, problems, and contradictions in modern society. Their opinions were of great help to me in the final text construction. Furthermore, in order to address some complex and important topics of a just society as thoroughly and accurately as possible, I quote the views of some prominent authors in a slightly extensive manner, which gives the book a chrestomatic note.

Positive critical evaluation, praise and support for this work, in a comprehensive written review, were provided by: Zoran Vidojević, Ph.D., philosopher and sociologist, and Srećko Djukić, Ph.D., a diplomat with the title of ambassador and political economist, for which I am sincerely grateful.

The motif for the subtitle of this book was the title of the article by Nobel Laureate Joseph E. Stiglitz, *After Neoliberalism* (Project Syndicate, May 2019).

This monograph includes the usual contents. In addition to the concluding remarks, it contains a list of bibliographic items that I used while writing the book (sources), literature, an index of personal names with basic information, and an author's note.

This work is not complete, much less perfect. Yet, the way it is, with all its flaws and shortcomings, I hope it may be interesting for readers who follow and study the complex social reality in which we live and work. It really does not matter whether they belong to the right or left hemisphere of society, or are somewhere in between, and whether they agree or disagree ideologically and politically with the views expressed in this work.

Any benevolent and creative critique is desirable and welcome.

David Dj. Dašić

1.

THE ERA OF NEOLIBERALISM, UNCERTAINTIES AND RISKS

Government is not the solution to our problem,
government is the problem.

Ronald Reagan

The period of social development in the world from the 1980s until now is called the neoliberalism era. The precise conceptual description of the coined term "neoliberalism," because of its complexity in economic, political, sociological, and legal terms, eschews any sort of generally accepted definition. Neoliberalism is commonly understood "as the ideological product of processes in which self-identified liberals, from the interwar period [between World War I and World War II—author's note] onwards, have attempted to renew liberalism as an ideology that claims to promote societal orders based on free markets and individual freedom. In other words, neoliberalism refers to efforts to construct new liberalisms" (Olsen 2019).

In fact, neoliberalism is the contemporary version of liberalism because it was founded

> ...on the values of classical liberal capitalism, glorifies the entrepreneurship of the private sector and advocates more radical limitation of the role of the state (decreasing state spending and the active participation of the state in business,

as well as limiting the state regulation of the market), and thereby ignores any sort of national distinctiveness, social responsibility, and moral and ethical principles (Dušanić 2016: 36–37).

Slightly simplified, one could say that liberalism is "the idol of the national bourgeoisie," while neoliberalism is "the ideology of the transnational bourgeoisie."

It is indisputable that liberalism, as a philosophical direction, has affirmed the personal freedom of man as one of the fundamental human values.

> The heart of the liberal philosophy is a belief in the dignity of the individual, in his freedom to make the most of his capacities and opportunities according to his own lights, subject only to the proviso that he not interfere with the freedom of other individuals do the same. This implies a belief in the equality of men in one sense; in their inequality in another. Each man has an equal right to freedom. This is an important and fundamental right precisely because men are different.... (Friedman 2002: 195).

The problem is, however, that freedom, like rights, can be abused. For example, the fetishization of the market in organizing business life is a form of abusing market freedom, known as market fundamentalism.

It is thought that the Great Depression—which began on October 29, 1929, with the Wall Street Crash in the United States (U.S.)—known as Black Friday—and lasted until 1941—was triggered by the classic economic liberalism of the day.

Also, the main cause of the outbreak of the global financial and economic crisis of 2007-2008 is attributed to the economic policies based on the premises of contemporary neoliberalism. The consequences of this crisis are felt to this day. However, regardless of the dimensions and consequences of this crisis, the essence of neoliberalism has remained unchanged, and it remains the dominant political ideology and economic practice in the modern world.

Historically, the emergence and rule of neoliberalism has most often been associated with the economic policies pursued by British Prime Minister Margaret Thatcher and U.S. President Ronald Reagan during their incumbencies.

The features of Thatcher's economic policies were: extreme economic liberalism, maximum respect for market laws, and the almighty "invisible hand" of the free market, with the deregulation of economic life and diminishing the state' s regulatory economic functions. State initiatives in the economic and social spheres were marginalized. The development of the private sector was comprehensively encouraged, and the state competencies were transferred to it. Such economic policies have been called *Thatcherism*.

Reagan's economic policies were characterized by: reductions in taxes and expenditures, abolition of social rights and privileges, fostering private entrepreneurship, affirmation of the free market, and stimulation of the international free trade. Such economic policies have been called *Raeganism or Reaganomics*. "Former U.S. President Carter was criticized by Reagan for advocating Soviet-type planning and confiscation, and Margaret Thatcher won the first election with a promise that she would release Great Britain of socialism" (Kuljić 2002: 35).

The common denominators of Thatcherism and Reaganism were uncompromising anti-communism and anti-socialism, the suppression of workers' movements and trade unions, the deification of private property and the free market, the maximum limit of the economic functions of the state, the demand for the broadest possible economic freedoms, but also the most championing of conservative social values, such as the emphasis on the awakening of Christians, mostly members of Protestant fundamentalism.

Systematic weakening of state power, reduction of its traditional role, and the transfer of the state functions into private hands are the most important determinants of neoliberalism. A process of direct entry of private enterprises into different traditional communal and municipal activities has been initiated in former socialist states, more or less, in the form of public-private partnerships, such as managing urban public transport. There is also an increasing role of the private sector in the sphere of specific public services, such as road maintenance, car parking, urban landscape maintenance, farmers markets, and the like.

At the epicenter of global neoliberal economic policy and reform, in addition to the monopoly of private property, "market fundamentalism" was established – a new dogmatic, almost religious teaching, according to which the market was a "promised land," even a "holy land," and private entrepreneurs, foreign and domestic investors, strategic partners, and managers were the "chosen people."

Serbian philosopher and sociologist Zoran Vidojević says,

> What is most commonly referred to as neoliberalism is not better in relation to the earlier practice of liberalism, but worse.... Neoliberalism is not just an economic phenomenon .... Moreover, *it is not even its main characteristic.* It is primarily a doctrine (heterogeneous within itself), *a global strategy and an expression of values of the interests of the largest capital, aimed at dominating the world to the fullest extent possible, or at dominating its most profitable and geostrategically most important*

areas, by all means .... Its most extreme and brutal variants are characterized by *social racism* towards lower classes and strata .... (Vidojević 2015: 31–33).

Due to such nature, as a contemporary sublimation of Thatcherism and Reaganism, by its general social definition, neoliberalism belongs to conservatism rather than liberalism in its original meaning. In fact, the real name for neoliberalism is *non-liberalism*.

In the absence of a precise, generally accepted definition of neoliberalism, other characteristics are also attributed to this term. For example, neoliberalism is equated with neocolonialism, i.e., with modern-age colonialism, when the world market became accessible to all. Likewise, neoliberalism is equated with Americanism, given that the U.S. played a major role in initiating and spreading the process of globalization of economy, law, and politics.

The rise of neoliberalism was also helped by the structural changes of capitalism caused by the information revolution, the transformation of Fordism into Post-Fordism, the era of digital and nano-technologies, the transition from industry to service sectors in developed countries, and the acceleration of globalization after the collapse of the European one-party socialist regimes.

In the West, the fall of the Berlin Wall on November 9, 1989, was seen as the "definitive collapse of communism" and the "end of the titanic ideological battle between communism and capitalism" that had lasted for seven decades, starting from the first day of the Great October Revolution in Russia on October 7, 1917, and the founding of the Union of Soviet Socialist Republics (USSR) in December, 1922. The Cold War was a geopolitical expression of this struggle in the years after the end of World War II in 1945. During this Cold War, capitalism sought to show and prove its superiority over socialism, especially its economic superiority, everywhere in the world and in every way possible. "The success of this order, and the attraction it consequently came to hold for countries outside of it, had made a substantial contribution to the collapse of communism in Europe, which put an end to the Cold War" (Mandelbaum 2005: 23).

After the collapse of European socialism, the collapse of the Soviet Union, and the final break with totalitarianism, former European socialist countries accepted capitalist values in their organization of their ociety and economy, rushing to promptly join the global neoliberal order led by the U.S.

Capitalism won its final victory over socialism during a long and fierce competition, primarily thanks to "open markets and Western liberal democracy," thus confirming its superiority over the applied methods of economic organization and development of socialist societies (America's 2016: 9).

Embracing capitalist values in the former socialist countries gave neoliberalism an additional ideological, economic. and political momentum. Hegemony of neoliberal capitalism has been established around the world with the exception of China, North Korea, and Cuba, to some extent.

Mainstream ideologists and politicians of neoliberalism, many of whom are affiliated with the Mont-Pèlerin Society—founded in 1947 and composed of eminent economists, philosophers, historians, intellectuals, and business leaders from around the world—are convinced that a "new stage of democracy" has emerged, that neoliberal capitalism has historically been proven to be the best possible social system, that this system has no alternative, and it is therefore eternal.

Opponents of neoliberal hegemony, on the other hand, say with conviction, "The age of uncertainty has arrived. We see a low-growth trap, rising inequality and populist movements. Neoliberalism, dominant since the late 1970s, has failed in many aspects. It has brought about widening inequality and financial vulnerability and boosted the emergence of far-right extremism" (Yokoyama 2017).

Assessing the general situation in today's globalized capitalist world, in the "era of neoliberalism, " one of the most significant contemporary Italian writers, Claudio Magris, among others, says, "I believe we are in fact in the World War IV. The Third ended by the victory of the West and the demise of communism. Everybody is now against everybody; we don't even know who against whom" (Magris 2017).

2.

THE FALL OF COMMUNISM OR THE FALL OF SOCIALISM?

*Even before the Berlin Wall was built,
Djilas had seen cracks in it.*

Muharem Bazdulj

DESTRUCTION OF THE BERLIN WALL AND COLLAPSE OF THE SOCIALIST (COMMUNIST) REGIMES

The destruction of the Berlin Wall in 1989 marked, on a global scale, the final victory of capitalism over communism, i.e. socialism, after decades of fierce competition between the two social orders. The capitalist system, based on the logic of the free market and the liberal-democratic ideology, has proven in practice that it is, locally and globally, economically more efficient and socially superior to the socialist system, which was based on central planning and one-party political domination.

Having massively and actively participated in the "colored revolutions," which contributed to the overthrow of the socialist order, fortunately without bloodshed, the citizens of European socialist countries rejoiced in the historic victory of capitalism, deeply convinced, thanks to intense Western propaganda, that the Western capitalist order was better, and more adequate than their former social system.

Newly formed political elites of the former European socialist countries embraced all the values of the Western world without hesitation and with enthusiasm, and suddenly, almost overnight, became newborn capitalist countries. Not only political elites, but also the vast majority of citizens were deeply convinced that a bright future of certain economic and every other prosperity awaited them. They were convinced that capitalism was a social order without any flaws, that all levels of its system, government, and management functioned flawlessly. At the time, they ignored the real economic, social, and political problems and contradictions inherent in capitalism.

Anti-communist and anti-socialist enthusiasm in former socialist countries gained momentum and became a key cohesion factor in the homogenization of broad social strata on a national basis. The inevitable product of that enthusiasm was primitive nationalism—a political phenomenon that was responsible for the outbreak of the civil war in Yugoslavia in the 1990s and the bloody war in the east of Ukraine, on April 6, 2014, which has not ended yet. "The collapse of socialism has revived that component of nationalism that cannot survive without a glorious past" (Kuljić 2011: 222). Thus, for example, Macedonians are looking for a non-Slovenian connection to Alexander the Great, Montenegrins are increasingly mentioning Dioclea, and Croats have deep ties to the Vatican (Ibid.).

Considering everything that happened in the world at the time of the demolition of the Berlin Wall and immediately afterward, the big question is: What really happened then? The fall of communism (socialism), or something else entirely?

In reality, all these countries which were called socialist and/or communist were very, very far from both socialism and communism as it was understood in the classical Marxist-doctrinal sense. The one true fact is that these countries had communist, socialist, or labor parties in power; that is, the most ideologically loyal and prominent members of these ruling parties were the specific executants of all forms of government in society.

SOCIALIST COUNTRIES WERE NOT COMMUNIST!

First, former socialist countries have never been communist, given that communism, in theory, involves a classless society. It is true that they liquidated the capitalist class through violent, revolutionary measures by the expropriation of expropriators. However, instead of the capitalist class, a new social class suddenly appeared in the socialist countries in the form of representatives of the powerful state-party apparatus: The ruling bureaucratic elite, called the polytocracy[1] or "red bourgeoisie," who lived a "high life." For example, eleven or twelve percent of the Soviet population, that is, the leading state-party elite, received fifty percent of the national income (Lazarević 2007: 33).

Milovan Djilas, close comrade-in-arms to Josip Broz Tito during the war and revolution, wrote about this new type of social class that had emerged in socialist societies in his famous work *The New Class*, published in London in 1957, in which he critically analyzed the system of communist government and the behavior of its state-party nomenclature. He noticed serious conceptual shortcomings in the functioning of this system. Namely, the party monopoly dominated all spheres of society and the state, as well as lives of ordinary people. A symbiosis between party and state was established. The executants of state-party government showed an insatiable greed for personal gain and comfortable life in their everyday behavior.

---

[1] Polytocracy is the ruling-administrative apparatus of a political party that holds all the levers of power in the country and imposes its concept of development imbued with bureaucratic methods of management and leadership

The demolition of the Berlin Wall and the events that followed completely confirmed Djilas' assessment of the regimes of power in European and other socialist countries at that time. The communist mantra of a "bright future," a classless society and universal equality of all people, despite all the efforts of the communist government, was nothing more than a utopia.

Unfortunately, Djilas' assessments are largely valid for almost all of today's post-transitional societies built on the ruins of socialism. Their right-wing political parties abducted the state and its institutions from the society and the people, created a de facto one-party or captive state in an incomparably more perfidious and dangerous way than those used by the left-wing, communist, socialist, and workers' parties during socialism/communism.

Secondly, no socialist country has even tried to realize the principle of the communist distribution of social income: "From each according to his ability, to each according to his needs." None of them were able to achieve an abundant production of goods and services, which, according to Marx, is the key condition for the realization of this principle. The actual production possibilities of all former socialist countries were limited. The economies they inherited were mostly technologically obsolete and underdeveloped. The concept of economic development they chose (pushing the development of heavy industry and energy sector at all costs, while neglecting the development of light industry and the production of consumer goods) did not enable them to produce goods and services in abundance. Many of them did not even have the natural or human resources necessary for such a production volume.

Slavery to the pattern of socialist development of the first country of socialism, the USSR, was "God's law" for other socialist countries, and any deviation from it was blasphemy and revisionism, which caused excommunication and pronouncements of anathema. Simply put, these countries largely did not know or were objectively unable to release man's creative power in a given socialist order—imposed from the outside—and to make his work more creative, venturesome, productive, and innovative in technique and technology. In that respect, capitalism was more successful and therefore managed to defeat the socialism of that time.

Instead of having the necessary abundance of consumer goods available as a condition for achieving "to each according to his needs" distribution, socialist countries faced shortages of such goods on a daily basis. They were, therefore, forced to find ways to meet the most basic needs of their citizens with a limited volume of consumer goods production. In this sense, they were often forced to distribute basic groceries, which were in short supply, to citizens based on a rationing system (vouchers, points, and quotas).

Everyday life of citizens in the socialist states was grim. Information about "well-being" could only be seen in film, read about in newspapers and magazines, heard on the radio, and watched on television. The effect of the communist agitation and propaganda—agitprop—on the "bright future," extremely "successful socialist construction," and information about regularly exceeding the goals of the five-year plans, were so suggestive that the vast majority of citizens did not pay much attention to their daily gloomy life. Intoxicated by the promised "bright future," the people perceived their suffering from poverty as a sacred sacrifice for the realization of the imposed "socialist construction" ideal.

These are the major reasons why, from the point of view of social theory and practice, it is not appropriate to talk about the fall of communism, because it really did not exist in any former socialist country. Many proponents and theorists of neoliberal capitalism, even those with the highest academic titles and prestige, simply overlook or consciously conceal this indisputable fact. Why do they persistently insist on the fall of communism and not socialism? Probably in order to completely destroy the idea of a classless society, inherent in communism, which makes them restless.

HOW SOCIALIST WERE THE SOCIALIST COUNTRIES?

In Marxist literature, before and after the socialist revolution, socialism was most commonly understood as a transitional social stage from capitalism to communism. It was considered that the countries that carried out the socialist revolution were on their way toward building a new classless communist society and that socialism was a "lower stage of communism," that is, a "path to communism."

The first measure taken by the communist authorities on their "path to communism" was the final showdown with the capitalist mode of production. Private property was abolished or radically limited. The state plan took over the role of the market, including the allocation of factors of production. Equality in society became more important than the lucrativeness of enterprises—making a profit in their business. Differences between socialist and capitalist countries were fundamental.

Socialist countries, due to the insufficient development of their productive forces and their limited economic development, were not able to apply the communist principle of distribution "to each according to his needs" in their distribution of social income. They were simply not able to produce the necessary goods and services in abundance. Therefore, instead of the communist principle of distribution, they were objectively forced to apply their own principle of distribution—"to each according to his contribution," called the "socialist principle of distribution."

However, former socialist countries ideologically obsessed with the communist ideas of economic and social equality were not satisfied with the principle "to each according to his contribution." The working abilities, innate or learned, of the individual are not equal. Also, the so-called "production conditions" vary from one company to another. In addition to the natural, technological and many other factors, business success of a company often directly depends, for example, on the macroeconomic measures of the state. All of this objectively led to economic and social inequality among people in socialist societies.

These were the main reasons why the former socialist countries, in addition to the principle of distribution "to each according to his contribution," introduced the principle of socialist solidarity into the system of social income distribution. In this way, they wanted to mitigate the social inequality produced by the "socialist principle of distribution" as much as possible, regardless of the fact that their material possibilities were limited. The principle of socialist solidarity, taking into account the "theory of equal stomachs," led to the rise of egalitarianism in society. Free education, free health care, as well as free social protection and other protections of citizens were an integral part of the socialist system as a whole.

In order to eliminate unjustified economic and social inequality in society, the state also prescribed relative wage relations for all employees (pay grades) and determined the range between the lowest and the highest wages, keeping the desired degree of social disparities in society under control to prevent extremely poor and extremely rich individuals. Equality and social solidarity were considered the highest goals. Economic and social equality in former socialist countries was achieved in conditions of relative general poverty. No former socialist country has managed to reach its desired level of economic development and social income. Economic construction of the former socialist countries was in the hands of their state-party bodies, which denied the laws of the market. Central plans prescribed what state enterprises should do, to whom, and at what price to sell manufactured goods and services. Economic planning directives had to be implemented without question. This was a moral obligation and "sacred duty" of everyone in a socialist society. In such social relations, workers' material motivation and creative initiative were objectively constrained. Productivity of their work was not enough. The available natural resources were not managed efficiently. Energy and reproductive materials were ruthlessly wasted.

No former socialist country has even reached a halfway point in achieving the socioeconomic goals of their envisioned socialist construction and prosperity. Even some economically more advanced capitalist countries with a pronounced social democratic tradition, such as the Scandinavian countries of Sweden and Norway, solved their citizens' existential economic and social problems more efficiently than the former socialist countries.

Having in mind all the economic, political and social problems that the former socialist countries were constantly facing, the question rightly arises today as to whether they were really socialists, how much authentic socialism was in their systems, and to what extent they managed to achieve fundamental socialist ideas and ideals, regardless of the fact that the very term "socialism" is not strictly defined in Marxist or any other political or sociological theory.

AN ATTEMPT TO CREATE A SOCIALIST SOCIETY

However, the argument that the former socialist countries were not "communist" and the following question about the extent to which they were truly "socialist" rightly bring up the question: What were they really? The one true fact is that they were not a capitalist, nor a capitalist-socialist social fabrication. The shortest answer to this question could be that former socialist countries made an *attempt to be socialist*, and this was an attempt that did not end successfully.

Why did socialism in the former socialist countries not manifest itself in a right and desired way? Because its practical application began in the wrong place at the wrong time. Simply put, historically speaking, the appropriate socioeconomic conditions were not met for all the generic forces of socialism to reach their full expression. Our present time, on the threshold of the third decade of the twenty-first century, is incomparably more suitable for the emergence of authentic socialism than the threshold of the third decade of the twentieth century. Over the past hundred years, thanks to tremendous technical and technological achievements, a high level of development of productive forces has been achieved, as well as a valuable experience in the functioning of both the capitalist and the socialist system.

Today, mankind needs even faster global development of productive forces and even greater social welfare for all, without the existing unnatural differences between the rich and the poor, without the exploitation of other people's work and living at other people's expense. Contemporary neoliberal capitalism is unable to ensure the timely and successful achievement of these strategic goals. This is why it is necessary to transform the ruling neoliberal capitalist system into a just, or at least, a more just society, with emphasized socialist-humanist traits with a human face. In this regard, the experience gained from the development of socialism in Europe and beyond, regardless of all its indisputable historical failures, can provide an appropriate theoretical and practical assistance in finding possible answers and solutions to outstanding issues, contradictions, and challenges of contemporary capitalism.

3.

VICTORY OF CAPITALISM: WESTERN TRIUMPHALISM AND EUPHORIA

> *Capitalism has survived communism.*
> *Now, it eats away at itself.*
>
> Charles Bukowski

Victory of neoliberal capitalism over all Eastern European socialist regimes was unquestionable. As a system, socialism did not have the necessary internal strength to resist fierce capitalist competition. The marginalization of the economic logic of profit and the suppression of private property and the market toward the periphery, and the outside of the social organization of labor were some of the crucial construction errors of the economic system in former socialist countries. Perhaps socialist Yugoslavia was somewhat of an exception in this respect because of its workers' self-management and state-owned enterprises with aspirations for a market economy and world market.

Socialism lost its battle with capitalism in the 1990s, not because of its ideas, but above all because of insufficient theoretical and practical knowledge of how and by what means instruments or mechanisms would make an economically efficient and a more socially just society achievable. In their search for these solutions, especially in defining their relationship to private property and the market, former socialist countries went "as through a mist in which the light which glimmers intermittently bewilders and deceives the eyes more than it shows the path" (Andrić 1982: 133).

Meanwhile, capitalism undisputedly ruled the world economic scene. The driving force of this social order has always been profit maximization in the market operations of enterprise, and the accumulation of wealth in the hands of the capitalist class. The rules of the game on the global economic stage, and in international economic relations in general, have been dictated by the most developed capitalist countries, led by the U.S.

The influence of the U.S. in shaping the world economic order after World War II was crucial, starting with the founding of the financial institution Bretton Woods (which created the International Monetary Fund and the World Bank) in 1944. On this American influence, Henry Kissinger says "In the twentieth century, no country has influenced international relations as decisively and at the same time as ambivalently as the United States. No society has more firmly on inadmissibility on intervention in the domestic affairs of other states, or more passionately asserted that its own values were universally applicable" (Kissinger 1994: 17–18).

Former socialist countries, with their failed anti-market economic systems, could not survive in a global capitalist economic and political environment, which is always anti-socialist and anti-communist. Simply put, in the given societal and market relations on the global stage, they were doomed.

The demolition of the Berlin Wall in 1989 was the symbol of the fall of communism in the world—more precisely, of the collapse of socialism and socialist regimes in the Soviet Union and Eastern European socialist countries in the 1990s—and the end of the Cold

War, were greeted triumphantly and euphorically in the capitalist West, especially in the U.S.

It was announced all over the world that contemporary liberal capitalism was the best social order, that it was eternal and with no alternative, that it represented the "end of history," that "nothing new" could happen anymore, that the "era of neoliberalism" had come, the "new era of democracy" based on the dominance of the free market and private property, and that humanity awaited a bright future of economic and every other well-being.

This new social situation is the subject of theoretical research and evaluation from different angles by researchers from diverse ideological backgrounds. U.S. scientists Francis Fukuyama and Samuel Huntington stand out among them, as well as the British-Pakistani writer Tariq Ali.

Fukuyama perceived the "fall of communism" as the "end of history."

> Liberalism's victory was declared to be unqualified and complete in 1989 in the seminal article 'The End of History' by Fransis Fukuyama, written following the collapse of the last competing ideological opponent...Fukuyama held that liberalism had proved itself the sole legitimate regime on the basis that it had withstood all challengers and defeated all competitors and further, that it *worked* because it accorded with humane nature...

> A main result of the widespread view that liberalism's triumph is complete and uncontested—indeed, that rival claims are no longer regarded as worthy of consideration—is a conclusion within the liberal order that various ills that infect the body politic as well as civil and private spheres are either

remnants of insufficiently realized liberalism or happenstance problems that are subject to policy or technological fix within the liberal horizon... (Deneen 2018: 28).

In other words, in Fukuyama's opinion, "what exists today as a form of social organization and a systemic solution in developed western countries is the last step in the millennial search for the better: the system of liberal democracy is the best possible, and no searching for a new system and striving for change will follow" (Ocić 2017: 53).

That is, with the fall of real socialism, capitalism became a universal form of social organization of work and people's lives on a global scale.

According to Branko Milanovic, a Serbian-American economist,

...for the first time in human history, a system that can be called capitalist, defined (conventionally) as consisting of legally free labor, privately owned capital, decentralized coordination, and pursuit of profit, is dominant over the entire globe. One does not need to go far back into the past, or to have a great knowledge of history, to realize how unique and novel this is. Not only was centrally planned socialism eliminated as a competitor only recently, but nowhere in the world do we now find unfree labor playing an important economic role, as it did until some 150 years ago.

Such is the hegemony of capitalism as a worldwide system that even those who are unhappy with it and with rising in e quality, whether locally, nationally, or globally, have no realistic alternatives to propose. 'Deglobalization' with a return to the 'local' is impossible because it would do away with the division of labor, a key factor of economic growth. Surely, those who argue for localism do not wish to propose a major drop in living standards or a Khmer Rouge solution to in e quality. Forms of state capitalism, as in Russia and China, do exist, but this is capitalism nevertheless: the private profit motive and private companies are dominant (Milanovic 2016: 92).

Analyzing the implications of the fall of communism, Tariq Ali, in his famous book *Clash of Fundamentalisms*, among other things, says,

> With the fall of communism, the state intellectuals of the American Empire began to debate glorious future. The ideological and economic triumph was complete, but was the world really conflict free? The first serious attempt to theorize the victory came in July 1989 with the publication of by Francis Fukuyama's essay 'The End of History?'...
>
> His basic theses, derived from the writings of Hegel and Kojève, was that with the defeat of fascism in the Second World War and the disintegration of the Soviet Union forty-five years later, the victory of liberal democracy marked the end of the ideological evolution of the humanity...It was the end because there was nowhere else to go...For a short time it [Fukuyama's essay—author's note] became [the] catechism of the new globalization... (Ali 2011: 297–299).

In the summer of 1993, in the leading journal *Foreign Affairs,* Samuel Huntington published his article "Clash of Civilizations," which, according to Tariq Ali,

> ...immediately ignited a global controversy...Essentially conceived as a polemic— against Francis Fukuyama and 'The End of History?'— Huntington's thesis argued that while the crushing defeat of communism had brought to an end all ideological disputes, it did not signify the end of history.

Henceforth culture, not politics or economics, would dominate and divide the world.

He listed eight cultures: Western, Confucian, Japanese, Islamic, Hindu, Slav-Ortodox, Latin American and, perhaps, African…The major divide was between 'the West and the Rest,' because only the West valued 'individualism, liberalism, constitutionalism, human rights, equality, liberty, the rule of law, democracy, free markets.' Therefore the West (in reality, the United States) must be prepared to deal militarily with threats from these rival civilizations…(Ibid.).

According to Samuel Huntington,

…the relation between the power and culture of the West and the power and cultures of other civilization. As the relative power of other civilizations increases, the appeal of Western culture fades and non-Western people have increasing confidence in and commitment to indigenous culture. The central problem in the relations between the West and the rest is, consequently, the discordance between the West's – particularly America's – efforts to provide a universal Western culture and its declining ability to do so.

The collapse of communism exacerbated this discordance by reinforcing in the West the view that its ideology of democratic liberalism had triumphed globally and hence was universally valid. The West, especially the United States, which has always been a missionary nation, believe that the non-Western peoples should commit themselves to the Western values of democracy, free markets, limited government, human rights, individualism, the rule of law, and should embody these values in their institutions. Minorities in other civilizations embrace and promote these values, but the dominant attitudes toward them in non-Western cultures range from widespread skepticism to intense opposition. What is universalism to the West is imperialism to the rest (Huntington 1997: 183–184).

Following the general euphoria and triumphalism of the 1990s, at the beginning of the twenty first century in the heart of neoliberal capitalism, some different thoughts and different approaches to assessing reality emerged from those exhibited by Fukujama and Huntington. Namely that

> ….when 'triumphalism' fosters complacency, it goes too far. It obscures the fact that the victories, more often than not, carry within themselves the seed of their own undoing. Enemies may disappear but historical processes rarely do: self-congratulation can get in the way of seeing what these are, where they are going, and what they may portend.

> Just because market capitalism and democratic policies triumphed during the Cold War is no guarantee that they will continue to do so. Capitalism still distributes the wealth and status unevenly, as Marx said it did…

> …If Marxism-Leninism generated so many internal contradictions that it ultimately collapsed, why should we regard democratic capitalism as exempt from similar tendencies? How do we know we are not living within a long historical cycle, one that may sweep us back to a world of authoritarians—although almost certainly not of the Marxist-Leninist variety—all over again? (Gaddis 1997: 295).

Assessing the current geopolitical situation and relations in the world, retired U.S. Army General Stanley McChrystal says, "I don't believe we have seen the end of history in 1989, it is more plausible we have only returned to old historic paths" (Miklaucic 2016).

On the contemplations about the "end of history," the British historian Terry Eagleton says "What bred the culture of postmodernism, with its dismissal of so-called grand narratives and triumphal announcement of the End of History, was above all the conviction that the future would now be simply more of the present. Or, as one exuberant postmodernist put it, 'The present plus more options'" (Eagleton 2011: 6).

Fareed Zaharia, an American political analyst, goes a step further and boldly states, "The future is already here" (Zakaria 2009: 182–183).

What were the results of the neoliberalism era?

It should be noted that, by historical standards, the neoliberal era has not had a particularly good track record. The most dynamic period of postwar Western growth was that between the end of the war and the early 70s, the era of welfare capitalism and Keynesianism, when the growth rate was double that of the neoliberal period from 1980 to the present.

...If its record of economic growth has never been particularly strong, it is now dismal. Europe is barely larger than it was on the eve of the financial crisis in 2007; the United States has done better but even its growth has been anemic...

...There is a widespread belief that another financial crisis may well beckon. In other words, the neoliberal era has delivered the west back into the kind of crisis-ridden world that we last experienced in the 1930s. With this background, it is hardly surprising that a majority in the west now believe their children will be worse off than they were. Second, those who have lost out in the neoliberal era are no longer prepared to acquiesce in their fate—they are increasingly in open revolt. We are witnessing the end of the neoliberal era. It is not dead, but it is in its early death throes, just as the social-democratic era was during the 1970s (Jacques M. 2016).

The social reality created after the "fall of communism," as they like to say in the West, has completely confuted Fukuyama and other endism theorists as well. One of them, for example, was the American sociologist Daniel Bell, a preacher of the "end of ideology"—a construct that "should mark the declining influence of classes on politics, where both the right and the left accept the peace between classes in a welfare state" (Ocić 2017: 53).

4.

GLOBAL ECONOMIC CRISIS OF 2007-2008: THE END OF EUPHORIA

*Economic growth without fairness and
environmental sustainability
is a recipe for disorder, not for well-being.*

Jeffrey Sachs

Euphoric enthusiasm in the West lasted continuously for nearly two decades, until the beginning of the summer of 2007. At that time, real estate prices in the U.S. fell sharply as a result of neoliberal economic policy implementation. This was the beginning of the 2008 global financial crisis.

Fictitious, speculative, and wandering capitals emerged to the surface of the financial market, created by the uncontrolled issuance of various banking derivatives without real coverage. The so-called "financial bubbles" created by the neoliberal financial system had to burst because counterfeit, fictitious, and usurious money could not have kept them alive forever. Many investment banks, burdened by their debts to creditors, were forced to go bankrupt. Among the first to go bankrupt in 2008 was the American financial corporation Lehman Brothers Holdings Inc., which existed in various forms since 1850 and was one of the four largest investment companies in the U.S. (behind Goldman Sachs, Morgan Stanley, and Merrill Lynch), and was once a symbol of the New York Stock Exchange.

The financial crisis then spilled over to other economic sectors, first into real estate due to the inability to collect loans from individuals and legal entities, and then into the real economy—i.e., corporations and other economic entities. The financial losses of manufacturing and other companies increased sharply. Laying off workers became a mass phenomenon. Many families lost their homes because they were unable to repay the housing loans they had taken out. The broadest strata of society became increasingly impoverished and more and more socially dependent on the state.

Sudden decline in economic activity in the U.S. in 2007 and 2008 announced not only a possible recession of their economy but also a recession of the Japanese, Euro-Atlantic, and global economy in general, bearing in mind the decisive influence of American economy on global economic trends.

The European Union (EU) has traditionally uncritically followed the ideology of Thatcherism and Reganism, orthodoxly and devotedly promoting neoliberal economic policies, and was therefore not spared by the financial and economic crisis.

Per the neoliberal agenda, there is no real remedy to stop crises like the 2008 crisis or to repair economic and other damage. The free market and the sacred right of private property were not able to cope with the global financial and economic crisis. This is why capitalist states were forced to resort to energetic interventionist measures—to set aside and allocate substantial financial resources for intervention in the banking sector and economy to save leading banks, corporations, and insurance companies from imminent chain bankruptcy, and thus became a co-owner in their property. Thanks to such state intervention, the consequences of the economic crisis were mitigated, but fears of a new crisis even more devastating than the last have not disappeared.

Economic and other results achieved since the historical changes in the 1990s until the outbreak of the global economic and financial crisis of 2007-2008 were below expectations, far from what was promised. They did not bring a good life to anyone. The 2008 crisis, which in many ways resembled the Great Depression of the 1930s, raised the issue and the need to critically re-examine the sustainability of the existing system of neoliberal capitalism, the main generator of the economic crisis.

The system of contemporary neoliberal capitalism is at a historical crossroads.

> Critique of capitalism has now become easier because it has got rid of the objection that it goes in favor of 'socialist totalitarianism,' and the capitalist system in the West has remained the only real subject of criticism. Capitalism has lost its 'totalitarian' rival, which had a purpose of constantly asserting itself as a mirror of freedom, and has been left without its strongest argument—the real communist danger (Kuljić 2002: 291).

Capitalism seems to have been more dynamic and energetic before the fall of the Berlin Wall and the "fall of communism." With the outbreak of the global financial and economic crisis of 2007-2008, the euphoria of the 1990s has simply dried up in the West. There is also much less triumphalism about that time.

Direct responsibility for the outbreak of the crisis is not the only sin attributed to the system of neoliberal capitalism: Generating inappropriate economic and social differences in society because it makes the rich even richer, and the poor even poorer, can also be attributed to neoliberal capitalism.

In his evaluation of the financial crisis of 2008 as the most traumatic global economic event, Nobel laureate Joseph E. Stiglitz argues, "Crises seem to be a part of modern capitalism. Put simply: it is apparent that the post-World War II capitalist system is neither efficient nor stable—and it is increasingly apparent that it is also not equitable, marked as it is with growing inequality" (Stiglitz 2018).

5.

THE RICH AND THE POOR

There isn't, nor can be a just wealth.

Mahatma Gandhi

When someone tells you he acquired wealth with his hard work,
ask him—whose work?

Immanuel Kant

The forces in a capitalist society, if left unchecked, tend to make
the rich richer and the poor poorer.

Jawaharlal Nehru

If a free society cannot help the many who are poor,
it cannot save the few who are rich.

John F. Kennedy

The Berlin Wall was indeed torn down,
but a wall between the rich and the poor was erected.

Todor Kuljić

The widening gap between rich and poor nations
accumulates for future troubles.

Niall Ferguson

Economic inequality among people—the polarization into the rich and the poor—appeared "as soon as human society had been born, because all human societies have been accompanied by differences in power and wealth" (Milanović 2012: 15).

According to Italian economist Vilfredo Pareto,

…income inequality is a social constant determined by forces that may be beyond human understanding and probably beyond human influence?

The founders of classical economies, Adam Smith and David Ricardo, were concerned with the distribution of income among what were then the three great social classes: workers, capitalists, and land-owners. They defined three factors of production: labor, capital, and land. The return to each factor was treated as the income of the respective social class.

Smith and Ricardo were interested in what determined the income of each groop relative to the total natonal income. Their theories predicted that as society progressed, landlords would become relatively better off and capitalists would become relatively worse off. Karl Marx had a different view. He predicted that as growth occurred, capitalists would become relatively better off and workers relatively worse off (at least until the whole capitalist system collapsed) (Lipsey&Steiner&Purvis1987: 324).

The famous English economic theorist Alfred Marshall, contrary to Marx, hoped that, with economic progress, the rich would become relatively poorer and the poor relatively wealthier (Ibid.).

All forms of inequality have culminated in the neoliberal era of contemporary capitalism, especially on the threshold of the third decade of the twenty first century. German political scientist Margit Mayer believes that neoliberalism "has caused an increase in social inequalities. The poor are being systematically pushed out, especially from urban centers, which, on the other hand, undergo the process of gentrification. People are getting poorer, especially since city administrations have been forced to take austerity measures. As costs are being reduced more and more, infrastructure, services, everything collapses" (Mayer 2016).

The worst feature of the neoliberal period is a massive rise in economic and social inequalities.

> Until very recently, this had been virtually ignored. With extraordinary speed, however, it has emerged as one of, if not the most important political issue on both sides of the Atlantic, most dramatically in the U.S. It is, bar none, the issue that is driving the political discontent that is now engulfing the [West]. Given the statistical evidence, it is puzzling, shocking even, that it has been disregarded for so long; the explanation can only lie in the sheer extent of the hegemony of neoliberalism and its values.

> But now reality has upset the doctrinal apple cart. In the period 1948–1972, every section of the American population experienced very similar and sizable increases in their standard of living; between 1972–2013, the bottom 10 [percent] experienced falling real income while the top 10 [percent] did far better than everyone else. In the U.S., the median real income for full-time male workers is now lower than it was four decades ago: the income of the bottom 90 [percent] of the population has stagnated for over 30 years.

> A not so dissimilar picture is true of the UK. And the problem has grown more serious since the financial crisis. On average, between 65-70 [percent] of households in 25 high-income economies experienced stagnant or falling real incomes between 2005 and 2014 (Jacques 2016).

The U.S., Great Britain, and other capitalist countries in the years after the "victory over communism" began to stumble instead of making even faster progress, which culminated with the outbreak of the global financial and economic crisis of 2007 and 2008. Along with the slowdown and decline in economic activity, there was a decline in their citizens' standard of living. "Today, four fifths of the American population has to spend twice as much time to earn the same salary as they did forty years ago" (Unkovski-Korica 2016: 2).

Unexpected and inexplicable wealth inequalities, which are constantly being created by capitalism, are the primary global political, economic, and social problems of mankind today.

> In our own time, as Marx predicted, inequalities of wealth have dramatically deepened. The income of a single Mexican billionaire today is equivalent to the earnings of the poorest seventeen million of his compatriots. Capitalism has created more prosperity than history has ever witnessed, but the cost— not least in the near-destitution of billions—has been astronomical. According to the World Bank, 2.74 billion people in 2001 lived on less than two dollars a day (Eagleton 2011: 8).

Thanks to the theoretical foundation of capitalism and its global neoliberal hegemony, the rich have gotten richer and the poor have gotten poorer.

According to Forbes, the planet was home to just over 140 billionaires in 1987 but counts more than 1,400 today (2013), an increase by a factor of 10…In view of inflation and global economic growth since 1987, however, these spectacular numbers, repeated every year by media around the world, are difficult to interpret. If we look at the numbers in relation to the global population and total private wealth, we obtain the following results, which make somewhat more sense. The planet boasted barely 5 billionaires per 100 million adults in 1987 and 30 in 2013. Billionaires owned just 0.4 percent of global private wealth in 1987 but more than 1.5 percent in 2013, which is above the previous record attained in 2008, on the eve of the global financial crisis and the bankruptcy of Lehman Brothers…This is an obscure way of presenting the data, however: there is nothing really surprising about the fact that a group containing 6 times as many people as a proportion of the population should own 4 times as great a proportion of the world's wealth (Piketty 2014: 305).

In contemporary neoliberal capitalism, the rich not only get richer, but they also get rich faster. For instance, "the number of billionaires in the United States has more than doubled in the last decade, from 267 in 2008 to 607 last year [in 2018—author's note]" (Jackson 2019).

These economic and social inequalities have caused a crisis of global proportions and created a very difficult, even unbearable social situation all over the world, especially in less developed countries. "One billion human beings are malnourished; 7 million children are dying due to the debts the countries they are living in have accumulated over time…Qualified workers are replaced by rented children. Two fifths of a chocolate being drank or eaten in the West is produced by the super-exploitation of child labour…This is the world we are living in…" (Ali 201: 315).

More than 70 percent of the world population is without adequate social protection (ILO 2014/2015). In 2015, about 10 percent of the world population lived on less than 1.9 dollars per day. Due to insufficient food production in the world and its inadequate distribution, the number of hungry people increased from 795 million in 2014 to 821 million in 2017, or 10.8 percent of the total world population. Insufficient progress has been made in prevention of stunted growth in children. Due to malnutrition, almost 151 million children under the age of five were too short for their age, compared to 165 million in 2012 (FAO 2018).

Every second, one human being in the world dies of hunger. It is estimated that about 36 million people worldwide will die of hunger in 2019, most of them children. "Into the 21st century hunger is still the world's biggest health problem" (World Counts 2019).

Accurate data on the number of people who are starving or have died of starvation in the world do not exist because official statistics are not reliable or do not exist at all.

> While the number of the rich and super-rich is exact and well-known, nobody knows the exact, actual number of people starving or dying of hunger, because in the countries where these events are [a] common reality, no statistic is made [on] who is hungry or not—we can only estimate their number by the GDP statistics on [the] number of people that *could be* starving. The poorest countries don't have any possibility to count people that have died—no matter what was the cause of their death, nor to make an estimate regarding the children,

since they are not inscribed in the birth, or death certificates (Matrix World 2011).

Dramatic differences between the rich and the poor are particularly striking in Brazil, the largest Latin American country. Brazil is among the three richest countries in the world in terms of available natural resources, and is the eighth largest economy in the world, with a gross domestic product (GDP)—measured based on purchasing power parity—that amounted to 3.24 trillion U.S. dollars in 2017 (World Factbook/1/2019). In Brazil, "[One percent] of the population, super-rich people own 99 [percent] of Brazil terrain" (Matrix World 2011).

In the twenty first century, Brazil is still facing social problems that are far more severe than poverty, with widespread penury and an extremely miserable economic position of individuals and some socially endangered social strata. Millions of Brazilians are still homeless, landless, without a steady income, and facing hunger. Former Brazilian President Lula da Silva won the 2002 presidential election with the slogan "Fight against hunger" (*Luta contra a fome*), emphasizing his main goal as president was that no Brazilian family goes to bed hungry. During his two presidential terms (2003-2011), da Silva managed to reduce the number of the poorest inhabitants in Brazil from about 40 million to about 20 million. Da Silva's policy against hunger in Brazil was continued by his successor Dilma Rouseff, which constantly conflicted with the interests of large capital and exponents of neoliberal politics in Brazil. Rouseff was impeached by the National Congress of Brazil in August 2016 on charges of misappropriating federal budget funds.

During the presidential election campaign in 2017, da Silva, while visiting the Brazilian state of Piauí, one of the poorest in the northeast of the country, criticized the sitting Brazilian government and

President Michel Temer, for their "lack of initiative" and the "return of famine in Brazil" (Lula 2017).

The current social situation in the European Union looks bleak. "Roughly 22 percent of EU citizens still find themselves at risk of poverty...while the richest 10 percent possess more assets than the bottom 90 percent in numerous countries" (Hubmann 2019).

In all former socialist countries, a part of the population also faces hunger and malnutrition. For example, in Russia, twenty million people live below the poverty line (Putin 2018).

In Serbia, according to its statistical office, "In 2016, the at-risk-of-poverty rate was 25.5 percent, and the at-risk-of-poverty and social exclusion rate was 38.7 percent, and such a situation is a push factor that prompts people to seek better working and living conditions outside their country" (Grečić 2019). According to the Eurostat—the statistical office of the EU—the greatest social inequality on the European continent exists in Serbia, the largest republic of the former socialist country Yugoslavia. About 650,000 of its inhabitants go to bed hungry every night. In Serbia, incomes of the richest 20 percent are nine times higher than the incomes of the poorest 20 percent, while the ratio at the EU level is 5.2:1 (Guzina 2018: 22). In 2016, half of the adult population in Serbia had a total monthly income of less than 213 euros, three quarters had an income of less than 312 euros, and 80 percent of people were paid less than 344 euros (Krek 2018).

Even the most developed countries in the world face the problem of hunger.

> In fact, according to the last statistics...30 million people in the United States are suffering [from] hunger. 30 million is a lot of people, and that means plenty of children...

...Hunger is 'surging' among the elderly: about five million older Americans, about 16 percent of the population over 60, are going hungry, they're malnourished, many of them are literally starving to death...Now, in the United States we don't have starvation the way they do in Haiti or Nicaragua or something—but the deprivation is still very real. In many places it's probably worse than it is in Cuba, say, under the embargo (Michell & Schoeffel 2002: 364–365).

Bernie Sanders, a U.S. senator from the state of Vermont, discussed the housing crisis and high rates of homelessness during his campaign for the Democratic Party nomination in the 2020 presidential elections. Sanders, during a campaign stop on February 10, 2020 at a former Ford assembly plant that was shuttered in 1955 in Richmond, California, said in front of a crowd of more than 6,000 that 'It is a moral obscenity that in our country tonight, 500,000 people will sleep out on the streets. Together we end that obscenity'" (Kaplan 2020).

Less developed countries in the global South are constantly lagging behind the rich countries of the North in economic development. The current difference between their levels of development poses a serious threat to the sustainability of the existing global economic system. "95 [percent] of the North has enough food and shelter… In the South, on the other hand, only 5 [percent] of the population has enough food and shelter" (Mimiko 2012: 47).

Assessing the social situation in the contemporary world, Zbigniew Brzezinski notes, "We have huge differences between those at the top and the average of everyone else, and that gap is constantly widening. In 1990, the earnings of those at the top were 17 times higher than the average American earnings. Today, they are 325 times higher" (Mišić 2012).

Such a social situation in the world is often criticized by Pope Francis, who accuses the global capitalist economic system of being insensitive to the needs of the poor and of not doing enough to share wealth with those who need it most. In an interview he gave to the Italian newspaper *Messaggero*, responding to criticism that when he criticizes capitalism and calls for radical economic reforms he sounds like a Leninist, Pope Francis said, "I would only say that the Communists have stolen our flag…The flag of the poor is Christian; poverty is at the heart of the Gospel." Citing passages from the Bible that speak of the need to help the poor and sick, Pope Francis went on to say that "communists say that it is all communism. Yes, but twenty centuries later. So when they speak, one can say to them, 'but then you are Christian'" (Pope Francis, June 29th 2014).

The gap between the rich and the poor has reached its peak in the middle of the second decade of the twenty first century. The international non-profit organization Oxfam—a confederation of 19 independent charitable organizations focusing on the alleviation of global poverty that works in more than 90 countries with thousands of partners, allies, and communities—at the annual World Economic Forum meeting held in Davos, Switzerland, on January 20-23 in 2016 and January 17-20 in 2017, published the following data, respectively:

- The richest one percent of the world population now own more than the remaining 99 percent combined (Oxfam 2016);

- The eight richest billionaires in the world (six Americans, one Spaniard, and one Mexican: Bill Gates, Warren Buffet, Jeff Bezos, Mark Zuckerberg, Larry Ellison, Michael Bloomberg, Amancio Ortega, and Carlos Slim) "own the same wealth as the 3.6 billion people who make up the poorest half of humanity" (Oxfam 2017);

- The "richest [one] percent bagged 82 percent of wealth created last year [in 2017—author's note]—[the] poorest half of humanity got nothing" (Oxfam 2018);
- The world's 2,153 billionaires have more wealth than the 4.6 billion people who make up 60 percent of the planet's population (Oxfam 2020); and
- The 22 richest men in the world have more wealth than all the women in Africa (Ibid.).

These and numerous other statistics confirm that "inequality is growing around the world. Every year, the gap between rich and poor gets even wider" (Oxfam 2019). Such a relationship between the rich and the poor in global wealth distribution "is unfortunate" (Piketty 2014: 307).

An extreme concentration of wealth in the hands of a small number of individuals on the one hand and an extreme poverty of the largest part of the world population on the other were created, without a doubt, by the international order established after World War II. However, regardless of such a situation, the leading circles of neoliberal capitalism insist on maintaining that order rather than changing it.

Social inequalities are increasingly pronounced, more or less, in all member states of the EU, even in the richest and most developed. A huge part of these countries' wealth has flowed into the accounts of a few owners of leading global corporations and large national companies. On the other side, an entire army of real proletarians who barely manage to feed themselves and their families with their regular earnings, often even working additional jobs, is being created. An army of migrants who have arrived in the EU in recent years are in a particularly difficult social position.

Economic inequalities are extremely high in the United States of America, especially when compared to the other richest countries in the world. In 2014, "the average U.S. adult income before tax and transfer was $66,100, but this figure masks huge differences in income distribution. Approximately 117 million adults, who make up 50 [percent] of the U.S. population, earned an average of $16,600 a year, representing only one-quarter of the average U.S. income" (Alvaredo 2018: 79).

Furthermore, living conditions for many children in the U.S. are extremely difficult. "Every third child in America, still the richest country in the world, according to David Harvey, lives in poverty. Many of them, as this author states, live in 'toxic environments, suffering from hunger and lead poisoning, being deprived of basic social services and opportunities for their education...'" (Jeffries 2017).

Despite the undoubtedly great social, economic, and technological achievements that capitalism has accomplished so far, the fundamental problem of this social order has always been the constant reproduction of poverty. This is why in contemporary capitalist world today, including in the most developed Western countries, there are too many poor people, beggars, homeless people, wanderers, and landless people, and this number tends to grow every day.

The latest report by the British Institute for Fiscal Studies (IFS) emphasizes that the widening and deepening of the gap between the rich and the poor in Western countries is "a threat not only to capitalism, but also to our [Western—author's note] democratic system" (Bienkov 2019).

Not only are people in the contemporary capitalist world divided into rich and poor, but so are countries, nations, and states into those that are the most developed, developed, developing, underdeveloped, and undeveloped. Since "the end of the 19th and the first half of the 20th century, income disparities between the rich world of Western Europe, North America and Oceania and the rest of the world (Africa,

Asia and Latin America) have exploded. It was actually the period in which what we call the 'third world' was born" (Milanović 2012: 98).

The differences between the rich and the poor have also created serious geopolitical uncertainty. The gap between rich and poor countries in the world has been constantly widening and deepening in the era of neoliberalism, becoming the largest in the first two decades of the twenty first century. Such a global economic situation in regards to relations between countries, nations, and states is one of the main causes of the emergence and flourishing of nationalism, extremist organizations, and terrorist movements around the world, such as the Islamic State of Iraq and the Levant (ISIL).

The existing dimensions of economic and social inequalities around the world in their own way reflect a possible pre-revolutionary situation quite similar to the one on the eve of World War II. It seems that the term "pre-revolutionary situation," although "historically outdated," defines the nature of existing problems and contradictions of the contemporary world more precisely than the terms such as terrorism, extremism, fundamentalism, nationalism, and the like, which are now widely used. After all, most historical revolutions broke out when nations were oppressed by poverty, when people had been hungry, barefoot, and homeless.

6.

WHAT IS GENERATING THE POVERTY?

The history of poverty, growing economic inequality, and social stratification in society is long and very complex, and its causes are numerous. "Throughout history, poverty has been portrayed as a state of misery and despair, or a vicious circle from which there is no way out" (Pantelić 2017: 107).

Economic and social inequality in society, as well as the birth of a vicious circle of poverty in the contemporary age, were primarily incited by the original accumulation of capital, carried out in the era of colonial imperialism after the fifteenth century, and even earlier. During this period, Western capitalist countries acquired invaluable wealth by plundering the resources of Africa, Asia, and Latin America, accumulating and constantly increasing their wealth on based on their interests.

Wealth has also been acquired through inheritance (one becomes rich by birth) and in various other ways—particularly tax evasion, usurious interests, corruption, trade of illegal goods (narcotics, weapons, etc.), and human trafficking.

Still, capitalist exploitation has been the main and inexhaustible resource for the increase in capital and the wealth of the capitalist class measured by this capital. Reducing the wages of employees and/or firing workers while transferring their workload to other workers has been the main source of profit for the owners of capital and the way to increase their wealth.

However, regardless of its origins, the wealth of capitalists has steadily increased as their financial capital was invested with high interest rates, and economic and social inequalities continued to deepen and widen. These inequalities culminated in the era of contemporary neoliberal capitalism with its exploitative social order during the last decades of the twentieth century, before and after the fall of socialist regimes, and in the current twenty first century. This order is dominated by the class stratification of society into those who own capital (the exploitative class) and those who are forced to sell their labor as a commodity (the exploited class) to the owners of capital.

Class stratification in society cannot be equated with the stratification produced and reproduced by technological progress, which differentiates jobs into those that are high- and low-paid. Differences in salaries and incomes between highly-skilled and unskilled jobs are objective. Highly-skilled jobs strongly encourage creativity and the emergence of new technological inventions, which are a key factor in economic growth and social progress. Social stratification in a society dictated by technology is not class stratification. Highly-skilled and well-paid employees do not exploit those with lower and low wages, but instead they are both exploited, the former even more so than the latter, by the class of capitalist employers, the owners of the capital.

Proponents of capitalism, including those with the highest scientific degrees, see the main causes of economic and social inequality in individual states and the world as outside the production relations of the capitalist social order, defending capitalism in every way from taking any responsibility. Consciously or unconsciously, they do not want to see that the main generator of growing inequality, although not the only one, rests within this order: that at the historical roots of growing economic inequality and social stratification is the capitalist exploitation of workers and all other working classes in society that forces them to sell their labor as a commodity to the owners of capital—that is, to the employers—so they can meet their basic needs.

The economic and social situation of workers in former socialist countries was extremely difficult not only in the years of the transition from socialism to capitalism, but remained difficult even after the completion of this socioeconomic transformation. The wild capitalism that prevails in all the former socialist countries, and the capitalist exploitation of workers, is even more ruthless, nefarious, and perfidious than in the eighteenth and nineteenth centuries. The increasing number of domestic and foreign owners of capital in former socialist countries, thanks to their strong political influence in society, dictate the conditions under which workers have to sell their labor force. As a rule, the price of hired labor is significantly lower than its real value. Workers' wages in EU countries are objectively higher than those in the former socialist countries due to the difference in their levels of economic development. However, the nature of their wage relation is identical. In the EU, due to the high unemployment rate, the supply of labor is also higher than the demand for it, so the price (wage) at which employers buy labor is objectively lower.

Economic and other inequalities in the contemporary world are also strongly encouraged by taxation policies, which are adapted primarily to the interests of the owners of capital, especially to the large ones, while undermining the overall position of the poor—especially of the very poor, i.e., the social strata who does not have ownership of the means of production (capital).

7.

MARX'S CONCEPT OF EXPLOITATION

Capitalism depends on the reproduction and
intensification of exploitation work.

Herbert Marcuse

Exploitation. This concept, once ubiquitous,
has almost disappeared
from the contemporary social sciences.

Razmig Keucheyan

First as a philosopher and then as a political economist, Karl Marx devoted his numerous scientific works, such as *Capital* (in three volumes), *Foundations of the Critique of Political Economy*, *A Contribution to the Critique of Political Economy*, etc., to the study of the capitalist social order. The ultimate goal of Marx's work on *Capital* was to "reveal the economic law of motion of modern [capitalist, bourgeois society - author's note] society" (Marx 1890: xxv). In this sense, Marx creates a comprehensive critical analysis of the capitalist mode of production. Among other things, he explains how capitalists—the owners of capital—exploit the labor of wage workers, i.e., how capitalists are constantly getting rich.

In order to consider and understand Marx's theory of exploitation, it is important to recall the basic economic categories and concepts that he uses in his analysis and critique of the capitalist mode of production.

MARXIST UNDERSTANDING OF COMMODITY

In his most famous work *Capital* (first book, first section, first chapter), Karl Marx begins his analysis of the capitalist mode of production by considering the notion of commodity. According to Marx, "the wealth of those societies, in which the capitalist mode of production reigns, presents itself as an 'immense heap of commodities'…The single commodity appears as the elementary form of this wealth" (Marx 1890: 2).

Commodity is the result (yield) of specific technological connections and combinations and the participation and consumption of basic factors of production: labor force, means of labor, and objects of labor. The means of labor are machines, technological, and other equipment. The object of labor are raw materials, reproduction materials, energy, etc. The means of labor and the object of labor are material factors of production and are also known as the means of production. The means of production are also identified with past materialized labor because they were created by the living labor of workers in previous reproductive processes. Since the main means of production in capitalist society are owned by capitalists, not by workers, they are also referred to as capital.

None of these three factors of production are, in and of themselves, sufficient enough to actualize the production of a given commodity, i.e., goods and services. In this sense, each individual factor of production is equally important. Human labor alone, no matter how skilled, cannot create a new product (commodity) if the other two factors of production are not included. Likewise, none of the material factors of production, however effective they may be, can create a new value, a commodity, without the proper cooperation of human labor.

The overall relations and conditions in which the "merging" of human labor and material factors of production, i.e. the means of production, take place to create new commodity values ultimately determines the very character of a given social system, as well as the overall political and socioeconomic position of the people in it.

Analyzing the "anatomy" of commodity, Marx discovers:

a) Two factors of a commodity: the use-value of a commodity and the exchange-value of a commodity. The use-value of a commodity refers to the properties of a commodity (goods and services) able to satisfy human needs. A thing that has no use-value has no exchange-value either. Exchange-value refers to a quantitative and qualitative relation in which one use-value is exchanged for another. The common denominator of all commodities in the process of their exchange is the human labor materialized in them.

b) Two-fold character of labor embodied in commodities: concrete and abstract labor. Concrete labor refers to the utilization of human labor in some purposeful form (the labor of carpenters, locksmiths, mechanics, etc.). Only useful concrete labor produces useful commodity values. Abstract labor represents the social character of human labor, i.e., the social unification of specific heterogeneous types of labor in the process of creating new use-values of the commodity, which abstracts the special characteristics of all types of concrete labor and is similar to average labor.

Marx also establishes the division of labor into necessary labor and surplus labor. Necessary labor is the labor of wage workers within working hours, which is necessary to produce the goods needed for the reproduction of that worker. Surplus labor is labor of wage workers after the required working hours.

The capitalist employer forces, obligates the wage worker to work beyond the time required for the worker's reproduction. Therefore, the wage workers, with their labor power, create a new value which is higher than the value of the wage the capitalist pays them. The capitalist strives to extend the surplus as much as possible beyond the necessary labor during the working day in order to provide a new value that is as high as possible—surplus value.

Marx bases his labor theory of commodity value on the dual character of human labor. According to this theory, the total amount of human labor, present and past, is the basic determinant of the value of each produced commodity and the main determinant of its market price, and not just its mere utility on the demand-side or scarcity on the supply-side.

c) Two-fold character of capital: constant and variable capital placed in the production of a given commodity, goods, and services. Constant capital is invested into the means of production. Variable capital is invested only in the wages of the hired labor force.

Marx divides the economic function of capital invested in the production process into fixed and circulating capital. Fixed capital is invested only in the means of labor, which transfers only an aliquot of its value to a new product. Circulating capital, which is invested into objects of labor and the wages for the hired labor force, transfers all of its value to a new product.

65

According to Marx, the economic structure of a commodity value (W) in the capitalist order consists of the cost of capital (C), wages (V), and surplus value (M), or $W = C + V + M$. Wages and surplus value $(V + M)$ create, Marx argues, a formula for the invested ongoing labor of hired workers.

The cornerstone of Marx's entire economic analysis is surplus value. He proves that the way of creating and appropriating surplus value is the backbone of the capitalist social system and its driving force.

ASPECTS OF CAPITALIST EXPLOITATION

Starting with the knowledge that the value structure of each manufactured commodity consists of the costs of constant capital, workers' wages, and surplus value, Marx finds that only the labor force has the ability to—with its ongoing newly added labor—to create value that is higher than the market price (wage, salary) the capitalist pays the hired workers. The ability to create value greater than its own is not characteristic of capital in the means of production (means of labor and objects of labor). The means of production can instead only transfer their own value to a new product and are therefore called constant capital, as opposed to the capital invested in the labor force (variable capital).

In fact, the capitalist will spend less on a produced commodity than it actually costs for the amount of surplus value, i.e., for the portion of the unpaid living, ongoing newly added labor of wage workers. In a market exchange, surplus value is depicted as achieved profit—what the capitalist gains. For wage workers, however, surplus value is nothing but their alienated labor. Such contradictory relations between the capitalists and wage workers are possible because in capitalism the value of manufactured goods is measured by expenditure in capital, not expenditure in labor. According to Marx, the actual cost of a produced commodity can only be measured by expenditure in the total amount of labor, past and present.

The capitalist private property monopoly on the means of production (the capital), which is institutionalized by the capitalist state, enables capitalists to fully appropriate the surplus value that their employees create through their ongoing work. In political economy and sociology, this process of appropriating the surplus labor of wage workers is referred to as the process of capitalist exploitation. Thanks to such exploitation, which is guaranteed by the capitalist social order, "the capitalist can live, and live from his capital" (Marx 1973: 314).

Because of the extent to which capitalists and the capitalist class increase their wealth based on the exploitation of wage workers, the real wages and the market price of labor force of the worker will decline or stagnate, not to mention the drastic decline in relative workers' wages.

On average, the price of the labor of exploited workers as a specific type of commodity is, as a rule, below its actual value, not because of technological progress, but because the labor force supply on the market is constantly higher than the demand for it due, more or less, to the very high unemployment everywhere in the world. In light of the conditions of the general economic treatment of the labor force on the market, the owners of capital, guided by their natural tendency to make as much profit as possible in their businesses, systematically reduce the salaries of their employees. Also, with the same goal, they systematically reduce the number of employees by firing them, requiring their remaining workers to perform jobs of the fired workers in addition to their own.

The owners of capital and their managers know perfectly well that a significant profit cannot be achieved solely on the basis of saving material factors of production (machines, raw materials, energy, and other means) in the production of goods and services. The level of consumption of these resources is largely pre-determined by specific standards and norms. As a rule, they are quite difficult to meet. Consumption of any material resource above the prescribed standards and norms potentially means a loss in business. This is why employers turn to a real "gold mine"—wage workers. They know very well that higher profits can only be achieved through lower wages for hired workers or by reducing the number of workers while performing the same workload.

Recent years in the development of neoliberal capitalism

> ...have proven the foresight of Kurt Vonnegut's first novel, *Player Piano* [published in 1952 – author's note], that an iron logic within market capitalism—namely the perpetual effort to suppress wages either by finding new low-wage markets or replacing humans with machines or computers—will increasingly reduce all but a few forms of work to drudgery and indignity (Deneen 2018: 140).

The constant reduction in the wages of workers and all other working classes of society who are forced to sell their labor force as a commodity—a consequence of the increasingly ruthless and cruel capitalist exploitation—directly leads to a decline in the purchasing power of these workers and their families. This is why consumables that no one can buy pile up on the shelves and warehouses of stores, shopping malls, supermarkets, megamarkets, etc.

Employers, the owners of capital, striving to make as much profit as possible at all costs, do everything they can to encourage their employees to work as much as possible and to exploit them as much as they can. Thus, for example, the most hardworking employees are given special material rewards and privileges and are awarded moral recognitions within the company in the form of public praise and honors. Such methods of additional exploitation of workers, based on the employer's insincere care for their workers, are irresistibly reminiscent of the former system of rewarding workers in former socialist countries.

The strategic goal of the capitalist class and its employers has always been the exploitation of each and every person in society, primarily workers, who are materially dependent on their employer's private capital. "In economic life the ideology of the ruling elite reduced workers to being humdrum or even lazy individuals, but who could be set in motion by giving them material gratifications. V. F. Taylor provided a classic formulation of this representation of workers and of the means of making them work for the maximum profit of the employers" (Touraine 2007: 48), while paying them the lowest wages possible. In this respect, nothing much has changed since the time in which Marx lived and wrote, regardless of the major social, economic, technical and technological changes that have happened in the meantime. The social nature of capitalist relations has remained the same. Capitalists today, in the twenty first century are getting rich in the same way as they have in previous two centuries by exploiting wage workers—i.e., by appropriating the unpaid portion of the workers' total living labor (surplus labor).

It is no exaggeration to say that the capitalist exploitation of workers on the threshold of the third decade of the twenty first century is crueler and more heartless than it was in the nineteenth century Marx wrote about. To verify the accuracy of this claim, it is enough to simply visit the Yura enterprise, a branch of the South Korean global corporation located in Serbia, and see that wage workers have to use diapers during work hours. Or, one could just ask the cashiers in Belgrade megamarkets how much they work, when their working day begins and end, how much they earn, and when they receive salaries.

Without any doubt, Marx's theory of capitalist exploitation of wage workers has, in contemporary conditions, become more existent and significant than ever before. Just based on his theory, it is possible to understand why the rich become richer and the poor become poorer, why the wealth of the capitalist class and the poverty of wage workers have reached dramatic proportions, and why wage workers have no "right to what they produce." In fact, the basic contradictions of nineteenth-century capitalism have, in essence, remained unchanged to this day.

A CRITIQUE OF MARX'S THEORY OF EXPLOITATION

The capitalist class, the owners of capital, employers, and theorists of capitalist social order argue that in capitalist society all citizens have equal rights and freedoms, that everyone, past and present, makes or made a living from their work because of their abilities, knowledge, and skills, and that employers do not exploit workers employed in their enterprises.

Employers reject Marx's theory of surplus value, the unpaid portion of ongoing work, and the exploitation of wage workers. For them, the wage they pay wage workers is the cost of doing business, just like the cost of any other factor of production. All profits, i.e. the surplus value that the owner of capital achieves over their operating costs, including paid wages, makes their business successful. Employer profit does not grow on trees—it is achieved through relentless competition in the market, and not through the alleged exploitation of wage workers. Profit is acquired only through the market, and relations inside their enterprises are by their nature strictly non-marketable.

Capital invested by an employer in the production of a given commodity has not only its value but also its market price. As a rule, it also involves a certain level of income reproduction of invested capital, which is nothing more than the profit that the employer expects to achieve through their business activities on the market. In addition to investing their capital, employers also recognize the invested living labor of their management team on the market, and often their own work contribution when they partake in the business decision-making process (living labor of the employer).

Wage workers hired by employers in the process of reproduction are not direct market participants; they do not bear the business risk, inherent to the market way of doing business, which is always borne by the owners of the enterprise. Any loss in the business of the enterprise directly affects the employer, the owner, and has a negative impact on their property (capital), while employees can be left without their salary or job.

Thanks to the systematic critique of Marx's theory of surplus value and exploitation, and in part to successful anti-Marxist propaganda in the West, the very concept of exploitation

> ...has almost disappeared from contemporary social sciences...The current trend, including among thinkers very much on the Left, consists in replacing the concept of exploitation by that of domination, which is supposed to be more inclusive and clear...The generalization of the concept of domination at the expense of the concept of exploitation coexists with the abandonment of the centrality of the conflict between capital and labor... (Keucheyan 2016: 220).

However, despite all the efforts of capitalist governments to replace the notion of exploitation with the notion of domination, the echo of exploitation has not yet disappeared. Discussing the "mystique" of labor and "exploited" labor, the American economist Thomas Sowell says that "echoes of this vision can still be found today, not only among a relatively handful of Marxists but also among non-Marxists or even anti-Marxists, who use such terms as 'unearned income' to describe profits, interest, rent and dividends" (Sowell 2000: 337).

Even with all the criticism of Marx's theory of surplus value and exploitation, whether partly justified or not, the question of the relation between labor and capital has remained open to this day. It strongly shakes the foundations of contemporary capitalist society from within. For this reason, the relations of production are not sufficiently natural, democratic, fair, just, or undisputable as the capitalist elite believes they are. In such relations, even the proclaimed fundamental human rights and freedoms do not have real substantive grounds, and they are objectively reduced, more or less, to a mere formality.

8.

OCTOBER AND OTHER SOCIALIST REVOLUTIONS

*What I hate more than communists are fanatical anti-communists
who know nothing about communism.*

Václav Havel

*Communism is an ideology, and anti-communism is a pathology,
that is, an ideology of idlers and swindlers.*

Anonymous

In the political history of the world, the exploited strata of society have always been the initiators of social revolts against exploiters. Social rebellions and socialist revolutions broke out in the twentieth century because the owners of capital overestimated the importance and role of their private capital and underestimated the value of the living labor of workers, ruthlessly exploiting them and pushing them to the periphery of society. Marx's critical theory of capitalism, called Marxism, became the ideological and political platform of these revolutions.

In the twentieth century, five authentic socialist revolutions were successfully performed: 1) the 1917 October Revolution in Russia under the leadership of Vladimir Ilich Lenin; 2) the 1941–1945 Yugoslavian revolution led by Josip Broz Tito; 3) the 1941-1945 Albanian with assistance from Yugoslav communists and led by Enver

Hoxha; 4) the 1949 Chinese revolution led by Mao Zedong; and 5) the 1959 Cuban revolution led by Fidel Castro.

Quasi-socialist revolutions were simulated in Poland, Czechoslovakia, Hungary, Romania, and Bulgaria, which fell under the sphere of Soviet influence after World War II. The USSR imposed its etatist socijalist order on Eastern European countries. Mao's socialism in China was, in essence, a replica of the Soviet model of socialism. North Vietnam and North Korea were influenced by Chinese socialist practices. Socialism in Cuba was under the ideological patronage of the USSR.

The main objectives of these socialist revolutions and their imposed socialist regimes were first to carry out an armed struggle of exploited workers, the working class (proletariat), and the poor peasantry against the exploitative capitalist class; second, the expropriation of expropriators—that is, to seize the means of production from the hands of the capitalists and transfer it to the hands of the socialist state as a revolutionary mechanism for the exploited masses in society; and third, to build socialism as a new socioeconomic and political system.

The October Revolution in Russia was launched in 1917 by the Russian proletariat—disenfranchised and exploited workers and peasants who were not even remotely able to provide a decent life for themselves and their families. The few enjoyed grotesquely large wealth while millions of people lived in poverty. In fact, the October Revolution, as well as the February Revolution that preceded it, were the "result of widespread popular discontent. This is what distinguished them from the coups that the right-wing historians so often like to pinpoint. It was, in fact, an unrestrained expression of the people's will that arose from hardship" (Nikolić: 2017).

The riddle that the October Revolution was meant to solve was: who could rearrange the world so that human labor can serve human needs? It failed to do so. It simply ate

> ...its own children (Trotsky, Kamenev, Zinoviev, Bukharin, and even Lenin, who was targeted by Fanny Kaplan), but even more tragically: it ate itself. People soon became bitter, suspicious, unable to celebrate October on an empty stomach. [And precisely because of this empty stomach, their hungry children and bare feet, that they rose up against the emperor, and not because they wore warm valenki in winter and ate hot porridge for lunch—author's note]. As the last act of a complete reversal, Lenin's untimely death followed, after which a hardened bureaucrat Joseph Vissarionovich Stalin came to power, although his predecessor, while still alive, suspected the kind of downfall the rise of Man of Steel would lead to. The rest is well known, and it is visible in the left neo-tsarism as it currently exists, for example, in North Korea (Ibid.).

Nevertheless, regardless of its unattainable ideals and unfulfilled expectations, the October Revolution was and remains a beacon of the primordial aspirations of man and humanity toward fundamental human justice, a dignified life for everyone, and fairness and equality for all people, free from all forms of exploitation and alienation. "We seem to have simply rejected the political values that had emerged from the October Revolution and followed more or less all other socialist revolutions in the 20th century: internationalism, solidarity, social equality, fraternity of peoples, equality of races" (Milošević 2017: 68 –69).

Nowadays, it is not only the teachings of Karl Marx (Marxism), but also the teachings of Vladimir Ilyich Lenin (Leninism)—especially his New Economic Policy (NEP), also known as Lenin capitalism—that are becoming inevitably unavoidable in seeking a way out of the impasse into which contemporary neoliberal capitalism has sunk into, both theoretically and practically.

9.

STALIN'S STATE (NON-MARKET) SOCIALISM AND ATTEMPTS OF ITS DEETATIZATION

Those who vote decide nothing.
Those who count the vote decide everything.

Stalin

STALINISM: THE STATE'S MODEL OF SOCIALISM

One of the fundamental values of the October Revolution was the affirmation of the idea of workers' control, understood as a contribution to the idea of workers' self-management of enterprise. This idea was realized for the first time in history during the Paris Commune (1871), when workers managed enterprises they worked in. In 1917, enterprises were introduced to a triple management system: factory committees, trade unions, and enterprise management. However, in the extremely complex political circumstances of the time—the outbreak of the counter-revolution, civil war, and foreign interventions in Soviet Russia—the triple management system was replaced in 1920 by an *edinonachalie*, which was a system of centralized state management of enterprises and the economy. This is the so-called war communism period, which started immediately after the victory of the socialist October Revolution.

At that time, all forms of economic construction were based on one fundamental principle which entailed removing the category of market from the economy, with all the value categories that accompanied it. Connection between the individual participants in the production was to be realized through direct distribution of total social product. As for the distribution of the product among the population, this task was being solved with a card system…The victory of natural deployment and natural distribution led to deformities of monetary economy….(Lisičkin 1966: 19th and 21st).

At the Tenth Congress of the Russian Communist Party (Bolsheviks), held from March 8-16, 1921 in Moscow, Lenin, the leader of the October Revolution, announced his New Economic Policy (NEP). NEP enabled commodity connectivity "between socialist industry and the individual peasant economy, temporarily allowing private initiative revival on a limited scale," establishment of a "market form of economic ties," and the widespread use of "laws of value in direct management of the socialist economy" (Ibid.: 23, 39, and 42).

In the years of NEP, "the Soviet Union's economy developed 2-3 times faster than all capitalist countries' economies combined…" (Ibid.: 41-42). Pointing out the importance of the NEP in the further socialist development of the Soviet Union, Lenin said, "Socialism should be learned from the major organizers of capitalism" (Ibid.: 43).

After the death of Lenin on January 21, 1924, Joseph Visarionovich Stalin came to power and ruled the USSR for the next thirty years until his death on March 5, 1953. "His death marked the end of one of the most contradictory periods in Russian history, which included heroism, enthusiasm, mass social creativity and stifling of dissent, forced country modernization and consolidation of command methods for its realization, thrust to democracy and the spread of totalitarianism" (Ivanov, B. J., et. al 2009: 205).

Having come to the helm of the USSR, Stalin decided with all his strength to build a rigid bureaucratic, centralized, statist model of socialism based on the fetishization of the role of the state in all segments of social reproduction, production, exchange, distribution, and consumption at the macro- and microeconomic level. In political theory, the system of government and the rule he created was named Stalinism. This term implies a totalitarian system of government, rule, a cult of personality, the suppression of all democratic actions of citizens and freedom of thought, liquidation of "unsuitable" party cadres ("cleansing"), and the formation of labor camps (gulags) for politically labeled opponents of the Soviet system of government and Stalin.

An important feature of Stalinism was the centralized and planned management of the economy and society. Through mass nationalization and collectivization—that is, by the expropriation of expropriators—the means of production (capital) and almost all agricultural land were forcibly taken away from their owners—capitalists and landowner—and ownership was transferred to the Soviet state. Private ownership of capital and land was replaced by state ownership. The entire economy was treated as one large state-owned enterprise. The state was the employer, and the workers were its de facto employees.

The market was replaced by the state plan and the marginalized market laws by planning. The central state planning agency of Soviet socialism, *Gosplan*, was directly responsible for decisions on what would be produced, how and for whom would specific goods and services be produced, what needs would be met, and how the produced goods and services would be distributed. Gosplan also determined the salary level for employees. Government agencies, enterprises, households, and consumers received detailed and precise administrative instructions from Gosplan on what to do and how.

State planners, using their indisputable scientific and statistical knowledge, were able to calculate everything that was needed—even how many neckties that needed to be produced in order to satisfy the needs of Muscovites. However, the planners were not able to calculate what color of necktie the Muscovites would like to wear because the market did not function based on what the consumer wanted, except in the farmer markets, and even then in a very limited way. Instead of meeting the basic needs and desires of its citizens-consumers, the political obsession of Stalin, and even Soviet leaders after his death, was to "reach and surpass the United States," the leader of the capitalist world, in order to show in practice that real statist socialism was a better social order than capitalism. "Stalin spoke about this for the first time in 1939, emphasizing that a higher industrial production per capita should be achieved: it is—he said—a 'basic economic task'..." (Boffa 1985: 395). And at the 21st Congress of the Communist Party of the Soviet Union (CPSUS) in 1959, Khrushchev "made his boldest promise: the United States would be reached and surpassed in both industrial and agricultural production per capita by 1970, 'perhaps even sooner.' This meant—he said later—that the Soviet Union would have the 'highest standard of living' in the world, and that it would become a country where people would 'live the best'" (Ibid.: 395–396). Khrushchev's optimistic predictions did not come true. History has denied them. The Stalinist statist system of socialism was not functional. It underestimated altogether the roles of the living labor of workers and the state capital and the means of production owned by the state, while it overestimated the role and power of the state-party apparatus in the management of Soviet society. It believed that "the state power was a miraculous force for meeting the needs of people in any proportions" (Lisichkin 1966: 20).

The fate of Stalin's statist, centralized administrative model of socialism was followed by other Eastern European socialist states that were in the "Soviet orbit."

As a political and social system, Stalinism left behind immense atrocities. According to official information published in 1954, from 1921 to February 1954, 3.8 million people in the USSR were sentenced for counterrevolutionary activity, out of which 642,980 were executed, 2.4 million people were sent to prisons and camps, and 765,180 people were persecuted or banished. According to some Western sources, the true number of Stalinist victims is much greater. It is estimated that millions of innocent Soviet citizens lost their lives in Stalinist repressions and purges on Stalin's "merit," and many family lines were ended. "There has not been a tyrant from Nero to Hitler who could be compared to him in the number of killings" (Antonov-Ovsejenko 1986: 353).

By order of Stalin, sixteen former leftists were liquidated in August of 1936, including two formerly prominent Bolsheviks: Lev Kamenev and Grigory Zinoviev.

> In January 1937, seventeen Bolsheviks were tried, thirteen of whom were shot, while four of them awaited a slow death in labor camps. These conspirators were allegedly in the service of Germany and Japan. In June, the Supreme Commander of the Red Army, Tukhachevsky [Red Napoleon—author's note], and seven other senior officers were secretly convicted and executed as spies and traitors, while Gamarnik, chief of the Political Department of the Army, committed suicide. In March 1938, twenty-one members of the so-called 'anti-Soviet bloc of right-wingers and Trotskyists' were tried, including

Bukharin, Rikov and the unengaged former commissar of internal affairs, and eighteen major transgressors were executed. At each trial, the defendants' only right was to confirm their earlier confessions extorted by the NKVD (Ibid.: 313–314).

According to Leo Trotsky's testimony, Stalin was the subject of Lenin's fears from the very beginning. During the 10th Congress of the Communist Party of Russia (Bolsheviks), held from March 8-16, 1921 in Moscow, Lenin said to his intimate associates about Stalin, "That cook will prepare only very spicy dishes." While thinking about resigning from his leadership position due to his seriously deteriorating health, Lenin gave the last piece of advice to the Party: "Remove Stalin from his position; he is capable of leading the party to its division and dissolution." According to Trotsky, "The party did not find out about this advice in time. A carefully selected apparatus concealed it" (Trotsky 1982: 342–343). It was perfectly clear to Lenin who should not succeed him. However, the course of history of the USSR went in a different direction.

The political system with the cult of personality that cast its the leader as "infallible," and the cadre policy that favored those who were "suitable," were important causes that led to the collapse of real socialism.

The statist model of socialism proved to be a negation of the idea of a just society when practiced by the socialist countries of the Soviet bloc, although their party leaders and communist ideologues were convinced that Soviet real socialism was a historical form of the only possible just society. "During the Stalinist period, it was real socialism to plenty of prominent, self-described socialists" (Niemietz 2018: 99).

KHRUSHCHEV'S ATTEMPT OF DE-STALINIZATION

In all the Eastern European socialist countries in the Soviet orbit, and even in Yugoslavia, which was not one of the Soviet satellite states, citizens were dissatisfied with the general social situation imposed by the Stalinist system of government and governance.

Just over three months after Stalin's death on March 5, 1953, while a fierce political fight for predominance was still going on in the USSR, a group of construction workers in East Berlin, Germany launched a protest on June 16. Initially, the workers' demands were economic in nature and aimed against the established high labor standards ("quotas"), but quickly grew into political demands. They raised slogans against the ruling Stalinist East German government, demanded the resignation of its leadership and free elections, and called for the "establishment of a revolutionary workers' government" in East Germany. The next evening, on June 17, an uprising of workers and citizens—thirty to fifty thousand—were suppressed by Soviet troops and the East German police.

Following the arrival of Nikita Khrushchev as the head of the USSR on September 14, 1953 and his election as the First Secretary of the Communist Party of the USSR, changes took place in the domestic and foreign policy of the USSR. These policy changes were called the de-Stalinization process, which was officially inaugurated at the 20th Congress of the CPSU, held on February 14-25, 1956. De-Stalinization began even before the Congress, starting immediately after Stalin's death, which was reflected in the weakening campaign of the Information Bureau of the Communist and Workers' Parties (known as the Informbiro or Cominform) against socialist Yugoslavia, the resumption of negotiations to end the Korean War in July 1953, the USSR's desire to improve overall relations with the United States, and the Soviet proposal for international negotiations on all contentious issues.

The process of de-Stalinization was essentially dynamized at the 20th Congress of the CPSU, where Khrushchev gave a "secret speech" titled "On the cult of personality and its consequences," which was soon disclosed. In it, he condemned Stalin's murderous tyranny, some of his crimes, especially those against the Party, and his "cult of personality."

> This speech was interpreted as evidence that the new people in power will not carry out terror against their own people. The ubiquitous portraits and paintings of Stalin, as well as everything else that seemed part of the cult, were removed. Places named after him gradually regained their previous names or got new ones, which were harmless and utterly unimpressive. Thousands of his surviving victims received some form of compensation, and thousands more were posthumously rehabilitated. Prominent dissidents, however, although freed of the most absurd accusations, were still politically anathematized (Vilets 2003: 326).

The Information Bureau was dissolved in April of 1956. In the announcement of this decision, in addition to the assessment that there were some serious errors in its work, the opinion included that communist and workers' parties would, "according to their needs and based on their specific working conditions, exchange opinions on common issues of the fight for peace, democracy and socialism..." (Štrbac 1982: 162).

Internally, "Khrushchev vigorously set to solve some of the most serious problems inherited from Stalin: slowness of the cumbersome and overly centralized bureaucracy, stagnation of the countryside, disobedience of the law by its enforcers, and the deepening gap between the privileged and the people" (Vilets 2003: 327).

Wanting to improve the living standard of his citizens, Khrushchev focused more on the production of household goods than on heavy industry. He fought against the housing crisis in the USSR and launched the rapid construction of millions of apartments in buildings without elevators, known as *Khrushchyovkas*. He also introduced a minimum wage for workers, following the example of some countries in the West. During the 1950s and 1960s, the USSR had higher rates of economic growth than most Western countries, despite its economic inefficiencies.

The process of de-Stalinization, initiated at the 20th Congress of the CPSU, at which Khrushchev announced the dissolution of Stalinist discipline and the start of life without fear of police and secret services, opened the perspective of new processes and relations in the countries in the USSR's socialist orbit and in the same region as the USSR. The events in these countries started to escape the traditional Soviet control of political party.

Workers in Poland began to openly express dissatisfaction not only with their existing financial position and working conditions in their enterprises, but also with the general situation in Polish society. The first mass worker protests against the Polish Stalinist government and authorities began on June 28, 1956, at the metal factory H. Cegielski and at several other large factories in Poznań in west-central Poland, in what came to be known as the Poznań June. With Khrushchev's consent, demonstrations of Polish workers were stifled on June 30, 1956.

Due to popular discontent with the general situation in the country, low standard of living, lagging economic development and the enhanced resistance to the Soviet bureaucratic regime, Hungary was swept by demonstrations that culminated in the outbreak of an armed popular uprising, that is, a real revolution of the people, on October 23, 1956. By November 4, 1956, Soviet armed troops had crushed the resistance of Hungarians and stifled their revolution. Numerous innocent lives were lost and there was considerable material destruction of the country.

At the 22nd Congress of the CPSU, held from October 17-31, 1961, Khrushchev made another criticism of Stalin's terror and purges, resulting in the Congress deciding to remove the body of the cruel dictator from Lenin's mausoleum for "grave violations of Lenin's principles, abuse of power and mass repression of honest citizens." Stalin's body was removed from Lenin's mausoleum and buried in the Kremlin Wall Necropolis, his grave marked only by a simple bust. The city Stalingrad was renamed Volgograd.

Khrushchev was removed from power on October 14, 1964. The main reason for his removal was the unanimous political assessment of the Presidium that the balance between domestic and foreign policy was negative during his rule. Furthermore, his failures and setbacks were emphasized, while his indisputable successes were not even mentioned. The Moscow-based and official Soviet state newspaper *Pravda* told its readers that new leaders did not accept Khrushchev's methods and manner of governance, emphasizing that his methods were the enemies of the Party created by Lenin: "subjectivities and deviations," "flaunting plans," "hasty decisions and plans that were not in line with reality," "boasting and empty talk" (Vilets 2003: 333).

According to later Soviet leader Mikhail Gorbachev, Khrushchev's merits were

> ....so significant that they far exceeded his mistakes. He started the fight against Stalinism, persistently promoted the policy of peaceful coexistence, rehabilitated millions of

innocent victims, and repealed Stalin's decisions to relocate entire nations to Siberia. The Karachays, Balkars, Ingush, Chechens, Kalmyks, and Crimean Tatars were displaced (Gorbachev 2014: 119).

Regardless of the historical assessment of Khrushchev's role, the fact remains that he failed to finish the process of de-Stalinization. Essential reforms of Soviet society were lacking. The Stalinist social system, in essence, remained unchanged. The state, the party, state property, and centralist planning continued to play a key role in the Soviet social and economic system, and the market, private property, personal initiatives and material motivations of workers were marginalized.

After the Khrushchev's removal, the first secretary of the CPSU, Leonid Brezhnev, was elected to be the general secretary of the CPSU, which was a title previously held only by Stalin. During his eighteen-year rule, by November 10, 1982, instead of de-statizing[2] the Stalinist system, Brezhnev was trying to further promote this system. Although Stalin's "mistakes" were not forgotten,

> Stalin's official reputation was constantly improving. The party press rejected the accusations of military incompetence made against him by Khrushchev and some generals. Historians studying the development of agriculture were warned not to be too critical in reviewing the process of collectivization. [The] revised edition of the one-volume *History of the Party* (1969) even described the Great Purge as a

---

2 Polytocracy is the ruling-administrative apparatus of a political party that holds all the levers of power in the country and imposes its concept of development imbued with bureaucratic methods of management and leadership. De-statizing is the rollback of this apparatus..

necessity...[with] which the Party protected itself from hostile elements and 'prevented actions directed against socialism and the interests of the Soviet state.' In the same year...Pravda characterized Stalin as a 'great theorist,' while also mentioning some 'mistakes that became serious during the last period of his life' (Vilets 2003: 334).

Brezhnev invented the theory of limited sovereignty, called *Brezhnev's doctrine*, which allowed Soviet military intervention and interference in the internal affairs of the Soviet satellite states in order to protect their socialism. The USSR applied this doctrine when it occupied Czechoslovakia using military force in August of 1968 and liquidated the so-called *Prague Spring*. With Moscow's support, Polish police brutally clashed with protesters across Poland during a student uprising known as "March 1968." Mass protests of workers in Poland in 1970 and 1976 were also suppressed by armed force. In contrast to their former practice of repressive actions towards strikers, the Polish government—in agreement with Moscow—did not resort to armed force in during the mass strike of workers at the Lenin shipyard in Gdansk on August 14, 1980, which then quickly spread to the rest of Poland. Instead, the government decided to reach an agreement with the strikers.

After the workers' strike in Gdansk, faced with political threats from the Polish labor union Solidarity—which was led by the workers' tribune Lech Walesa—and its increasingly intense activity and growing influence in Poland, Brezhnev considered military intervention to be the only solution in the "Czechoslovak" scenario that would allow the pacification of the situation in Poland. However, in December of 1981, Yuri Andropov, as the chairman for the Committee for State Security (KGB) with great political influence, regardless of his previous role in Hungarian and Czechoslovak events, convinced Brezhnev not to resolve the crisis in Poland by armed force, arguing that Soviet occupation of Poland would be counterproductive. This was the de facto end of Brezhnev's doctrine of limited sovereignty.

ANDROPOV'S VISION OF SELF-MANAGEMENT

After Brezhnev's death, Yuri Andropov was elected General Secretary of the CPSU Central Committee on November 12, 1982, and President of the Supreme Soviet of the USSR on June 16, 1983. Despite his many years working in the KGB, with all the specifics of that service fighting the "enemies" of the Soviet order, Andropov understood the gravity of the social problems the USSR was facing, as well as the historical significance and political message of the social riots that shook the Soviet satellite countries in Eastern Europe after Stalin's death and after the 20th CPSU Congress.

The common denominator of social riots in the Soviet satellite countries was the open resistance against the ruling bureaucratic centralist social system, and the workers' and nations' aspirations and fight for better working and living conditions. In 1953, protesters in East Germany demanded the "formation of a revolutionary workers' government." Polish workers, striking in Poznań in 1956, spontaneously founded workers' councils in their factories, which the Polish communist government, under strong pressure from workers, had to recognize as official governing bodies, at least temporarily. In 1956, Hungarian revolutionaries fought for the democratically elected workers' councils to be the main body that would run the factories and for the interconnected workers' councils to form a workers' government throughout the country. Advocating for "socialism with a human face," leaders of the Prague Spring fought for workers' rights to self-management and for liberal, market socialism. The Polish independent "self-managed trade union" Solidarity, with its program of being a "Self-managed republic," saw the future of Poland in the workers' self-management in factories and society.

Although he belonged to the Soviet political nomenclature, Andropov ultimately assessed the phenomenon of workers' and people's riots in the satellite countries differently from Khrushchev and Brezhnev. For Khrushchev and Brezhnev, these riots were an attempt to turn these socialist states to the right, toward capitalism, and they prevented that "turn" by armed force. Andropov, on the other hand, saw in these riots the aspiration of insurgent workers and citizens toward a new possible socialism, different from the Soviet "real socialism" where the party, the state, society, and people would be governed by administrative and centralist methods.

Having followed, studied, and evaluated the historical processes and events in the countries in the Soviet orbit— especially the self-governing practice of Yugoslavia, which was outside of the Soviet sphere of influence, and where workers' councils were pillars of its socialist order—soon after his election as KPSS secretary general, Andropov announced his intention to improve the socialist social order of the Soviet Union. In his study, titled "The Teachings of Karl Marx and Some Problems of Socialist Construction in the USSR," Andropov clearly and precisely theoretically conceived the basic direction Soviet leaders needed to go in building socialism in the USSR and the way out its economic lag and other ways it was falling behind (Andropov 1983).

Starting with the "ideal of communist self-management," as Marx had imagined it, Andropov pointed out in this study that the most important thing was that the Soviet socialist social system

...works and improves, finds new forms and methods of developing democracy, expands economic rights and opportunities of the working man in production, through social and political practice—from parliamentary commissions and popular control to regular production meetings. This is the real socialist self-management of the people.... It primarily refers to the revival of local initiative and its wider use, to greater organic involvement of all work collectives in public affairs" (Andropov 1983).

Andropov's vision for a new form of socialism, not only in the USSR, but also in the world, was a "real socialist self-management of the people" *("действительное социалистическое самоуправление народа")*. Unfortunately, Andropov did not manage to put his vision into practice and realize it in the social practice of socialism. Death was faster than him. He passed away only fifteen months after taking over the highest party office in the country, on February 9, 1985.

Andropov's death was a huge and irreplaceable loss for the USSR, its society and citizens, and not only for them. "Undoubtedly, Yuri Vladimirovich Andropov was an exceptional person, versatile, naturally gifted, a true intellectual. He resolutely opposed everything we called Brezhnevism—favoritism, secret battles, corruption, moral depravity, bureaucracy. All this corresponded to the people's expectations" (Gorbachev 2014: 328).

GORBACHEV'S "PERESTROIKA" AND "GLASNOST"

Yuri Andropov's successor, Konstantin Chernenko, was the head of the CPSU from February 13, 1984 to March 10, 1985, even shorter time than Andropov.

Chernenko was succeeded in his role as the general secretary of the CPSU by Mikhail Gorbachev, a representative of the younger generation of Soviet leaders who were born after the October Revolution. When Gorbachev became the head of the USSR, he seemed very promising—that is, a lot was expected of him not only in the USSR, but also worldwide.

Andropov contributed to Gorbachev's rise by supporting him during Brezhnev's time and especially during his mandate. However, by becoming the head of the USSR, Gorbachev did not follow Andropov's political course; he did not follow the path of "real socialist self-management of the people" that Andropov had traced from the enterprises and local communities to the top of Soviet society. This political option was most likely not ideologically close to Gorbachev because he did not particularly address the theoretical questions and problems of socialist development. During most of his political career—by his education as a lawyer and agrarian economist—Gorbachev was predominantly, and very successfully, engaged in the development of Soviet agriculture. Among other positions he held, he was the secretary of the Central Committee of the CPSU for Agriculture.

In his autobiography *Memoirs*, Gorbachev mentions Andropov on over 60 pages in various contexts, but does not mention Andropov's theoretical work "The Teachings of Karl Marx and Some Problems of Socialist Construction in the USSR," nor his coined expression of "socialist self-management of the people." In his book, Gorbachev only says, "My thoughts, and my conversations with Andropov, gave me the idea that 'more democracy' would mean 'more socialism'" (Gorbachev 2014: 379). Commenting on the appearance of the "Andropov phenomenon" as the beginning of general and deeper changes in Soviet society, Gorbachev apodictically claimed that "Andropov would not have sought for radical changes, just as Khrushchev could not have done it. And perhaps it was destined for him to die without facing the problems that would have inevitably stand in his way, and lead to disappointing others and disappointment in himself" (Ibid.: 329–330).

Instead of accepting Andropov's concept of "socialist self-management of the people" as the starting point for changes in the Soviet social system, the Soviet leadership, headed by Gorbachev, declared in April 1985 a course to "accelerate the socioeconomic development" of the Soviet Union as a way out of the crisis. This orientation was based on using the full potential of the socialist system—strengthening work discipline and the intensive exploitation of production resources. However, the economic and social effects of this "acceleration" were not successful.

The inherited problems of stalled economic growth, low productivity, and economic inefficiency remained open and continued to hinder and threaten the socialist development of the Soviet Union and its position on the global political scene. After months of intensive talks with workers in enterprises and citizens in regions throughout the USSR, at the plenary session of the Central Committee of the CPSU in June 1987, Gorbachev initiated *perestroika*, that is, the realignment, reform, and modernization of Soviet domestic and foreign policy. Assessing the historical moment of its launch, Gorbachev said, "I witnessed a huge desire of people for change, and the indifference of leaders to change" (Gorbachev 2014: 402).

Internally, perestroika legalized private property for the first time since Lenin in order to develop the private sector; it allowed "individual labor activity" and the creation of cooperatives in the service sector and the consumer goods sector; eliminated the monopoly of the minister of trade in transactions with foreign countries; allowed foreigners to invest in the USSR and own up to 49 percent of shares, and for Soviet citizens to be directors of enterprises. The law on state-owned enterprises that went into effect on January 1, 1988 expanded the rights of enterprises, but retained the powers of ministries and other departments of state administration. Despite these measures, there was a decline in national income, which had a negative impact on the material position of the population. In 1989, a wave of socioeconomic strikes swept across the USSR. "In such conditions, Gorbachev's leadership recognized the need for a gradual transition to market economy, but did not take any real steps in that direction" (Ivanov, et al. 2009: 215).

The overall effects of perestroika at the national level were not in line with the optimistic expectations of citizens because the promised increase in their standard of living was not delivered.

However, the effects of perestroika on foreign policy were more specific and more visible. It transformed the foreign policy of the USSR. Gorbachev announced the formal end of Brezhnev's doctrine of limited sovereignty. At the end of 1988, a decision was made that allowed members of the Warsaw Pact to determine and regulate their internal affairs at their own discretion, guided by their national interests. This initiated the process of far-reaching political, economic, and social changes in socialist countries across Eastern and Central Europe, the beginning of the end of the Cold War, and the removal of the Iron Curtain between the East and the West. USSR Foreign Ministry spokesman Gerasimov named the new Soviet foreign policy "Sinatra's doctrine," alluding to Frank Sinatra's famous song "My Way" because the USSR allowed members of the Warsaw Pact to go their own way. Gorbachev's new course in the foreign policy positions of the USSR was crucial for the events that followed in 1989 and 1990 because it enabled a different direction of world history.

Thanks to the results achieved in the pursuit of new Soviet foreign policy, initiated by perestroika, Gorbachev gained broad popularity all over the world, especially in the West. He was gladly received and welcomed everywhere, often greeted with applause from ordinary citizens on the streets of the cities he visited, and spontaneously called "Great Gorby." He was awarded the Nobel Peace Prize on October 15, 1990.

However, the internal grinding of perestroika worried Soviet leadership, led by Gorbachev. "According to the general opinion, things got stuck because of the gigantic state-party apparatus, which became a barrier on the path of reforms and any changes in general" (Gorbachev 2014: 403). Perestroika failed to reform the deeply rooted bureaucratic centralist system of managing the Soviet economy and society, or to modernize enterprises' dealings in accordance with the requirements of the domestic and foreign markets. The old state-party apparatus openly and covertly resisted the implementation of perestroika in the economy.

In 1988, faced with such a political situation and relations in the country, Gorbachev

> ...advocated the introduction of 'loudness' (openness) in the practice of social life. The realization of the principle of 'loudness' ensured the ideological preparation of political reform. Issues of history and development perspectives of Soviet society were discussed in the press, at gatherings and conferences of different kinds, in discussion clubs. In 1988, a constitutional reform was carried out. The Congress of People's Deputies, which elected the Supreme Soviet, became the highest authority (Ivanov, et al. 2009: 216).

At the first Congress of People's Deputies, held in May and June of 1989, Gorbachev was elected president of the Supreme Soviet, and in 1990, became the president of the USSR. This was a time when tensions in the relations between the center and the federal republics began. The main causes of their disputes were the bad economic effects of perestroika, which started to lose its political power as early as 1990, and the already critical economic situation in the Soviet Union. With the demise of perestroika, the optimism of Soviet citizens and their faith in a "bright future" melted away. On December 21, 1991, the Soviet Union disintegrated into fifteen independent states, and Gorbachev resigned as president of the USSR on December 25, 1991.

In much of public opinion worldwide, the responsibility for the disintegration of the USSR is widely attributed to Gorbachev, the last Soviet leader, and especially to his policy of perestroika. Gorbachev failed to use perestroika to reform the Soviet economic system designed in Stalin's time, to modernize the Soviiet way of doing business, to increase productivity and efficiency in business operations, nor managed to improve the living standard of his citizens. In the end, Soviet citizens were simply disappointed in both Gorbachev and his perestroika.

Gorbachev participated in the June 16, 1996 presidential election in Russia as an independent candidate and self-proclaimed social democrat, and won only 1 percent of the vote. This vote confirmed the greatest possible indignation of Russian citizens towards Gorbachev, their former leader who gambled away their expectations. However, in the West, Gorbachev has remained "Great Gorby," and his statesmanship and political merits have been praised to the skies.

On the back cover of the aforementioned book *Memoirs*, Gorbachev presents his ideological and political credo to the public by saying, "My goal was to liquidate communism and dictatorship over the entire nation." This actually means that the introduction of a capitalist social order into the USSR, into Soviet society, was Gorbachev's vision and the strategic goal of his perestroika. The USSR could not survive on such a political platform—it had to disintegrate because the internal cohesion threads that kept the USSR together as a state and social community were anti-capitalist and non-capitalist, derived from an ideological interpretation of Marx's notion of socialism and communism. It could have only survived by finding a new form of socialism and a socialist society tailored to the USSR, that would have been more advanced, more just, and humane not only compared to the given Soviet statist model of socialism, but existing neoliberal capitalism as well.

Historians and historical science will, sooner or later, give a final judgment and assessment of Gorbachev's place and role in twentieth century world history, especially in the social history of the former USSR's geopolitical space. In this context, the Soviet and Russian historian Dmitri Furman gives the following assessment, "We do not have a powerful liberal historical tradition, but we had perestroika. We had Stalin, but we also had Anti-Stalin—Gorbachev, whose epoch is the one of disintegration and 'the greatest geopolitical catastrophe' for the traditional mind, and the epoch of conquered freedom and the real greatness of Russia for the new democratic mind" (Furman 2011: 599).

10.

STATE SOCIALISM IN YUGOSLAVIA

In the first five years after the end of World War II and the liberation of Yugoslavia from its occupiers, who were there from 1945 to 1950, the social system of government in socialist Yugoslavia was administrative and centralist—a fairly faithful copy of the Soviet model of socialism. The overall socioeconomic and political system and how the country, its economy, and other areas of social labor were managed were determined by the state ownership of the means of production. The Federal People's Republic of Yugoslavia (FPRY), proclaimed on November 29, 1945 (previously known since November 29, 1943 as the Democratic Federal Yugoslavia), adopted on January 31, 1946, its first constitution, which, following the example of the Soviet constitution, institutionalized state property as the dominant form of ownership in the new socialist society.

MASS NATIONALIZATION: CREATION OF STATE CAPITAL

During and after World War II, revolutionary measures of *mass collectivization* were implemented in Yugoslavia, such as nationalization, confiscation, and sequestration, and partly even agrarian reform. These reforms were based on the transformation of property from privately-owned enterprises and the property of individual owners, to state property. The most important measure in this regard was nationalization.

The first nationalization measures in 1946 transferred 100 percent of industry of federal and republic importance, 70 percent of industry of local importance, overall banking, all foreign trade and domestic wholesale trade, all means of transportation, and 90 percent of retail trade into the hands of the state (FPRY). Due to the second nationalization of 1948, about 3,100 companies of local significance passed into the hands of the state (FPRY): 10 mines, 65 power plants, 280 brickyards, 250 different industrial enterprises, 200 printing houses and lithographies, 800 warehouses, 180 cellars, 300 sanatoriums and hospitals, 550 hotels, 40 bathrooms, 15 resorts, 530 mills and 100 cinemas.

Based on nationalization and other measures of mass collectivization, the dominant form of ownership in Yugoslavia became state property. Its monopoly was untouchable. The titular of the entirety of state property was the socialist state. Its management was entrusted to socialist state enterprises, which operated in accordance with the guidelines of the state authority in charge of central planning. At that time in the Yugoslav administrative-centralist social system, private property also existed, but it was completely marginalized. Landholdings of peasant households and backyards were limited to ten hectares (land maximum), which was insignificant economically and marketwise. Craftsmen were allowed to work in their small family shops, and doctors were allowed to have private practices. The attitude of the government toward the private sector, however, was very restrictive. The state did not allow it to flourish, with the explanation that private property was a relic of capitalism and a source of the exploitation of workers. There was also cooperative property in the form of peasant labor, agricultural, and craft cooperatives, but their role was also marginal in relation to the dominant status of state property and enterprises in this form of ownership. Personal ownership by citizens of goods intended for their personal consumption was guaranteed.

BUREAUCRATIC-CENTRALIST GOVERNANCE

The economy was managed by the principle of revolutionary-democratic hierarchy and in a strictly centralist manner. The whole economy, in all of its activities and sectors, was huge and cumbersome, but was a unique economic organism headed by a state body, the administrative-operational leadership (AOL), which had great authority.

> This body was in fact a college of ministers of all economic departments, a kind of board of directors of a giant trust that makes up the entire national economy. Each line minister was, in fact, a director general for the management of 'his' trust, a group or branch of the economy entrusted to his management and leadership...Each economic ministry formed several main and general directorates for direct administrative and operational management of a group of similar enterprises (Bilandžić 1978: 119).

State-owned enterprises were managed by a director. He was the state commissioner and the most responsible person for the work of the enterprise, was appointed and replaced by the AOL, and had only the AOL to answered to. All workers and employees in the enterprise were accountable to the director, who was their disciplinary officer. The workers' and officials' only task was to blindly execute all planning directives. They had no decision-making rights in their work or in the operations of the enterprise, except for some advisory influence regarding the protection of their social interests.

The centralized state budget was the financial plan for the entire economy. It regulated all cash flows in the country. The state had an absolute control over the distribution of social products into the necessary labor and surplus labor. All available funds for development (accumulation) were poured into the budget and distributed in accordance with the established planned priorities. At the bottom of the pyramid of the centralized budget system was the financial plan of enterprises, which expressed real revenues and expenditures and existed under the control of the state.

State authorities directly determined the salary grades of workers in enterprises and employees in state agencies and the economy, and their salaries were prescribed in advance. Instead of the former private owners of the enterprise—capitalists—workers and employees in the socialist state-owned companies were in a de-facto wage relationship with the director of the company, the AOL, and the state, and were thus passive and insufficiently materially motivated to work.

The state also introduced a system of moral incentives. For example, the following honorary titles were introduced for the labor exploits of individuals: shock worker, champion of socialist labor, hero of socialist labor of the people's republic, hero of socialist labor of the FPRY, meritorious farmer, meritorious cooperative farmer, prominent cooperative farmer of the people's republic, and prominent cooperative farmer of the FPRY. There were also special honorary titles for enterprises and cooperatives.

In the years of its administrative-centralist system, Yugoslavia fought against hunger and general poverty, and thus introduced the mandatory purchase of agricultural products and the planned distribution of available quantities of agricultural and industrial products. Their prices were administratively determined by the responsible state bodies.

Export/import transactions and foreign exchange operations were subjected to the most rigorous state control, greater than in any other area of economic activity at the time. Initially, only state-owned enterprises of federal importance were engaged in foreign trade.

Through the higher prices of industrial products and the lower prices of agricultural products—the price scissors—the state collected the missing funds for the realization of their plan of industrialization and electrification of the country, which led to the deteriorating economic position of the village in relation to the city and the uncontrolled migration of the rural population into the cities.

The administrative-centralist system of managing the economy and society did not allow for the building of authentic socialist relations conceived at the time of the Yugoslav socialist revolution and the People's Liberation War. The most obvious product of this statist system was the general bureaucratization of economic and social life from top to bottom.

VOLUNTARY WORK ACTIONS IN THE POST-WAR RECONSTRUCTION OF THE COUNTRY

The only bright spot in the administrative-centralist period of governing society was the mass participation of the entirety of Yugoslav working people, especially its youth, in rebuilding the war-ravaged and devastated country. Despite numerous difficulties and general poverty, thanks to the primarily voluntary youth work actions organized throughout New Yugoslavia under the slogan "No rest for progress," the reconstruction of the country was carried out faster than any other European country that had suffered in World War II, and they did it almost entirely on their own. In less than two years, the severest consequences of the war were removed, even though very modest material resources were available.

The largest constructions were built, almost as a rule, by the youth. For example, in 1946, over 60,000 young people (brigadiers) participated in the construction of the Brčko-Banovići railway, and in 1947, over 217,000, of which 5,683 came from abroad, took part in building the Šamac-Sarajevo railway. About 503,000 brigadiers took part in local work actions in 1948. From 1948 to 1950, 320,000 young people from all parts of Yugoslavia participated in the construction of the Zagreb-Belgrade section of the Brotherhood and Unity Highway. It was a time of unprecedented enthusiasm and hard work of the masses. The work enthusiasm of the masses was a direct expression of the fact that they "felt that, with the final victory of the people's government, the liquidation process of exploitation of man by man was being launched. If the working masses had not felt that, no one would have been able to lead them or force them to perform such miracles of work heroism" (Kidrič 1960: 347–348).

11.

SOCIALIST SELF-MANAGEMENT: TITO'S MODEL OF LIBERAL (MARKET) SOCIALISM

Free development of each is the condition
for the free development of all

Manifesto of the Communist Part
(Karl Marx and Friedrich Engels)

Freedom is the heritage of liberalism, and equality of socialism.

Jovo Bakić

Titoism is a contrasting background necessary to distinguish
between good and evil,
desirable and undesirable, "Tell me what you think about Tito, and
I will tell you who you are?"

Todor Kulić

Nationalism is the worst human construction.

Mario Vargas Llosa

After Josip Broz Tito's conflict with Stalin in 1948, the Yugoslav party
and state leadership led by Tito vigorously opposed Stalin's hegemonic
pretensions and decided to leave the administrative-centralist system of

managing the economy and society, embarking on its own path of socialist construction. That path was an orientation towards socialist self-management.

THE ROOTS OF SOCIALIST SELF-MANAGEMENT

The idea of self-management was not born out of the conflict with Stalinism, but was a strong motive for the country to properly value its own revolutionary experiences and the experiences of the workers' movements in the world. Namely,

> ...self-management was not invented by Yugoslav theory and practice, even though some people insist on giving us undeserved credit—or blame—for it. The idea of self-management is as old as the idea of humanism, as old as the international workers' movement, its class struggle and socialist practice. It is the culmination of man's eternal aspirations for freedom and free creativity, for mastery over the objective laws of nature and society, for a better life (Kardelj 1980: 9).

During the socialist revolution in Yugoslavia, citizens organized themselves into various committees of national liberation, which independently took care of maintaining order in liberated territory and securing a minimum standard of living for the people. In the years spent rebuilding the country after the devastation of war, the work enthusiasm shown by the masses was, in fact, authentic revolutionary self-management.

The utopian socialists Charles Fourie, Robert Owen, and Louis Blanc were particularly preoccupied with the idea of self-management. Karl Marx and Friedrich Engels envisioned their new socialist society as a self-managed and democratic community of free and equal manufacturers. In all of their works, they paid special attention to socialist self-management. Their ideas of direct workers' management in enterprises were practically implemented in the Paris Commune, the first workers' state to exist in Paris from March 18—formally from March 26—to May 28, 1871. In the regulations on the workers' cooperative association in the workshop for weapon repair and modification at the Louvre, the mechanism of workers' self-management was elaborated on in great detail and was published in the *Official Gazette of the Commune* on May 3, 1871.

In his conception of Soviet government, Lenin gave an elaborate and extraordinarily far-sighted vision of self-management and self-managed democracy, which he saw as the direct participation of working people in the management of society through their delegates, who were constantly accountable to the base that elected them. He paid special attention to the issues of workers' participation in enterprise management. In Stalin's time, Lenin's conception of Soviet government was changed.

In 1949, in his article "On People's Democracy in Yugoslavia," Edvard–Bevc Kardelj presents "a fundamental critique of Soviet statism. There was a danger that the party and the state would merge, become independent and place themselves above society. In 1950, together with Milovan Djilas, Boris Kidrič, Moša Pijade and Vladimir Bakarić, he drafted the Basic Law on State-Owned Enterprise Management" (Čalić 2013: 238).

The exact authorship of the idea of self-management cannot be determined. It was conceived in the circle of Djilas, Kardelj and Kidrič (Ivesic 2016). Djilas argues, "The initial idea of self-management was mine, but it was later elaborated by Kidrič and Kardelj, not me" (Djilas 2016). "But if it was Djilas and Kardelj who first spelled out the political bases of a self-managed society, it was Kidrič, the then-chief of the planning commission, who first developed a model of operational decentralized socialism" (Dyker 1990: 27).

TRANSFORMATION OF STATE PROPERTY INTO SOCIAL OWNERSHIP

The bill of the Basic Law on Management of State Economic Enterprises and Higher Economic Associations by Work Collectives was adopted on June 27, 1950 and was known as the Law on Self-Management. According to this law, the social ownership of the means of production, self-management of direct manufacturers in the economy, and self-management of working people in municipalities, cities, and districts were proclaimed to be the basis of socioeconomic and political organization of the country. The administrative-centralist order of the country based on state property, as defined by the constitution of the People's Republic of Yugoslavia of 1946, was thus fundamentally altered.

Administrative and operational leaderships (AOLs) were abolished. Centralist planning was abandoned, but state planning was not in its entirety.

> The Planning Commission, transformed into a Federal Planning Institute, continued to elaborate plans, initially just on an annual basis The means of production (state capital) were transferred from the hands of the state to direct manufacturers in enterprises under the motto 'Factories for the workers.' Direct manufacturers were given the right to, instead of the state, manage enterprises and all of their business activities on behalf of the social community, according to the social economic plan. They exercised this right through their self-managed apparatus: assemblies of working people,

workers' councils, management boards, workers' control, and other self-managed agencies. Enterprises were declared commodity manufacturers and were obliged to obey market laws and the laws of supply and demand. In 1957, the whole tax system was revamped. The most important change in principle was in the accounting base of the system. The old category of *dobit*, not very different from the capitalist concept of profit, was dropped. From now on enterprise taxation would be based on the concept of *dohoda*k, or net income, which netted out costs of material inputs, etc., but not wage payments. This effectively meant that 'profit' tax now taxed wages as well as profit...At the same time, however, the authorities introduced a progressive tax on distributions (Dyker 1990: 30–31).

On the basis of the Law on Nationalization of 1958 (the third nationalization), rented residential and business buildings became social property, and construction lands were nationalized in cities and urban settlements. There was more freedom in the formation of prices and the exchange rate. Directive and detailed planning was replaced by general planning. In essence, the orientation of Yugoslav society toward socialist self-management meant its firm commitment to "market socialism," that is, to liberal socialism, a socialism fundamentally different from Stalin's statist socialism.

Instead of state property, social property was given, formally and legally, the central place in the new state organization of labor based on direct workers' self-management. It is a complex idea whose theoretical definition is:

Social ownership—like any type of ownership—is a system of relations among men and not [the] relationship between man and things. It is a system of relations in which no individual subject in society, including the state, work collectivity or individual worker, can claim a monopolistic title to it. It is the common property of all those who work, therefore the property of every individual working man to the extent to which it gives him a title to work using socially-owned resources, together with all other inalienable rights which are linked with this basic right to work. These include the right to resources for personal and collective consumption according to work performed, on equal terms with other workers. Socialist ownership is thus expressed in the right to work using socially-owned resources, and in the responsibility of each worker to exercise this right in full equality with every other worker who has the same right, together with all other rights and responsibilities that go with this basic socioeconomic right of the worker. In this manner social property becomes nobody's and everybody's, both collective and personal.

This concept, however, does not do away with the principle of ownership, does not abolish all those property relations arising from appropriation on the basis of labor, but merely changes its socioeconomic content. Since social property is the common property of all people who work, in the last analysis of all members of society, no one on the basis of this ownership can appropriate this property on behalf of an individual or group nor acquire a position of control in relation to other workers (Kardelj 1980: 22).

In his well-known study "The Contradictions of Social Property in Contemporary Socialist Practice," Kardelj says,

The historical meaning of social property under condition of socialist self-management is that it overcomes the alienation of labor from social capital. For social property brings about the integration of labor and social capital. This integration cannot be achieved through any form of property monopoly on capital which, under capitalism, leads to appropriation of 'surplus-labor' by capital, and under socialism manifests itself in the residual form of the state-property right to social capital and the subordination of labor and workers to this right. *The integration of labor and capital can only be achieved by workers exercising direct control over the objective material condition of their labor, that is, through socioeconomic unification of 'living' and 'past' labor materialized in the means of production and social capital in general* (Kardelj 1975: 46).

Concretizing his understanding of the essence of social property in the conditions of socialist self-management, Kardelj explicitly emphasizes, "Social property is at the same time a form of the worker's 'individual' property without which neither he, nor his labor can be free" (Kardelj 1982: 41).

The importance of social property in the development of self-managed socialism was especially affirmed by the Yugoslav Constitution of 1963, which transformed the Federal People's Republic of Yugoslavia into the Socialist Federal Republic of Yugoslavia (SFRY).

The transformation of state property into social property was a historic form of socialist privatization, since the means of production passed from the hands of the state into the hands of free workers: i.e., went from being state property to the "individual property" of workers, as Kardelj used to say. The strategic goal of such far-reaching social changes was to create the necessary socioeconomic and political preconditions for building a socialist society that would be more just and prosperous than a Soviet society dominated by state property, as well as more just and prosperous than a capitalist society dominated by private property. This goal was not successfully accomplished. It was, at best, half-achieved.

OBSTACLES IN IMPLEMENTING SELF-MANAGEMENT IN BUILDING A JUST SOCIETY

The system of socialist self-management in Yugoslavia was mostly successful until the mid-1980s. In the West, especially in the U.S., Yugoslavia was considered the most economically prosperous country in the Eastern socialist bloc, and even a consumer society. However, serious weaknesses in the system of socialist self-management emerged, primarily in Yugoslavia's economic relations with foreign countries. Namely, the constitutional amendments of 1971—and especially the Constitution of 1974—gave the republics and provinces the right to obtain foreign loans, but their obligation to repay these loans was not determined. The foreign debt of Yugoslavia increased by two billion U.S. dollars from 1965 to 1971, then increased by 6.3 billion dollars in the following six years, rising to 9.5 billion by the end of 1977. In the next three years, from 1977 to 1979, the foreign debt of Yugoslavia doubled, rising from 9.5 billion to 18.4 billion dollars (Gnjatović 1991: 330-331).

After Tito's death on May 4, 1980, Yugoslavia faced an economic crisis of unexpected proportions. In 1982, the foreign debt of Yugoslavia reached about 21 billion U.S. dollars—or about 30 percent of their gross social product—which in and of itself was not much. However, its expensive refinancing was a big problem because interest rates were high at the time and export revenues were insufficient due to the trade deficit.

In the absence of Tito's unquestionable authority, a consensus of the republics and provinces on key state issues could not be reached. The leaders of the republics and provinces became the main political actors. Suppressed nationalist and separatist aspirations surfaced more and more frequently, which were latent in Tito's time and occasionally suppressed by his authority and the measures of the communist party.

In fact, Yugoslavia began to sink into a debt crisis immediately after the tragic death of Prime Minister Džemal Bijedić, on January 18, 1977 (i.e., the president of the Federal Executive Council of the SFRY), a competent and pragmatic statesman who had direct communication with President Tito. In January 1977, the foreign debt of Yugoslavia was just over six billion U.S. dollars, and its regular repayment did not burden the state's balance of payments. With Tito's personal support, Bijedić effectively prevented the republics and provinces from excessive borrowing abroad, instructing their leaders and members of the federal government, who were constantly putting pressure on him, to discuss the matter with Tito, which none of them dared to do. The Yugoslav Constitution of 1974 did not present any obstacle for Prime Minister Bijedić, who continued to hold the reins of federal executive power.

The federal government headed by Prime Minister Veselin Đuranović from 1977 to 1982, however, was unable to counter the persistent pressures of the republics and provinces, which sought to obtain as many foreign funds as possible and to freely borrow abroad in their own names, but at the expense of the federation, which would repay their debts.

After Tito's death and the premature passing of Edvard Kardelj— one of Tito's closest long-term associates and the creator of all constitutional changes in post-war socialist Yugoslavia—on February 10, 1979, at the age of 69, there was no political will or theoretical knowledge to embark on making new far-reaching changes to the Yugoslav Constitution of 1974, the shortcomings of which were obvious. Among other things, the autonomous provinces of Vojvodina, Kosovo, and Metohija became constitutive elements of the Yugoslav federation, but also remained part of the Republic of Serbia. With such a constitutional solution

> Serbia's position was anomalous: it had two autonomous provinces (Kosovo and Vojvodina) with voting rights in most federal institutions (such as the federal [presidency]) on a par with the republics, and Serbia's right to change the Serbian constitution depended on the assent of the assemblies of the two autonomous provinces, thereby giving them an effective veto. By contrast, the autonomous provinces could change their own constitutions without the consent of the republic of Serbia. This was a source of resentment that was to be fully exploited later (Roberts 2016: 6).

The 1974 Constitution and the Law on Associated Labor was treated like the Bible by Yugoslav state and party leadership, which was an expression of loyalty to the life and work of President Tito. The newly formed presidency of the SFRY—a collective body composed of one representative from each republic and province, with the president of the collective presidency rotating each year—did not have the state capacity for further reforms or a vision of how to pursue Yugoslav policy.

Searching for a way out of the economic crisis, Yugoslav leadership decided to adopt the Long-term Program of Economic Stabilization, conceptually based on the Constitution and the Law on Associated

Labor of 1976, instead of making changes to the 1974 Constitution and the systemic legislation passed under it. However, this program did not legally bind anyone to it, and everyone interpreted and implemented it as they saw fit. The effects of its application were far below expectations and the effort invested in its preparation. It did not offer operational, pragmatic solutions on how to reschedule external debt with creditors, commercial banks, individual states, and international financial institutions, or how to provide the foreign exchange necessary to pay for the import of many reproductive materials and the equipment for manufacturing in enterprises which were technologically dependent on foreign countries.

The federal government, headed by Prime Minister Milko Planinc, who took office on May 16, 1982, was faced with the impossibility of regularly meeting the obligations to foreign creditors.

> In the spring of 1983, the Yugoslav government called on foreign creditors to urgently negotiate a postponement and extension of debt repayment...In October 1983, the Yugoslav authorities were required to make a public announcement that the country was unable to pay its foreign debts.
>
> After Yugoslavia had publicly declared its lack of creditworthiness, an international operation began to save the interests of Yugoslav creditors...The Yugoslav state guaranteed repayments of all loans, regardless of who had used them. In 1983, an expensive debt rescheduling operation began, which took away eight billion dollars in foreign exchange from Yugoslavia by the end of 1990...

> By saving the interests of foreign creditors, the interests of the republican and provincial governments were also saved... (Gnjatović 1991: 332–333).

The debt crisis thus caused an energy crisis because there of the lack of necessary foreign exchange funds to supply oil, oil derivatives, and gas. There was also a shortage of basic goods important to the living standard of citizens and the quality of life in general: detergents, oil, coffee, chocolate, and many other products. Economic activity stagnated. Losses in the enterprises' operations grew. Inflation became a serious threat to living standards, general economic stability, and development.

The problems of the country's economic stabilization were strongly addressed by the federal government headed by Prime Minister Branko Mikulić, who took office on May 15, 1986, trying, like the previous two federal governments, to find a way to preserve and develop Yugoslavia without making significant changes to its self-managed social order and legacy of nonalignment. This was not achieved by the government of Prime Minister Mikulić, and he resigned on March 16, 1989, before his four-year mandate expired.

When it became clear that Yugoslavia no longer had the geopolitical importance it once had for the West and the U.S. and given its domestic political situation and the new international environment formed before and after the fall of the Berlin Wall in 1989, Yugoslavia's social system and foreign policy had to change. Radical economic and political changes in Yugoslavia's social system and a new concept of its foreign policy were proposed by Ante Marković, the successful long-time director of the Rade Končar enterprise, who was elected the new president of the Yugoslav government on March 16, 1989.

The government of Prime Minister Marković sought support for resolving the Yugoslav crisis primarily through the political and economic assistance of the U.S. and Western Europe. That is why it had the best chance of succeeding. The prime minister immediately launched a program of economic reforms—the world's first comprehensive project to transform a socialist economy into a market economy—and began to turn social property into private property by issuing shares to workers, using the advice of the world's preeminent economists such as the American economist Jeffrey Sachs. He also announced constitutional changes, namely, the transformation of Yugoslavia into a multi-party parliamentary democracy and its introduction into European Community (EC) institutions. The SFRY was then at the entrance of the EC. Prime Minister Marković's program was supported by broad sections of people throughout Yugoslavia. It was also supported by the U.S. and the EC, regardless of the fact that they were no longer interested in actively dealing with the problems of Yugoslavia, but on the conditions that it was supported by the Yugoslav republics and provinces, in which the government was located, and that it was backed by a strong Yugoslav-oriented democratic party.

However, Prime Minister Marković, like previous federal governments, encountered resistance from the top positions of the authoritarian republic governments, especially Serbia, Montenegro, and Croatia because they all had conceptually different visions of the Yugoslavia's future and the form of its possible state organization. Marković was forced to end his term as prime minister on December 20, 1991, before his four-year term expired.

DISINTEGRATION OF SOCIALIST YUGOSLAVIA IN 1991-1992.

In the end, Yugoslavia was unable to preserve itself, internally or externally. It was doomed because of its non-visionary nationalist and separatist leaders burdened with the myths of incorrectly read history and atavistic national programs and prejudices. The leaders of the Yugoslav republics and provinces were not able to agree on the conditions for the implementation of the people's right to self-determination. Instead of reaching an agreement, a solution was sought on the battlefield. They were the gravediggers of Yugoslavia.

The followers of the non-socialist defeated political forces from the time of World War II, Chetniks, Ustashas, and others understood the demolition of the Berlin Wall as their historical victory and took up arms in a bloody war in which everyone was against everyone until extermination: the Serbs against Muslims (Bosniaks) and Croats, the Croats against Serbs and Muslims, the Muslims against Serbs and Croats, and even Muslims against Muslims in Velika Kladuša, in the northwest of Bosnia and Herzegovina (Dašić 2015: 649).

The war in the territory of Yugoslavia was waged from 1991 to 1995. What can be said now is that it was, first and foremost, a true fratricidal war in which, by unwritten rule, injuries were deep, slow to heal, and the scars remained for all time, as a warning, but also as a real threat.

Fratricidal war in Yugoslavia probably could have been avoided. Yugoslavia could even have been preserved, but only with more intelligence, wiser and more capable leaders, and with more attention and more effective support from the international community. And if its disintegration could not have been stopped, it could certainly have been carried out in a peaceful way, without bloodshed. In state and society, and in more accountable places in the federation and republics, however, there were no open-minded people who could see farther, who were selfless, loyal to the nation's unity and to making changes in the state exclusively in a peaceful manner, or to going their separate ways to avoid war and preserve the basis for good relations between the nations, which was important for the future.

The inevitable death of socialist Yugoslavia was also sponsored by external factors. Yugoslavia was betrayed by the West and the international community, although it first betrayed itself. A severely ill Yugoslavia was treated with medicine which could not help it recover. It seems that, at that time for the West—for the U.S., and the EU—it was still more important, at any cost and as soon as possible, to fully wipe out the remaining traces of a socialist—that is, communist as Yugoslavia was considered—state from the political map of Europe than to prevent its chaotic disintegration and the bloodshed of Bosniaks, Serbs, and Croats in a timely manner through the use of consistent measures and energetic actions. Simply put, "Yugoslavia was not to be allowed to remain a socialist alternative to capitalist development" (Bakić 2008: 233).

The International Peace Conference on Yugoslavia—which began in November 1991 in The Hague and continued in Brussels on January 10, 1992 with a discussion on Lord Carrington's plan for resolving the Yugoslav crisis, which was unveiled on October 17, 1991—did not give the expected results. Subsequently, the EU, the United Nations (UN), and other members of the international community launched new peace initiatives from 1992 to 1995 and proposed more peace plans to stop the war conflicts in the territory of former Yugoslavia. Such plans included: the Vance Plan of February 2, 1992, the Cutileiro Plan of February 23, 1992, the Vance-Owen Plan of early 1993, the Owen-Stoltenberg Plan of July 30, 1993, and the Contact Group Plan (i.e.,

France, Germany, Russia, Great Britain and the U.S.), published on July 5, 1994.

Regardless, however, of diplomatic and other efforts made in the preparation and implementation of these attempted peace plans, none of them were able to stop the war conflicts and bloodshed in the territory of former Yugoslavia. This was not achieved until late 1995, after peace talks in Bosnia and Herzegovina. Talks conducted from November 1-21, 1995 at the Wright-Patterson Air Force Base near Dayton, Ohio, under the auspices of the U.S., resulted in the Dayton Peace Agreement. This agreement was formally signed on December 14, 1995 in Paris, ending the civil war in Bosnia and Herzegovina after three and a half years of relentless warfare.

An argument can be made that the strategic goal of the North Atlantic Trade Organization's (NATO) bombing of the Federal Republic of Yugoslavia (i.e. Serbia and Montenegro), in the spring of 1999 was to create the necessary political conditions for the final cleansing of Europe of the remnants of "communist leprosy." This goal was achieved on October 5, 2000, when Slobodan Milošević and his totalitarian regime were removed from the Serbian political scene by a "colored" bulldozer revolution.

The disappearance of socialist Yugoslavia from the geopolitical map of Europe and the world had catastrophic consequences for all South Slavic peoples and beyond.

> Regardless of our position and intentions, when we think of Yugoslavia, the inevitable conclusion is that it was, in both of its lives, a framework for emancipation and modernization of all Yugoslav peoples, that future republics, which are states today, were constituted in it, and that the biggest take-offs of all individual peoples were achieved precisely in this country.

According to Marie-Janine Calic, Yugoslavia was the most serious modernist endeavor in this area, and everything that has happened since the late eighties, and what is happening today, is essentially anti-modern and takes us back a century. The return to strict national prohibitions, all of that is some kind of a dark [nineteenth] century and it is in total opposition to everything we had in both Yugoslavias (Vučetić 2017).

Regarding Yugoslavia and its socialist order, prominent German historian Marie-Janine Calic says,

The Yugoslav model of socialism combined a variety of ideas and concepts, originating from nineteenth- and twentieth-century thinkers, social reformers, and politicians on ways to cope with the challenges of modernity. The notion prevailed that entire societies could be designed and constructed on the basis of reason – one of the basic intellectual assumptions of modernity. Socialism committed itself explicitly to the attempt to achieve justice and modernity by way of comprehensive social intervention. On one hand, its ideals were inspired by the Enlightenment and nineteenth- and twentieth-century reform movements that emphasized values such as rationality, efficiency, education, hygiene, prosperity, and social security. These ideas fit into the Europe-wide context of a world permeated by science and technology. On the other hand, its ideals were substantially influenced by communist dogma: the Marxist ideology, a radical humanism, atheism, collectivism, and patriotic virtues such as friendship between peoples and 'brotherhood and unity.' Last but not least, the Yugoslav social model also incorporated liberal-bourgeois values, principles, and practices into its modernizing strategies, including—within limits— the market economy and private property, consumer goods fetishism, and the free movement of labor. The system even tolerated the fact that a segment of its citizenry submitted themselves to the laws of capitalist wage labor by working abroad. So Yugoslav modernity after 1945 consisted of a particular combination of various norms, values, and practices, on the basis of which the multinational state formulated its own unique response to the challenge of the new age (Calic 2019: 325).

One of the most prominent contemporary philosophers and sociologists in Germany and the most significant representative of the second generation of the Frankfurt School of Critical Theory, Jürgen Habermas, says about Yugoslavia,

> Yugoslavia was a wonderful project. I always thought it should remain as such. Genscher [former German foreign minister—author's note] made the terrible mistake of premature recognition of Croatia...It was beautiful there. Those were fantastic times. I could talk about that for hours. But I can't, too much memory, too much excitement for someone my age" (Habermas 2018).

The great French philosopher Jean-Paul Sartre said the following about socialist Yugoslavia: "Tito's Yugoslavia is the realization of my philosophy" (Mandić 2017: 147).

Another well-known French philosopher, Alain Badiou, says, "I deeply regret the disappearance of the former Yugoslavia, and I do not believe at all that the existence of some ten states in its place represents progress" (Badiou 2017).

The following assessment of Yugoslavia has a special significance:

Yugoslavia was, in fact, one of the greatest cultural and human experiments in history. Formed in the crucible that was the conflict in between the Austro-Hungarian Empire and the Ottoman Empire, Yugoslavia melded together people's of both cultures, and in ways not seen since the time of Alexander the Great's assimilation of peoples after immense conquest (Butler 2016).

Badiou even thinks that Yugoslavia will reunite, that it is only a matter of time (Badju 2019).

TERMINATION OF YUGOSLAV SELF-MANAGEMENT

When the SFRY ceased to exist, so did its system of liberal (market) socialism, i.e. socialist self-management, after four decades of its existence. "Academic interest in self-managed socialism was swept away with the Berlin Wall in 1989. The demise of the communist experiment was extraordinarily rapid…" (Estrin & Uvalic 2008: 666–667).

The new sovereign states that emerged from the ruins of the SFRY immediately renounced multinational socialism and embraced national capitalism. Not only did they renounce the Yugoslav system of socialist self-management, but they anathematized it. It was deemed responsible for the economic and social crisis that led to the disintegration of Yugoslavia.

Socialist self-management was not an ideal social system. It often greatly overestimated the role of workers and their labor and underestimated the role of social capital (the means of production in state property). Workers were guaranteed extensive economic and social rights, regardless of the results of their work. Capable enterprise directors who advocated greater work discipline in manufacturing were often declared technocrats—that is, obstructers in the development of socialist self-management. In such relations, it was not possible to reach the necessary level of economic efficiency required by the market.

On the other hand, social property, due to its conceptual imperfections, socialist self-management blurred the economic relations between individual workers in self-managed associated labor, the individual organizational parts of the same enterprise, and between the Yugoslav republics and provinces. The blurred material relations between the federal units constantly fueled suspicion that they were exploiting each other and that some were living at the expense of others. This contributed the most to the rise of destructive nationalist and separatist tendencies within the Yugoslav community, which objectively led to its disintegration.

In fact, the central problem in the functioning of the system of socialist self-management was not so much the concept of social property in itself, but the statist paternalism, aspirations, and ambitions of the state to have earned income and surplus labor of associated workers in socially-owned enterprises at the state's disposal, and for the state to decide how the results of the work of workers should be managed and where and in which projects development funds should be invested. A large part of state workers' income and surplus labor were constantly being taken away from them under the pretext of "higher social interests." Because of such systemic conditions and socioeconomic relations imposed from the top of the state, workers never perceived the assets of socially-owned enterprises—i.e. socially-owned means of production (capital)—as their own, nor believed that those assets really belonged to them. They perceived these assets as if they were someone else's, like they were constantly slipping out of their hands, regardless of the fact that these assets created with their own work, their own personal sacrifices, and not by the state or the agile officials who personified them.

This was a critical point of the Yugoslav system of socialist self-management: the beginning of its breakdown from within and its final disintegration, including, eventually, the very disintegration of the Yugoslav socialist federation. Simply put, the vast majority of self-managed government workers were deeply disappointed with their working and self-governing status in socially owned enterprises, and in society as a whole. The power of bureaucratic and technocratic structures increasingly dominated social enterprises inside and out, pushing the self-management of associated workers to the margins. This is why, when the state turned socially owned enterprise property into state property in the transition from socialism to capitalism, self-governing workers did not try to prevent it, nor did they particularly resist the privatization of this property. At certain moments, workers even strongly condemned socialist self-management, blaming it for everything, hoping that the state and the new private owners of the enterprises would provide them with a better working, economic, and social position than the one they had in the "self-managed system of associated labor."

The process of transition—that is, the transformation of socialist self-management relations into capitalist relations—shows and confirms that social ownership in the system of Yugoslav socialist self-management was never truly the common property of free associate workers who worked using socially owned means of production. That is why self-management as a system of qualitatively new socialist relations in society could not survive.

LEGACY OF SELF-MANAGEMENT

Yugoslav socialist self-management, known as "market socialism" and "liberal socialism," with all its successes and failures, all its virtues and disadvantages, provided the world with a new dimension to socialism and important social content. "The distinct Yugoslav path to socialism found admirers around the world. In Eastern Europe, the combination of market socialism and self-management offered a model for anti-Stalinist reformers. In the capitalist West, democratic socialists hopefully viewed the experiment as a more 'human' socialism" (Robertson 2017).

Many eminent theorists around the world considered socialist self-management to be a possible alternative not only to Soviet real socialism but also to Western neoliberal capitalism. It was even called the "hope for humanity." Indeed, without exaggeration, it could be said that Yugoslav socialist self-managed society was on the trail of practically realizing great ideas about human freedom and justice. It was, in economic and social terms, an "attempt of a just society." "The whole EU today is reminiscent of self-management. Its vocabulary, its Newspeak and bureaucratization show that it hides behind almost the same terms" (Cvjetičanin 2017: 6).

Socialist self-management has never ceased to be a subject of study, research, and practice. For example, within the Morning Star Company—a California-based agribusiness and food processing company founded in 1970 and the largest tomato processor on the planet, supplying 40 percent of the U.S. tomato paste and diced tomato markets—was built on the foundational philosophy of self-management. Their Self-Management Institute was formed in 2008 as a research and education organization focused on the development of superior systems and principles of organizing people.

Self-management is an organizational model wherein the traditional functions of a manager (planning, coordinating, controlling, staffing, and directing) are pushed out to all participants in the organization as opposed to a select few. Each member of the organization is personally responsible for forging their own personal relationships, planning their own work, coordinating their actions with other members, acquiring requisite resources to accomplish their mission, and for taking corrective action with respect to other members when needed (Morning Star Self-Management Institute 2019).

In his famous work *Die Zeit-Messungen*, the German philosopher Herbert Marcuse writes that "After the sixties [of the twentieth century—author's note], the factory settings and the notions of self-management in manufacturing and distribution regained their importance" (Marcuse 1978: 43).

The French philosopher Bruno Latour, one of the most prominent modern thinkers, says on self-management, "I am very...surprised how relevant the notion of self-management is again." Serbia has a long history of self-management; it was a great thing in the time of Yugoslavia. It is not needed to take everything from the past, just some recipes from this laboratory" (Latour 2017: 20).

Edmond Maire, a prominent French trade union leader, believed in the future of self-management. "If the future belongs to us, then it is up to us to build it so that we can be happy in it. Not because of some happiness that will be determined by a moral or social authority, but because a self-managed society will create conditions for everyone to develop according to their own predispositions and abilities in general and individual freedom. This is already our task today" (Maire 1977: 137).

T. Piketty, a French economist, says on self-government,

> If there had been no war [in Yugoslavia in the 1990s—
> author's note], we might have discussed the Yugoslav model of
> self-management much more. The society that existed before
> the war was relatively equal, thanks to the socialist model of
> public and semi-public ownership and the model of self-
> management that worked to some extent, certainly better than
> the socialist model of the Soviet type (Piketty 2015: 14).

All in all, Yugoslav socialist self-managed society, with all its
problems, difficulties, and contradictions it constantly faced in its
development, truly strived to create a potentially freer and more just
society in its internal and external historical circumstances. That is why
a more comprehensive scientific study on the experience of the former
Yugoslav liberal (market) socialism (i.e., Tito's self-management),
could be helpful in finding possible alternatives to contemporary
neoliberal capitalism in order to create a just society.

Keeping in mind the Yugoslav socialist self-managed experience, in
a future democratic society—freer and more just than existing
neoliberal capitalist society—social property would have to be *the true
common property* of freely associated workers operating with the means
of production of their form of property. In addition to the direct self-
management of associated workers in their socially owned enterprises,
a "gradual withering away of the state in the favor of direct self-
management of society" would be ensured by the current
socioeconomic and political system (Badiou 2017).

YUGOSLAV IDEA

The Yugoslav idea managed to survive two extremely difficult challenges in the twentieth century: the collapse of the Kingdom of Yugoslavia in 1941 and the 1991-1992 disintegration of the SFRY. Even after everything that had happened in the territory of former Yugoslavia, it still has its admirers among all South Slavic peoples, although their admiration is more silent than declarative. The Yugoslav idea used to be

> ...a signpost in history for the South Slavs, sometimes a light that shone in the darkness. It was born, developed and it collapsed in various ways, as a cultural, political or state-building idea. It carried the hope that together we would be more free, more independent and stronger than we were under the foreigner. The disintegration of Yugoslavia, the way it had played out and the consequences it had left behind, pushed this idea to the edge of the past. It is still preserved in the memory of many citizens. It is not uncommon for people today to admit that we lived better in Yugoslavia. In the 1970s and 1980s, standard of living was pretty high, unemployment was negligible, social security was expanded, pensions were guaranteed, education was free, and health care was available. Life was, despite different restrictions, more dignified than in the countries of Eastern Europe, which suffered under totalitarian regimes, marked by Stalinism. Year after year, progress was noticeable, it inspired a certain confidence, it encouraged (Matvejević 2014: 2).

The Yugoslav idea has survived the disintegration of socialist Yugoslavia because the South Slavic peoples are ethnically, linguistically, and culturally very close, and they need each other in every way, especially economically and marketwise, because they are deeply interconnected by thousands of threads—regardless of their nationalist madness and retrograde ideologies that unfortunately dominated the area of former Yugoslavia for too long. The overall socioeconomic development and political relations over the past three decades in the Western Balkans region, the so-called *Yu-region*, have largely confirmed the thesis that the mixture of aggressive nationalism and backward political consciousness is an explosive mass equal to the destructive power of an atomic bomb.

The disintegration of Yugoslavia did not bring any good to any newly created South Slavic state. All of them were better off when they were a part of Yugoslavia than they are now, both domestically and externally.

Political and economic relations in former Yugoslavia, the Balkans, and Southeastern Europe have become extremely complex, burdened with unpredictable risks and threats to peace and general security, and not only because of the open and very complicated issue of Kosovo. All previous efforts by the administrations of the global centers of power—and the international community in general—to establish a "sustainable order" in the Balkans have not proved effective enough. The policies that these centers are now pursuing in the Balkans are not able to provide a long-term solution for the problems that were created by allowing and even enabling the disintegration of Yugoslavia. Simply put, the "Balkanization" of the Balkans is not the way to solve the life problems the Balkan peoples face on a daily basis, and instead only serves to constantly sow discord among them and govern them from the sidelines.

It seems that the only right and possible solution to get out of the vicious circle of the "Balkanization" of the Balkans is for all South Slavic and Balkan nations to turn to each other to look at the future, and not at their difficult past. The Yugoslav idea, which guided Serbia in waging the Great War of 1914-1918 for the liberation and unification of Serbs, Croats, and Slovenes, is needed by the South Slavic peoples now more than ever before on the threshold of the third decade of the twenty first century. This idea, which is historically democratic and libertarian, is now re-emerging as the only guideline for overcoming the impasse at which the South Slavic peoples and their fragmented states find themselves. Such as they are, they do not have and can never individually have a place on the global political and economic scene as it was held by Yugoslavia and its peoples together.

The future of the South Slavic peoples lies in the affirmation of the modern Yugoslav idea of the twenty first century; in its revival and redesign; in its free and democratic return to real political life in the Balkans, as it happened after the bloodshed of World War II, when Tito's second Yugoslavia was built on the Yugoslav idea of the twentieth century. Initiating the process of creating a *new, modern democratic community of all South Slavic peoples* and beyond is the only real option for the exit of the Balkan peoples from their current deep economic crisis and for sustainable future development. The formation of such a democratic community would be appropriate for a new time of the globalization of economy, law, and politics, which are primarily oriented toward closer economic, infrastructural, and technological connections and the integration of the South Slavic and Balkan peoples.

Of course, any possible attempt at the automatic reconstruction of the Yugoslav state, which fell apart in 1991 and 1992, would be equal to utopia and foredoomed to failure.

> Common state is not the only precondition for cooperation with other nations, near and far, especially with those with whom our destiny, language and history were interconnected. The permeability of borders and the exchange of goods, material and spiritual, the encounters of people and meetings of cultures,

the flow of ideas and the transmission of experiences, the confrontation of creators and their works have become the criteria of modern civilization. They do not diminish identities in any way and do not endanger the independence of nations. Whoever does not know how to recognize them and does not want to accept them is condemned to relive the past, its worse part (Matvejević 2014: 10).

12.

TRANSFORMATION OF SOCIALIST SELF-MANAGEMENT INTO CAPITALISM

There comes a time when wisdom is quiet,
ignorance starts speaking and corrupt become rich.

Ivo Andrić

After the disintegration of socialist Yugoslavia, the newly formed states—to be precise, the tiny states that emerged from the SFRY's ruins—were faced "with looting and corruption on a large scale, with unprecedented privatization, with debts for which there was no coverage, with daily increase in unemployment which increasingly affects the younger generation in particular" (Matvejević 2014: 2).

MASSIVE PRIVATIZATION: LIQUIDATION OF SOCIETAL OWNERSHIP

The Federal Republic of Yugoslavia (FRY) was established on April 27, 1992 by Serbia and Montenegro, two republics of the former SFRY. The FRY immediately began making radical changes in the existing system of property relations, transforming socialist social relations into capitalist social relations. The means of production (capital) of social self-managed enterprises, which were in social ownership mode, were transferred into state ownership. Legally and at short notice, socially owned enterprises became state-owned enterprises. The responsibilities of self-managed organizational bodies of socially owned enterprises (workers' councils and the executive bodies of workers' councils) were transferred to the responsible state institutions. That was only a temporary solution, however. The main goal was the transformation of state-owned enterprises into private, capitalist enterprises. It was the next ultimate step: selling the assets of state-owned enterprises—that is, former socially owned enterprises—to private enterprises and entrepreneurs at a certain price.

In order to carry out this operation as successfully as possible, the state set up the Privitization Agency of Serbia. Its job was to sell the property of state-owned enterprises to interested private enterprises and entrepreneurs—domestic or foreign. Through measures of mass privatization—tender and auction sales, mass voucherization, and free allocation of internal shares to employees and pensioners—the assets (capital) of state enterprises passed into the hands of new private owners. That action was largely reminiscent of the original accumulation of capital from the time capitalism was born.

The central problem in the process of state capital privatization—to be exact, capital taken by the state—was determining its real selling price. Unlike workers, self-managers in socially owned enterprises knew the value and price of this capital very well because they created it through working for many years, which was not the case with civil servants in the Privatization Agency. Objectively, the employees in the Privatization Agency were not able to realistically estimate the value and determine the selling price of state capital because they did not directly participate in its creation. Apparently, that wasn't that important. The most important task was to strictly adhere to and consistently implement the neoliberal motto of the ruling party and state structures in society: "Privatize, privatize as soon as possible, it doesn't matter how you do it, it is essential that you do so immediately and radically" (Komazec 2008: 51).

Therefore, in the process of privatization, the most important task was to transfer state capital from the state into private hands as soon as possible and at any cost, regardless of whether those hands were clean or dirty or whether the funds used to make those purchases came from legal or illegal sources. The end result of such an approach to privatization was negative. The property (capital) of state-owned enterprises was sold, i.e. privatized, at a price which was, as a rule, well below its market value. The effects of privatization would have been incomparably better if the decisions about the sale of social (state) capital were made directly by workers—self-managers in socially owned enterprises—instead of government officials in the privatization agency. After all, in the history of real estate trade, it is well-known that the price of a house is always lower if it is sold by the son who did not build it than if it is sold by the father who built it. This was similar to the relationship between civil servants in the Privatization Agency and self-managed workers in socially owned enterprises during the privatization process of their social (state-owned) capital.

All privatization contracts were more or less concluded to the detriment of the state, society, and ultimately to the detriment of the workers from whom this property was forcibly taken. In almost all privatized enterprises, former self-managed workers were immediately dismissed as redundant, lost their jobs very soon after privatization, or were constantly harassed by their new private owners. A large number of workers found themselves in an incomparably worse economic and social position than before—not only in comparison to the time of socialist self-management after 1950, but to the years of post-war state socialism after 1945. Even after World War II, when the new Yugoslav socialist (communist) government by revolutionary measures confiscated and nationalized the assets of private, capitalist enterprises and transformed them into property of state-socialist enterprises, with "just compensation," workers mostly did not lose their jobs.

Thus, the fate of former self-managed workers was definitely sealed. Their economic and social situation deteriorated dramatically. They soon realized that they were wrong not to try, in an energetic way, to prevent the state from transforming socially owned enterprises into state-owned enterprises and then in turn selling them to private entrepreneurs. It was a unique historical form of capitalist expropriation of the assets (means of production) of self-managed workers and the liquidation of their social ownership and socially owned enterprises, which was directed, of course, by the post-socialist state—and more precisely, by the anti-socialist state. The state's attitude toward former self-managed workers was, and still is, disingenuous, even humiliating, because it left the fate of self-managed workers to the unpredictable and uncontrollable whims of "newly minted capitalists."

The buyers of most former socially owned enterprises were private individuals who made a fortune through "getting by" in the murky waters of the 1990s. The "original accumulation of capital" was achieved by financial speculations in times of hyperinflation (foreign exchange hedge, etc.); robbery in the years of civil war in the territory of the former SFRY after its disintegration in 1991-1992; the smuggling of scarce goods, oil, cigarettes etc., often on behalf of the state at a time of international sanctions against the FRY; drug and white slave trade; tax evasion, etc.

Numerous "quasi-businessmen" emerged to the surface of society, becoming politically very active and influential. Many of them, however, were not qualified to manage the property purchased from the state in an economically rational manner. Their businesses did not operate successfully, and they were forced to sell quickly, leaving workers unemployed. In such relationships, the negative effects of privatization were inevitable.

Among the purchasers of state-owned enterprises who were "prone to business," were quite a few socially privileged individuals: former ministers, their assistants and advisers, banking officials—from vice governors, to sector directors and heads of banking departments, directors of some socially-owned enterprises and their close associates, local government officials, as well as officials of some political parties.

Only a small number of state-owned enterprises (former socially owned enterprises), passed into the hands of real businessmen and authentic entrepreneurs who created and increased their own private capital solely through their own work and dedication to business. Through their knowledge, giving up and saving, these businessmen earned their success through relentless competition in the domestic and foreign markets. Such privatizations were mostly successful and turned out to be socially justified. However, some true local businessmen were not interested in buying state-owned enterprises, considering state-owned capital to be "cursed" and believing it could do no good to anyone, instead only causing problems.

An important element in the process of the transformation of socialist into capitalist relations was, and still is, *the restitution of private property* confiscated after World War II because of the implementation of nationalization and other measures of liquidating capitalist ownership in Yugoslavia. In accordance with the law, the state undertook the obligation to return the confiscated property to the rightful owners in its original condition. If, for objective reasons, this was not feasible, the state was then obliged to provide financial compensation for the lost property. This rectified a great injustice that the post-war Yugoslav socialist government had inflicted on private owners who earned their property through honest work.

TURBID PRIVATIZATION: APPEARANCE OF WILD CAPITALISM

Many privatizations of state-owned enterprises were carried out in suspicious ways, with not only dirty but also fictitious capital behind them. "Resourceful individuals" bought these enterprises with no capital of their own. Thanks to their state and party connections, they were able to take out short term loans, which provided them with the necessary funds for the purchase of the enterprise, and then they would immediately pay these loans back using bank loans obtained based on a pledge (mortgage) on the property of the already-purchased enterprises. In the process of selling state-owned enterprises, the responsible state authorities did not inspect the origin of the capital used for their purchase, and objectively, they could not have done it. In the transition from socialism to capitalism, the Social Accounting and Auditing Service (SDK) had been abolished, which was the only agency able to control the total cash flows in the country. Thus, in the years of transition after the "fall of communism," the birth of wild capitalism was legally enabled.

The new owners of privatized enterprises generally did not know how to manage them properly or how to maintain their manufacturing process. None of these owners managed to create a single new product that would be recognizable on the market—not even on the domestic, let alone global, market. They only knew how to import goods and sell them on the domestic market at a much higher price than their import cost. The state has also helped enterprise owners in this by selling them foreign currency from the national bank at the lower official exchange rate than the real, market rate. Thus, many important industrial manufacturing enterprises have been shut down, and only ruins and industrial graveyards are all that remains of the once successful and good socially owned enterprises.

In the years of the euphoric transition from socialism to capitalism, individuals acquired their initial private capital and wealth by hunting in the murky waters of false, predatory privatizations rather than by their knowledge and work. Out of the murky waters of these privatizations, which were pervaded with corruption, a new layer of wealthy individuals, the "new capitalists," have emerged to the surface of society, a group who has grown into a new expropriatory and exploitative economic and political class. The members of this "new capitalist class" became increasingly rich as they stole property from workers, society and the state—that is, their wealth grew while employees in privatized socially owned enterprises and society became poorer.

Such enrichment of some and impoverishment of others in society has taken place on the basis of laws created according to the selfish and predatory interests of the newly created political party elite, which identified itself with democracy and declared itself the bearer of democratic social changes.

TYCOONIZATION OF SOCIETY

Most members of this social stratum or class of "new capitalists" were labeled in society— especially in the cultural public—as tycoons and controversial businessmen. A large part of the financial power of society poured into their hands. Their influence on the decision-making process at the top of society in government and parliament remains exceptional even today. Such relations and the situation created in the economy and society are referred to as *tycoonization*—a term which mainly denotes the engagement in private business by war profiteers and privileged party and state cadres starting in the 1990s.

Tycoons and controversial businessmen have become a serious social problem. Some of them have already been identified. Criminal and other court proceedings have been initiated, conducted, or are being conducted against such persons with the aim of confiscating the property which they have "legally and legitimately" stolen from the working people, society, and the state in the years of transition from socialism to capitalism. Due to inefficiencies of the courts, the outcomes have not been as expected.

13.

WAS THE CAPITALIST PRIVATIZATION NECESSARY?

Today, at a sufficient historical distance from the "fall of communism" and the disintegration of Yugoslavia, the question can be asked whether the privatization of successful socially owned enterprises was necessary. Professor Branko Horvat, Ph.D, a Nobel Prize in Economics nominee in 1983 and one of the most talented Yugoslav and Croatian economists, once advocated for a model of market socialism and was explicitly against the privatization of socially owned, self-managed enterprises.

Professor Horvat claims that the

> Yugoslav economy was the most private economy in Europe, because the members of the workers' councils and boards of directors were private individuals, not civil servants. Therefore, there was nothing to privatize. And yet, it was done in such a way that the state first seized all the social capital, and then sold it to foreign capital and its favorites, often at bargain prices. This is where two different privatizations can be noticed, the capitalist and the socialist. Capitalist privatization is being pushed by IMF. In Yugoslav countries, it is mainly reduced to the sellout of people's property to foreign capital. Socialist privatization was carried out in 1950-1952, when state-owned enterprises were handed over to employees'

management, that is, when self-management was introduced. Socialist privatization led to extremely rapid economic development. Capitalist privatization has led to backwardness (Horvat 2002).

From the standpoint of economic efficiency and rationality instead of capitalist privatization, it would have been incomparably more useful if socialist privatization had been finalized—if the workers of socially-owned enterprises had essentially become, in the formal and legal sense, co-owners of the means of production, that is, of the social capital in "their" enterprises.

The list of successful Yugoslav socially owned enterprises—which should not have been privatized according to capitalist principles—that were well-known and recognized in domestic and foreign markets was really long. For example, the Belgrade construction work organizations Energoprojekt, Trudbenik, Rad, Planum, Napred, PIM-Ivan Milutinović, and others in the construction business communities (consortia), such as INGRA from Zagreb, were very successful competitors to many large global companies in public procurements in Africa, Latin America, and Asia. The annual foreign currency income of Yugoslav construction operations reached up to three billion U.S. dollars.

The factory Prva petoletka from Trstenik (PPT), with almost 20,000 employees, exported about 40 percent of its hydraulic systems and other high-tech products to more than thirty countries on several continents, and intensively cooperated with large global companies such as Boeing, Bugatti, Lucas, Bendix, Daimler, Martin Merkel, Paul-Mott, Orsta Hydraulik, Wabco Westinghouse, Linde Guldner, Ermeto and ZF Friedrichshafen. Agricultural Combine Belgrade (PKB) was one of the largest and most successful agricultural companies in Europe. Goša from

Smederevska Palanka was a giant of the Yugoslav economy and machine building.

Energoinvest from Sarajevo is a world-renowned enterprise, especially in the design and production of expensive and specific energy equipment for nuclear power plants. Geneks from Belgrad had, at its peak, about three hundred offices around the world. In New York City alone, there have been over sixty offices of various Yugoslav enterprises and several Yugoslav banks. Men's suits from Beogradska konfekcija (Beko) from Belgrade and Mura from Murska Sobota were highly valued in Manhattan, the heart of New York City. Parachute fabric produced by the Belgrade factory Kluz was among the best in the world. Metalworking machines with built-in electronics, produced by the socially owned company Ivo Lola Ribar in Železnik, Belgrade, were highly valued in Germany. Ivo Lola Ribar were among the first to start producing computers. Skis from the enterprise Elan, due to their indisputable quality, are among the most sought after on the global market, and the world champion alpine skier Ingemar Stenmark has skied on them.

In a unique production technology chain, Yugoslav socially owned enterprises have manufactured fighter jets and tanks, which proved to be among the best in the world in desert warfare. Yugoslav shipyards have manufactured ocean, sea, and river boats sought after on the global market. The socially owned enterprises of Yugoslavia produced wagons and locomotives, designed and built hydroelectric power plants, thermal power plants, and other energy facilities, designed and built ironworks, opened mines, and have been highly engaged in geological research.

The "Belgrade hand" and "Belgrade knee prosthesis," created at the Belgrade School of Robotics at the "Mihajlo Pupin" Institute in Zvezdara, Belgrade, left a permanent mark on the global field of humanoid robotics. Nuclear scientists worldwide have closely followed the results of the research and work of the Yugoslav nuclear institutes Vinča in Belgrade, Ruđer Bošković in Zagreb, and Jožef Stefan in Ljubljana.

Some other successful Yugoslav socially owned enterprises were: Litostroj, TAM, Tomos, Gorenje, Iskra, Rade Končar, Rudi Čajavec, Vutex, Torpedo, TAS, Šipad, IMT, Minel, MIN, Crvena zastava, IMR, Zmaj, IMK 14. oktobar, Ikarus, Insa, Utva, EI Niš, RIZ, Jugometal, FAP, Prva iskra, Barič, HIP Petrohemija, Jugodrvo, Robna kuća Beograd, Centroprom, Jugoeksport, Centrotekstil, Radoje Dakić, KAT (KAP), EI Obod, Galenika, Hemofarm, Pliva, Krka, Alkaloid, and many more.

The stories of almost every one of these aforementioned Yugoslav socially owned enterprises have a sad ending. These and many other successful socially owned enterprises have fallen victim to the strict, uncritical, and reckless implementation of the mass privatization policy imposed by the Washington Consensus.

Of course, socialist Yugoslavia also had unsuccessful enterprises and economically failed investments whenever political and nationalist interests were put ahead of market demands—when political and nationalist interests were given more importance than the real supply and demand relations on domestic and global markets. Nevertheless, the number of successful socially owned enterprises in socialist Yugoslavia was incomparably higher than the number of unsuccessful ones. Furthermore, only unsuccessful enterprises—if there were no appropriate material or other conditions for their lasting economic recovery through social ownership—should have undergone capitalist privatization, and even then, only after their preparation for this form of privatization.

In the Federative Republic of Brazil, for example, when a strong state economy sector was formed after the fall of the military dictatorship (which lasted from 1964 to 1985), the new democratic government—especially under President Fernando Henrique Cardoso in the 1990s—carried out the privatization of insufficiently successful and unsuccessful state enterprises by technologically, economically, and organizationally improving them before selling them to foreign and domestic private partners, thus raising their sale price. In the states created after the fall of the SFRY, however, the prevailing practice was to sell unsuccessful and successful socially owned enterprises at a price that was, as a rule, lower than their real price after the disintegration and abandonment of the socialist self-managed system. Thus, a huge part of social capital was legally drained and poured into private ownership.

14.

IMPLICATIONS OF THE WASHINGTON CONSENSUS

*Liberalize as much as you can, privatize as fast as you can
and stay firm in your fiscal and monetary policy.
Do what we say, not what we do.*

Washington Consensus Directives

The transformation of socialist productive and social relations into capitalist relations after the historic victory of the capitalist West over "communism" in Eastern and Southeastern European countries—including the USSR—took place in accordance with the ten principles of the Washington Consensus. These principles were "served" as recommendations to former socialist countries as a guide for their future economic and social development on the basis of neoliberal capitalism. The West did not leave the transformation of socialist to capitalist relations to the autonomous will of authorities in former socialist countries or to any spontaneous development of these relations.

The ten principles or ten recommendations of the Washington Consensus, originally stated in 1989 by English economist John Williamson, were:

1. Low government borrowing. Avoidance of large fiscal deficits relative to GDP;

2. Redirection of public spending from subsidies ('especially indiscriminate subsidies') toward broad-based provision of key pro-growth, pro-poor services like primary education, primary health care and infrastructure investment;

3. Tax reform, broadening the tax base and adopting moderate marginal tax rates;

4. Interest rates that are market determined and positive (but moderate) in real terms;

5. Competitive exchange rates;

6. Trade liberalization: liberalization of imports, with particular emphasis on elimination of quantitative restrictions (licensing, etc.); any trade protection to be provided by low and relatively uniform tariffs;

7. Liberalization of inward foreign direct investment;

8. Privatization of state enterprises;

9. Deregulation: abolition of regulations that impede market entry or restrict competition, except for those justified on safety, environmental and consumer protection grounds, and prudential oversight of financial institutions;

10. Legal security for property rights.

(Williamson 1990, Williamson 2003, Williamson 2004; Bukvić 2011).

These ten Washington Consensus recommendations are usually summarized into three general requirements: (1) macroeconomic stabilization, (2) price liberalization, and (3) massive privatization.

The Washington Consensus principles/recommendations have been accepted by the World Bank (WB) and the International Monetary Fund (IMF), which are leading Washington-based international financial institutions, as well as by the U.S. Department of the Treasury, giving the Washington Consensus principles/recommendations a special global and globalist dimension. All former socialist countries in which communist regimes fell during the "colored" revolutions were de facto forced, and often conditioned in financial and other ways, to strictly adhere to the principles of the Washington Consensus when pursuing macroeconomic policy and in their overall development.

Sovereign states created by the disintegration of socialist Yugoslavia, as well as most other former socialist states in Europe, uncritically and wholeheartedly accepted the recommended principles of the Washington Consensus and mostly mechanically implemented them. No matter how much the new authorities in these formerly socialist states were in favor of and attached to these principles, which ideologically and politically symbolized the neoliberal concepts of capitalist order and development, and no matter how economically logical they sounded, came into conflict with the given economic and social reality of these countries. The desired economic and other effects expected from the transition and transformation into capitalist relations were not achieved. Why? Because the principles of the Washington Consensus were turned into a political dogma of universal significance and were unadjusted to the real economic situation, conditions, and specifics of the social environments in these formerly socialist states.

Economically successful socially owned enterprises run directly by workers through workers' assemblies and indirectly through workers' councils should not have been privatized. These enterprises were constantly adapting to market demands, especially after the Yugoslav social and economic reforms of 1965, and struggled with private capitalist enterprises on demanding world markets. They strived to get to know the markets' nature, strengths, and weaknesses, respecting the practice of free market pricing and the objectivity of the "world price" criterion, striving to find out what could be sold or bought in foreign markets under the most favorable conditions and took into account consumer preferences, not only in domestic but also in foreign markets.

After a new democratic government was created in Serbia on October 5, 2000 that was formed in the Democratic Opposition of Serbia (DOS), mainly in Serbia and partly in the former FRY, the Serbian government, instead of providing comprehensive support and assistance to social enterprises which were successful on the market, decided to strictly implement the directives of the Washington Consensus, privatizing not only these enterprises, but everything they could.

Why was the mass privatization of successful socialist socially owned enterprises one of the main political priorities for the new DOS government? Because those enterprises were the embodiment of socialist self-management and its economic validity and market vitality. In practice, they were an insurmountable obstacle for the practical implementation of the Washington Consensus recommendations. That is why the ideologues and theorists of neoliberalism and the responsible executive holders of political power insisted that all successful social enterprises, beyond any economic justification and business logic, should be removed from the political, economic, and market scene, regardless of their destiny—that is, the destruction that awaited them.

On the other hand, however, the attitude of official liberal capitalist ideology and politics toward unsuccessful social enterprises has been quite different. The process of privatization has been incomparably slower. Some of these unsuccessful enterprises, even though they have been bankrupted for a very long time, have still not been privatized or liquidated. They are now taken care of by well-paid so-called state bankruptcy trustees. The long-term maintenance of failed social enterprises in whatever condition possible is further evidence for neoliberal apologists that the self-managed economic system is not economically valid and should be forgotten and not even mentioned anymore. The only valid system for them is the capitalist economic system. Meanwhile, the emergence of economically unsuccessful private enterprises in this system does not call into question its foundations.

Judging by the overall economic results achieved in the past three decades in the formerly socialist Yugoslavia, an argument can be made that the liberal capitalist economic system based on the domination of private property and embraced by sovereign states created after the dissolution of Yugoslavia has not shown its economic advantage over the earlier Yugoslav socialist economic system, which was based on social ownership and self-management. On the contrary, the self-managed economic system was incomparably more fruitful than the current capitalist system. Sovereign states created in the ruins of socialist Yugoslavia, when looked at as a whole, have not yet managed to reach 40 percent of the Yugoslav industrial production of 1989. The total foreign debt of the former Yugoslav republics today is more than ten times higher than the Yugoslav debt in 1992—and effectively must be at least two to three times higher when taken into account that world currencies, including the U.S. dollar, have lost their former real value in the meantime (i.e. they have been devalued). None of these new states have managed to launch any product that would make them recognizable on the global market. Very few CEOs of private companies in these countries today can, in terms of their professional abilities and business achievements, compare themselves with the directors of many of the most successful socially owned companies in socialist Yugoslavia, who were the modern socialist managerial elite and highly valued in global business circles.

The consequences of implementing the mass privatization policy inaugurated by the Washington Consensus have been extremely painful for the workers of numerous socially owned enterprises in addition to the huge material damage done to the economy. By hastily turning socially owned enterprises into state-owned enterprises, the state simply excluded workers from negotiating the terms of their privatization and sale, even though the assets of those enterprises were directly created by the workers, not by the state and its officials. It was an act of real expropriation of the social property of associated workers.

In fact, the ultimate goals and effects of privatizations carried out in the transition of former socialist countries was to push workers to the social margin, to create as powerful a capitalist class as possible, and to transform common social wealth, accumulated over centuries, into the private property of members of that class, especially in its contemporary generation of tycoons.

In the parliamentary elections held in Serbia on May 6, 2012, the democratic government constituted after October 5, 2000, personified by the Democratic Party and led by then-president Boris Tadić, suffered an electoral defeat. Many citizens who were victims of the mass privatizations of socially owned enterprises simply did not support the policies and achievements of the Democratic Party. The coalition Let's Get Serbia Moving, headed by the conservative Serbian Progressive Party and led by its then-president Tomislav Nikolić, won the election convincingly and has been in power in Serbia ever since.

The Democratic Party has been blamed, justifiably or not, for the great plunder of the property of socially owned enterprises and the collapse of the Serbian economy in the years when it was in power. The Progressive Part of Serbia capitalized on this sentiment very successfully, which worked in its favor. Meanwhile, the ratings of the Democratic Party and other political parties that were once aligned with the DOS, which was the bearer of political and democratic changes in 2000, have fallen very low, and some have disappeared entirely from the political scene.

According to the results of a public opinion survey in Serbia, conducted in November of 2019 by the National Democratic Institute (NDI), an American non-profit, non-partisan and non-governmental organization, with support from the U.S. Agency for International Development (USAID), the coalition around the Serbian Progressive Party is supported by 34 percent of the citizens, and the coalition that would include the Democratic Party, the Party of Freedom and Justice, the Serbian Movement Dveri, the New Party, and the Social Democratic Party is supported by just six percent of respondents in the upcoming elections. Seven percent of citizens said they would vote for the electoral list of the Socialist Party of Serbia and United Serbia. Most small political parties are below this threshold (Stojanović 2020).

15.

IS THE RESTITUTION OF PROPERTY STOLEN FROM WORKERS POSSIBLE?

The situation in post-socialist states is economically, politically, and socially unsustainable. It must change. Any privatization of a socially owned or state enterprise found to be predatory, unjustified and unjust, or have stolen property (social capital) from workers, society, or the state, should be annulled and the process of its restitution should be initiated (i.e., the process of giving back to those who had created this property in their enterprises). There are relevant accounting records of all such privatizations based on which restitution can be carried out, provided, of course, there is an appropriate political willingness to do so.

The property of any controversial businessman determined by appropriate legal procedures that it was acquired illegally should be placed under the legal order of sequestration, and stay under it until there is legal evidence of its origin (i.e. until it is proven how, through which channels, and by what means it was acquired). This would be one of the desirable measures necessary for the political, economic, and social recovery of post-socialist societies such as Serbia.

The return of property seized from workers could be carried out in accordance with a model similar to one recently applied in Serbiain cases of restitution of property expropriated from its owners at the end and after World War II by the measures of mass collectivization—nationalization, confiscation, and sequestration.

Restitution of social property expropriated from the workers would be, in fact, the expropriation of expropriators under the new conditions. Its benefits would be manifold. The society and the state would collect part of the missing domestic monetary accumulation, which is currently being spent unproductively by owners of socially owned enterprises with the mentality of "if you got it, spend it." These owners boast luxury yachts, private planes, luxurious villas, and the most expensive cars and travels around the world. In Serbia today, for example—as well as in almost all post-transitional societies in general—no one mentions the importance of domestic accumulation, simple and extended reproduction, or the need to rely on the state's own forces in economic and social development, which are the preconditions for sustainable development and the exit from the maze of contemporary neocolonial economic and political dependence.

Increasing the volume of domestic accumulation would significantly reduce the need for foreign investments and foreign loans. In the long run, reliance on domestic sources of accumulation is the only guarantee of the stable and dynamic economic development of a society. Every foreign loan—even cheap ones with low interest, an appropriate grace period, and long repayment period—is a material burden on the current and future working generation that they have to pay back. As soon as the repayment of the foreign loan principal begins, regardless of how favorable the interest rate is, foreign debt becomes expensive, especially when such a loan is not rationally invested economically or when the developed capacity does not bring adequate income results, which is often the case.

Is it possible to return the property expropriated from the workers?

It is a fact that expropriated workers, many of whom have already died or retired, have almost no social power to fight for and win their material rights expropriated by false and predatory privatizations.

Therefore, there is not a single authentic political party on the side of labor, while there are many on the side of the capital.

It is also more than likely that the national and global centers of neoliberal capitalist power, and especially those in the West, would be fiercely opposed to such a systemic measure because it directly materially interferes with the essence of established capitalist relations in all former socialist countries in Eastern Europe. The rich, tycoons, and even the state, which is in the hands of the rich and the tycoons, would not be willing to accept such a solution.

Only in more radically altered social relations, if the power passed from the hands of the political right into the hands of the political parties of the true left, could the restitution of property stolen from workers by false and predatory privatizations be possible. Such restitution would be a measure of a new expropriation of the property of the newly created expropriating capitalist class, which they had acquired by stealing socially owned and state-owned enterprises in the murky waters of privatization.

16.

EXPROPRIATION OF ASSETS INVESTED INTO THE PENSION FUND

Old age and poverty, one of these two troubles suffice.

Chinese proverb

Some of the biggest losers of the transition in Serbia and the biggest victims of the privatization of state enterprises are workers who reached the end of their working lives and retired, i.e., pensioners who are, economically and socially, in the most vulnerable social stratum. Pensioners in Serbia and other former Yugoslav republics have been especially impacted by the material and other consequences of these social changes and suffered because of them. During their working life, they usually lived with relatively low personal incomes because they tended to set aside a big part of their earned income for investments in their enterprises, in new technologies, and in economic and social development, believing that such dedicated behavior would pay off manifold in their retirement. With such an attitude toward development, by "tightening their belt," they managed to create numerous highly successful economic organizations (enterprises) and economic conglomerates (consortia), well-known and recognized not only in domestic but also foreign markets. In the first fifteen years of socialist Yugoslavia, at times up to 65 percent of domestic national income was allocated for investments. New factories, power plants, mines, roads, bridges, hospitals, schools, colleges, apartments, and

155

entire cities were built across the country as a result of millions of workers' efforts. It is the life's work of the current generation of retirees and many workers who are no longer alive.

The expectations of pensioners, however, have not come true. Many successful socially owned enterprises have disappeared entirely from the economic scene. Most private enterprises that emerged from the ruins of socially owned enterprises, as well as those created independently from the privatization of socially owned enterprises, have not been able to stop the decline in industrial and other production or the obsolescence of the technological basis of the economy, and there has thus been a general falling behind in development and a drastic decline in social gross product. This has been largely contributed by many other factors: the economic sanctions of the international community against FRY in the 1990s, the disintegration of Yugoslavia and the destruction of its common market, the civil war in former Yugoslavia from 1991-1995, and the NATO bombing of the FRY in 1999.

A direct consequence of the decline in social gross product has been the increase in the state budget deficit. In order to consolidate the unsatisfactory budget situation in the country, the state has taken away a part of the pensions of higher-income pensioners by administrative measures—through bureaucratic force, bypassing the legal system. During their working life, these workers allocated the most funds from their gross income for retirement insurance and invested them in the state pension fund. The state thus took away a part of these pensioners' monetary property, which had been earned by their dedicated work and accumulated in the pension fund.

There are exact bookkeeping and statistical records on pensioners' assets—that is, part of their lives' work—accumulated in the pension fund. The data clearly shows, individually and specifically, how much someone allocated from their gross income for retirement insurance during their active working life. The amount of the insurer's retired pay, determined at the end of his working life, is based on this data. Furthermore, there are exact statistics of when, to whom, and for what purposes the accumulated funds paid were paid from the Pension Insurance Fund (PIF). When it comes to state property, this data cannot be mystified and must be made available to the public so everyone can see who made contributions to create this property, and how much have they individually contributed.

Pensions are the monetary right of pensioners acquired during their working life by making regular payments, which were required by law, to the state pension fund. Therefore, the obligation of the state is to guarantee not only the acquired right of the retiree to a pension, but also to the real amount of their pension. The claim that "retirees are entitled to a pension, but not to its amount" does not have a legal, scientific, or ethical foundation. Moreover, the pension cannot be simply compared or equated with some other asset, such as inherited land. Pension is the monetary asset of retirees in a pension fund acquired through their work. It can be compared only to the funds from a savings account in a bank, and the pension payments to retirees from the pension fund can be compared to the withdrawal of a certain funds from the savings accounts.

No matter what political party forms the government in society, the duty of every responsible state is to pay retirees a real aliquot of the amount of money that they regularly paid every month in their working life to their pension fund and to respect the principles of solidarity in the pension insurance system in an appropriate manner. That is why pensions are not charity from the state or an expression of its generosity, but instead are the explicit material obligation of the state to retirees, which has a specific legal definition. The obligation of the state to retirees is the same as it was when it was obligated to pay depositors their savings in dinars and foreign currencies.

The state cannot transfer its indisputable and immediate material obligation to retirees to the current generation of employees. Repayment of pensions is not the responsibility of current employees. They do not support retirees—they work for themselves and their family, and by making payments to the pension fund, they are materially insured for their own old age. Bidding for the relation between the number of retirees and the number of employees in a country, which is often the case in Serbia, does not contribute to anything, but only pits these two generations in society against each other for no good reason.

If, on the other hand, the state mismanaged funds that flowed into the pension fund and spent them inappropriately, and therefore the funds for current pension payments were lacking, only the state must bear the responsibility for such behavior. It must provide all the missing funds for the payment of pensions and not reduce the pensions of innocent retirees because that would be stealing their earned assets.

Faster economic growth of the country and higher growth rate of gross social product is the only real method of ensuring an increase in cash flow into the pension insurance fund, which is needed for the payment of earned pensions. Additionally, a portion of those funds could possibly be provided by the restitution of employee assets from former socially owned enterprises that were confiscated from them by unjust and unjustified privatization. Among the possible options for providing the necessary funds for the full payment of pensions is an announcement of a national loan and taking out a special-purpose foreign loan.

The state and its government, current and future, should, in their relationship with retirees, always keep in mind the wise old saying, "If old age is not happy, the youth that comes after cannot be happy either."

17.

EXPLOITATION AS PRIVILEGE: PRECARIZATION, SLAVE-WORK AND PENURY

If workers are more insecure, that's very 'healthy' for the society, because if workers are insecure, they won't ask for wages, they won't go on strike, they won't call for benefits; they'll serve the masters gladly and passively. And that's optimal for corporations' economic health.

Noam Chomsky

Not to be exploited is no longer an ideal, but to be employed and constantly exploited.

Todor Kuljić

The systemic collapse of the socioeconomic position of workers in capitalist enterprises and society as a whole began in the time of Thatcher and Reagan, and continued and intensified after the "fall of communism." The exploitation of workers, working people, and the working nation in general has been drastically intensified by the constant underestimation of the role of labor and the overestimation of the role of capital in the creation of new values and their distribution. Daily living and working conditions of the broadest working strata in society have been constantly deteriorating and becoming increasingly difficult in every respect. Protection of workers, their rights, and their interests has fallen to the lowest possible level. Workers live in economic uncertainty and social insecurity. They are unsuccessfully fighting for the realization of their basic economic and social rights. For example, according to statistics published by Tanjug, a news agency from Belgrade, on March 6, 2016 there were about 40,000 labor disputes pending before courts in Serbia in 2016.

Millions of people around the world work occasional, temporary, undemanding, and poorly paid jobs with short-term or uncertain contracts and the constant threat of losing their jobs. When starting a new job, there is a practice of requiring a signature on a blank resignation so that the employer can dismiss the employee at any moment, without any consequences. Employers, the owners of capital, usually hire workers only to perform temporary and occasional jobs—not permanent ones. Working hours are part-time or rotating. Employees do not know when they work or how much they work. Owners force employees to work even 24 hours straight. Workers are "overjoyed" if their boss allows them to work 60 hours a week, under any conditions. The workers' right to a five-day or shorter working week is mentioned almost nowhere.

Workers' incomes are unpredictable; their wages are irregular and uncertain and they do not know how much they are being paid or when their pay day is. They are generally denied a number of benefits that were normal for previous generations: paid annual leave, paid sick leave, free or subsidized vocational training, cash transfers in case of losing their job, or retraining. The prospects for workers' professional advancements are very limited. Many workers are denied the right to annual leave by their bosses, and paid annual leave is considered a luxury. The owners of capital lay off workers on short notice, and workers often do not know the reason why. The position of female, pregnant, and disabled workers is especially difficult (Ružica, February 27–28, 2016).

In contemporary neoliberal capitalism, instead of workers (proletarians) and the working class (the proletariat), there are an increasing number of so-called precariats. The precariat is a new social class that is economically, socially, and politically most endangered, and often includes the social stratum that Marx once called the lumpen or the lumpenproletariat.

> In a trend parallel to the financialization of capitalism, and as a consequence of changes in technology and market organization, there has been discernible fragmentation of work, including of wage labor, in space and time. Whereas in the Federal Republic of Germany in 1970, the ratio between workers in fulltime employment and all others in the workforce doing part-time and short-time work or are temporarily and marginally employed—in other words, workers in so-called atypical employment conditions—was 5:1, this shifted by 1990 to 4:1 and to 2:1 by 2013. Every third person in 2013, then, was working either part-time, temporarily, on subcontract, or in a mini-job. The elasticity of gainful employment and the fluidity of working conditions are on the rise (Kocka 2016: 140).

The appearance of labor fragmentation, employment flexibility, and the fluidity of labor relations produced by the capitalist order further worsened the economic and social security of everyone in society living exclusively from their living labor—which are primarily the security of workers and the working class.

The process of precarization, which denotes a condition of job insecurity and diminished non-existent labor rights and protection at work, began in Europe in the 1970s with the gradual disintegration of welfare state. The introduction of atypical forms of employment, such as fixed-term employment, temporary, occasional, and incomplete forms of employment has not only cut labor costs for the owners of capital, but also allowed them to lay off employees more easily or to reduce their number in case of declining demand or cyclical market disruptions. Special agencies dealing with the "traffic" of workers in the country and abroad have also been legalized.

After the 1990s, workers, the working class, and other strata of working people have been the biggest victims of the "fall of communism" and the mass capitalist privatizations of state and socially owned enterprises. Their position has become socially and politically unbearable, and they are exploited perhaps even more than workers under nineteenth century capitalism. They have reached a state of complete penury, extreme poverty, and social misery. Even "the loss of their dignity and respect hits them almost harder than losing their job" (Harvey 2018: 196).

The greed of capitalists for as much profit as possible at any cost and by any means has no limits. In the continuing era of neoliberalism, the capitalist class has managed to impose "democratic" shackles of slave labor on working people in order to force them to work as much as possible with the same or lower wages, and to secure as much profit as possible for themselves, through the unpaid labor of workers.

Pope Francis frequently points out the acuteness and severity of the problem of slavery and slave labor around the world. In his message on the 48th World Day of Peace, he said, "Slavery is a terrible open wound on the body of contemporary society" (Pope Francis 2014/August 21).

Slave labor has become the central political, economic, social, and moral problem of contemporary neoliberal capitalism. The precariat armies around the world, created by existing neoliberal capitalism, are in a far worse economic and social position than the proletarians of Marx's time, whom he described in his scientific works. The precarious workers are left in the lurch. There is almost no one left in society to adequately protect them—neither the state, nor trade unions, which are becoming more and more powerless and bureaucratic. For instance, "only about 10 percent of American workers are in labor unions" (Rosenberg 2019). The governments of many states have become the boards of directors of big capital, caring only about the interests of the most powerful owners—capitalists and tycoons—and not about the interests of oppressed workers, the working class and all working strata in society.

Employers are free to do whatever they want. They can get away with anything or almost anything. They keep their workers "on a short leash," mistreat them, mob them, blackmail and underestimate them, force them to work overtime in difficult and dangerous conditions, dismiss them when they are seriously ill, do not pay them for months and years, and do not pay taxes and benefits. This is not a depiction of just some individual cases in many privatized enterprises, but of the general state of mind in most former socialist countries.

The position of workers and the working class may be even more difficult in some branches of global corporations that have located their capital in former socialist countries. The South Korean company Yura and the Croatian company Idea are examples of exploitative capital invested in Serbia. In these companies, workers do not know which is worse: their wages or their rights. They are at the same level as migrants who fled headlong from their countries affected by the chaos of war, behind which are the selfish interests of devoured global capital.

Firmly embraced by large capital, the state cares less and less about the basic needs of the owners of small and medium-sized private enterprises who created their capital exclusively through their own work, knowledge, and savings—and not by privatization of the state and social capital, regardless of their indisputably great economic importance and role in the development of society.

18.

MAO'S COMMUNISM AND DENG'S TRANSFORMATION OF CHINA

It doesn't matter whether a cat is white or black,
as long as it catches mice?
Let some people get rich first.

Deng Xiaoping

After a lengthy and persistent political and armed struggle and, ultimately, a triumphant victory over Chiang Kai-shek's army on October 1, 1949, the definitive victory of the socialist revolution in China was announced. On that day, the People's Republic of China was created as a united state led by Mao Zedong, the first prime minister of the central government of China. Regardless of the independence and originality of the Chinese socialist revolution, Chinese leadership was convinced that by looking to the Soviet experience in building socialism, China could be transferred as quickly as possible from its pre-revolution state as a semi-enslaved, semi-feudal, and semi-colonial country into the socialist-communist era (Mao Zedong 1968: 15 and 20).

In the late 1950s, however, the Communist Party of China introduced two new political methods into the process of building socialist Chinese society: the Great Leap Forward and the Great Proletarian Cultural Revolution.

The Great Leap Forward was the government takeover of the commanding heights of the economy—including the forced collectivization of agriculture—and an attempted industrialization campaign, comparable to Soviet economic policies in the 1930s. The Cultural Revolution was a program of purging society of 'counterrevolutionaries', 'saboteurs', and remnants of 'bourgeois' traditions, vaguely comparable to Stalin's Great Terror...

The period from, roughly, the beginning of the 1960s to the mid-1970s became the honeymoon period of Maoism...

This was, of course, a period during which millions of alleged 'saboteurs' and 'counterrevolutionaries' were executed, or worked to death in the Chinese version of the Gulags, the Laogai. The Great Leap Forward led to what may well have been the worst famine in human history. Taken together, Chinese socialism was responsible for about 65 million deaths, according to one estimate...

The claim that Maoist socialism was not 'real' socialism is a post-hoc fabrication. It *was* 'real' socialism. Until it was not (Niemietz 2019: 100–101 and 115).

The global crisis of socialism, which became drastically obvious at the end of the twentieth century, did not bypass the People's Republic of China, the leading Asian socialist country. The crisis in China, however, was resolved in a different way than in European socialist countries. Unlike these countries, China did not have a "colored revolution." The Chinese communist authorities used military force to prevent such reform of their social system.

In early June 1989, before the demolition of the Berlin Wall, mass peaceful student demonstrations erupted in China demanding a radical change of the situation and relations in communist China. The initial impetus of the students' massive protests was the sudden death of a prominent Chinese revolutionary and reformist Hu Yaobang, who had died of a heart attack on April 15, 1989. Many protestors believed that Yaobang's death was related to his forced resignation in January 1987. The demands of the leadership of the student movement were as follows: the full political rehabilitation of Hu Yaobang; revival of his legacy; affirmation of his views on democracy and freedom; acknowledgement that party campaigns against the "spiritual pollution" and "bourgeois liberalization" had been wrong; publication of information on the income of state leaders and their family members; enabling privately run newspapers and cessation of press censorship; increase in education funding and raise in intellectuals' pay; ending restrictions on demonstrations in Beijing; and providing objective coverage of students in official media. In short, the students demanded more freedom at the university, as well as full democratization and far-reaching political reforms throughout the society.

The domestic and international public encouraged Chinese students to persevere in their demands. It was precisely in those critical days that Soviet leader Mikhail Gorbachev paid a historic visit of reconciliation with Chinese leader Deng Xiaoping. He was given a ceremonial welcome at the airport, instead of Tiananmen Square or the Gate of Heavenly Peace, where foreign leaders had always been welcomed according to the Chinese protocol. Although he was not given the opportunity to come to Tiananmen Square, students cheered Gorbachev. They placed the sculpture "Goddess of Democracy," which visually resembled the Statue of Liberty in New York Harbor, in

Tiananmen Square. In addition to Beijing, protests broke out in more than 340 cities across China, even where there were no universities or students. Workers gave support to the students.

At the top of the Chinese state-party, there were major disputes between the two political currents, which were tentatively referred to as "liberal," led by the then-Secretary-General of the Central Committee of the Communist Party of China Zhao Ziyang, and "conservative," led by then-Chinese Prime Minister Li Peng. Ziyang opposed the use of force against students and their peaceful protests. Peng was the biggest ideological opponent of Ziyang and the late Hu Yaobang, who was also considered an advocate of the "liberals" among the leaders of China. Among the "liberals" were advocates of more radical political reforms, referred to as the "Western type," who claimed they would further accelerate the progress of the country. Many intellectuals advocated the "wholesale Westernization" of the Chinese society (Huntington 1997: 105)

Peng claimed, citing available intelligence data, that the student demonstrations were induced, inspired, and supported by the West, primarily by the United States, the place for the "Goddess of Democracy" was in New York Harbor and not Beijing's Gate of Heavenly Peace, a risky shift in reforms should not be rushed, student demonstrations had led to the destabilization of the county, and that force should be used against the protesters.

It was up to Deng Xiaoping, the great Chinese communist reformer, to make the divisive decision as an undisputed political authority in China. At the time, China was already reaping the fruits of liberal economic policy reforms and opening up to the world, which had been advocated for by Xiaoping in the late 1970s. Although he was close to the "liberals" in his beliefs, Xiaoping decided to energetically crush the student uprising and remove the sculpture the "Goddess of Democracy" from Tiananmen Square in Beijing. This was the last straw for the people at the top of the Chinese state-party, including Xiaoping himself (Stanojlović 1999).

On the evening of June 3, 1989, the army was ordered to enter Beijing to break the "counter-revolutionary uprising" and "clean up Tiananmen Square before dawn," but to "treat the students reasonably." Peaceful student demonstrations in Beijing ended tragically on June 4, 1989, when the Chinese army and police tanks ran over a large number of unarmed young people and innocent citizens, not only in Tiananmen Square, but in cities across China. The exact number of people killed is unknown. China officials stated that 218 civilians had been killed, while Western journalists in Beijing reported the deaths of several thousand protesters.

During the tumultuous June event, Ziyang left China's political scene and ended up under house arrest, where he remained for fifteen years.

Two years after Ziyang's death in 2005, Gene Sharp, an American political scientist—known as the Machiavelli of nonviolence and the Clausewitz of nonviolent warfare, a figure thought to be involved in violent and nonviolent regime changes around the world before and after the demolition of the Berlin Wall—admitted that he had been active even in China and that he was in Beijing on the Tiananmen "three or four days before breaking the students rebellion" (Pal 2007).

The events in Beijing's Tiananmen Square have been subjected to historical evaluations for three decades. In China, with the exception of Hong Kong, the student movement of June 1989 is still regarded as a "counter-revolutionary rebellion," and the outbreak of student demonstrations in Tiananmen Square "as just another foreign imposition" (Huntington 2000: 106).

Following the bloody Tiananmen event, China continued the route traced by Xiaoping by retaining the leading role of the Communist Party in managing the society and state, the sophisticated application of the classic capitalist style of business in Chinese social and economic conditions, and continuing China's opening to the world.

The People's Republic of China innovated its social system. It accepted many values of the Western social order, such as private property and free market, but kept its one-party communist system and state property in its economic system. China has built its own model of economic development derived from its social being and experience. Unlike the former socialist countries of Eastern Europe, China has not taken for granted the neoliberal economic philosophy, according to which only private property and the "invisible hand" of the market are guarantees of economic development and social wellbeing.

In the years after the Tiananmen democratic stampede, China has made steady economic and technological progress year after year, combining a strict communist-party dictatorship and classic capitalist-industrial discipline. The combination of these two essentially opposing styles of organizing society and state is incomprehensible and unacceptable to many outside China, but not inside. This combination has been operating successfully in China for almost three decades. The phenomenon of human rights is understood differently in China than in the West. The Chinese state-party leadership is proud of the fact that over the past two or three decades it has managed not only to save over four hundred million people from starvation, but also to create the material basis for an even better life, considering it the highest respect for human rights.

Thanks to Xiaoping's leadership skills, farsightedness, and agility, China has changed radically; it is very different than it was in the time of Mao Zedong. Ideologically, China has been able to timely break free from the Marxist dogma of the monopoly of state property in socialism. Private property has been systematically enabled and the development of the private sector has been encouraged in communist China while its system of state ownership and its state sector of economy have been simultaneously maintained, preserved, and developed, and remains very powerful—more precisely, superior. In addition to institutionalizing private property, China has also opted for commodity and market production but has not given up on long-term planning for its overall development. The consistent pursuit of long-term planning goals of socioeconomic development has remained the strategic ideological commitment of the Chinese Communist Party and a binding ideological and political task of all Chinese communists in their practice.

The Chinese communist government and Chinese capitalists have managed to reach a strategic agreement on China's long-term interests and what is best for their state at the present time and in the future. Modern China affirms day after day that mutual understanding between capitalists and communists is not only possible, but necessary for the country. The simultaneous existence of the private and state sector and their mutual competition has proved to be beneficial to China's economic revival and progress.

British historian Timothy Garton Ash, at a lecture held in Belgrade on February 13, 2019, said that China was the country that benefited the most from "the fall of communism."

> The communist rulers of China have learned a lesson from the fall of the Soviet Union and said 'we will not repeat the same mistakes.' That is why they have developed what we might call Leninist capitalism, combining the dynamics of the free market with the foundations of the Leninist political

system. Nobody even dreamed about that in 1999 (Radišić 2019).

The Communist Party of China remains the "leading political force of China" (Qinmin 2015: 203).

Despite the far-reaching changes that have taken place on a global scale in recent decades, China officially still adheres to Marxism as its leading political ideology and continues to publicly declare itself a communist country. Part of the global political left of Marxist orientation doubts that the Communist Party of China is still truly a communist party and suspects that current Chinese leadership pays more attention to capitalist than socialist values in the economic organization of Chinese society.

By introducing private property into its communist socioeconomic system with its doors wide open, China has enabled the organization of authentic capitalist forms of doing business, which has proven to be a very economically justified solution. Thanks to substantial changes made in its socialist system, China's economic development has been very dynamic during the last two or three decades, and in the middle of the second decade of the twenty first century, it managed to economically overtake the U.S. and the EU according to GDP, which is measured by purchasing power parity, and is set to become the leading economic power in the world.

It is estimated that GDP in 2017 was 23.2 billion dollars in China, 20.9 billion dollars in the EU and 19.4 thousand billion dollars in the U.S. (World Factbook/I/2019). Total GDP is, of course, not the only parameter on which the level of economic development of a country is measured. For example, it is estimated that in 2017, GDP per capita in the U.S. was 59,800 U.S. dollars and 16,700 U.S. dollars in China (World Factbook/II/2019).

Chinese experience seems to suggest that the future will be inclined toward societies and states that are not ideologically obsessed with capitalism, ex-socialism, the dogma of ownership, or the absolutization of one form of property to another—in other words, the future is not inclined to societies and states that allow their economic entities (enterprises, companies, and corporations) to operate in any possible form of ownership (personal, private, state, social, common, and collective), without any administrative hurdles, i.e., completely free.

Instead of uncritically embracing the neoliberal dogma of private property monopoly in designing its economic development strategy and implementing far-reaching economic reforms, China has resolutely opted for property pluralism, which authentically reflects the essence of the ancient Chinese wisdom: "Let a thousand flowers bloom." The historical depth of that wisdom was best understood by Deng Xiaoping, who tried to implement it in the Chinese state and economic reality as much as possible.

"The two major long-term goals" of contemporary China are: "building a modern prosperous society by 2020 and a modern socialist country by 2049." (Qingmin 2015: 8).

On a theoretical level, there are open questions about the real nature of the social system in contemporary China: is it truly a communist, socialist, or capitalist country, or the country with two different systems—socialist and capitalist—or something completely new and unknown to political history and science? According to the French philosopher Alain Badiou, "China has become a neocapitalist and bureaucratic state" (Badiou 2014).

Well-known contemporary Slovenian philosopher Slavoj Žižek believes that in China and Vietnam there is a "fusion between despotic communism and cruel capitalism" (Jacobson 2020).

With its positive trends, uncontested economic achievements, and accomplishments in other spheres of society, China has become a country of the very rich and the very poor, with threats of social and regional economic inequality.

The systemic reforms that have been implemented so far have moved China away from it being objectively possible that a just or more just, socially responsible or more responsible society can exist there. The social system in China is not "communist" if communism implies a classless society. Contemporary Chinese society is class-divided into private owners of capital and wage workers, despite the fact that China is still dominated by a political party that is called "communist."

In China, especially at local levels of state and social organization, discontent and resistance are increasingly noticeable because of the created social inequalities and constant differentiation of Chinese society into the rich who are getting richer and the poor who are getting poorer. "Chinese wage workers today certainly experience commodification, capitalist instrumentalization, uprooting, and exploitation in a manner that is roughly comparable with what European workers suffered during the first phase of industrialization, even if the Chinese experience has been compressed into a shorter time, making it especially disruptive." (Kocka 2016: 138).

The number of urban and rural poor people in China is increasing. Resistances are emerging and movements are being organized against such a social situation in the country. It is a threat and a challenge for current Chinese party and state leadership, and could, if China does not change for the better faster and more radically, be the cause of wider political discontent of the poor social strata, spontaneously or in an organized manner, with all the negative consequences which may arise.

In addition to social inequality, another urgent problem facing modern Chinese society is corruption, which is, above all, a product of the Chinese dual economic system. Practice shows that trade and cash flows between the private and the state sector entities are not being successfully subjected to control by the responsible state authorities, especially when individual civil servants succumb to bribery.

All in all, with the problems facing modern China and the justified and unjustified criticisms directed at China and China's social and economic system, China has, although it is not clearly defined in ideological and political terms, become a very serious competitor to neoliberal capitalism. Economic, technological, and other achievements of China, globally admired by many, are at the same time present a great challenge for some of the leading countries in the world. For instance, the current U.S. president, Donald Trump, openly states that contemporary China is not a partner of the U.S., but their rival.

A thorough study of the political and economic system of contemporary China and a more complete knowledge of its overall identity and accumulated experience, both positive and negative, could be of great practical use to many states seeking and tracing possible directions for their future socioeconomic development. All the more so because China has always been, to a large extent, enigmatic and unpredictable for the rest of the world. Fundamental values of the contemporary world order, such as democracy, human rights, and freedoms, do not have the same meanings in China and the rest of the world, and above all in the capitalist West. Throughout the long history of civilization, their philosophies and the paths of their social development have been different.

19.

CHANGES IN THE STRUCTURE OF SOCIAL LABOR

Science, scientific research, and education have become predominant productive forces and the generators of economic and general progress of society. Scientific achievements have resulted in, among other things, the technical and technological improvements of the production process and the use of robotic and digitized machines in the process of production of material goods and services. In the factory halls of some branches of the process industry—for example, in the automotive industry—robots have taken over or are taking over parts of traditional worker jobs. Robots have already become a competition to workers and in the future, near or far, they will be an even bigger competition. For example, a working hour of a welding robot is two to three times cheaper than a working hour of a welding worker. Robots reduce capital expenditures that would have traditionally been used for paying workers, and thus reduce the total operating costs of an enterprise. In addition, robots perform planned operations faster and more accurately compared to workers because they are technologically "more reliable." Moshe Vardi, an Israeli mathematician and computer scientist, "proclaimed robots could wipe out half of all jobs currently performed by humans as early as 2030" (Weller 2016).

The progressive reduction of the relative share of living labor and the increase of the relative share of materialized past labor in the structure of total social labor is an objective economic law and a global development megatrend. A job once abolished by robots can no longer be regenerated. It is an irreversible process.

Even with all the technical and technological progress, it is not possible to robotize all types of work, and often not even that many manual jobs. Regardless of the fact that robots are increasingly replacing worker labor and that people are losing their jobs because of it, living labor of a certain quality will always exist to a greater or lesser extent. In the era of current and future automation, robotization, and digitalization of production processes, the control of these processes in the final instance must be in the hands of specially trained professionals.

Another result of technical and technological progress is the progressive increase in the participation of intellectual work and decrease in the participation of manual work in the total work in society. The demand is objectively decreasing not only for new, but also for the existing productive labor force—that is, for workers who are already employed.

The share of the tertiary sector (various services) has unexpectedly increased, and the share of the primary sector (industry and agriculture) has decreased in the creation of products of social labor, which has led to the progressive reduction of productive labor and an increase of non-productive labor in the overall structure of social labor. The tertiary sector already participates in making the GDP in more industrialized countries, contributing over 60 percent of total GDP on average. This sector will gain more and more economic importance in future development and there will be far more room for hiring new workers in the tertiary sector than in the primary sector of the economy. Already today, for instance, less than two percent of the total working age population is engaged in U.S. agriculture, and the U.S. is still among the largest producers of agricultural surpluses in the world.

In the structure of total social labor, the participation of personal labor, which uses citizens' personal funds, is also progressively increasing. Economic domains with traditionally personal labor are numerous and both productive and non-productive (service) activities, such as: agriculture (farmers), crafts (craftsmen), construction (masons, carpenters, painters), the catering industry (caterers), tourism, intermediary (agency) activities, the protection of life and property, intellectual services in science, culture, art, education, publishing, health, etc.

In recent years, the digital economy— based on the use of new information technologies in the work process—provides promising opportunities for the faster development of the personal work sector. It is estimated that there are about 16.8 million programmers (IT professionals) in the world, of which around 43,350 are in Serbia (Rangelov 2017). Although reliable statistics are not available, it is believed that a considerable number of programmers are employed in the personal work sector ("self-employed").

Workers who were made redundant by the robotization of work processes in factory plants and the digitalization of jobs in state and societal services, seek and often find new employment in the production and service sectors based on personal work—either continuous, temporary, or periodic. In this regard, new forms of economy, such as the gig and Uber economy and the Airbnb business network (the world's largest community of vacation rental hosts), offer a wide range of alternative employment opportunities for workers whose permanent jobs were abolished by robotization and digitalization.

In the coming years, work will become less tied to permanent jobs and the traditional border between the employed and the unemployed will fade. Many low-wage workers are forced to do extra work in order to survive. The unemployed also get by in different ways, performing different non-permanent jobs in order to earn a living: driving for Uber, completing tasks online, and other freelance jobs. These are the so-called "gig jobs" and "gig workers."

According to the U.S. Bureau of Labor Statistics, "55 million people in the US are 'gig workers,' which is more than 35 [percent] of the US workforce. That number is projected to jump to 43 [percent] by 2020." (Swaniker 2019).

Changes in the structure of social labor also leave a strong mark on the class structure of society (i.e., to social stratification).

20.

CLASS STRATIFICATION OF CONTEMPORARY SOCIETY

*Capitalism always recreates new classes
and a new global distribution of wealth.*

Todor Kuljić

Philosophers, sociologists, and political scientists have long been drawn to the study of the social stratification of society (society's division into groups or classes) due to its importance and exceptional complexity. This is still an open and very current topic.

DIFFERENT THEORETIC APPROACHES TO THE CLASS STRATIFICATION OF SOCIETY

In terms of defining the class stratification of society, several theories have been formulated, different in their theoretical and methodological approaches to studying this topic and their need to politically defend society's economic and social situation or to justify the material interests and status of a social group or class. "Social scientists use three common methods to define class—by occupation, income, or education—and there is really no consensus about the 'right' way to do it." (Draut 2018).

The English philosopher John Locke divided the world into two kinds of people: "the industrious and the rational" and "the querulous and contentious." (Deneen 2018: 136).

According to the British economist Adam Smith and British political economist David Ricardo, there are three great social classes in society: workers, capitalists, and landlords.

Karl Marx and Friedrich Engels define the class structure of capitalist society in in the *Communist Manifesto* in the following way, "Society as a whole is more and more splitting up into two great hostile camps, into two great classes directly facing each other—Bourgeoisie and Proletariat." (Marx & Engels 1848: 15).

Max Weber, the German sociologist, argued that in capitalism there are four major social classes: upper class, white-collar workers (bureaucracy), the petty bourgeoisie, and the manual working class (blue-collar workers).

In contemporary capitalist societies, three main social classes are usually emphasized: upper class, middle class, and lower class. The upper class qualifies as the class of the rich, the lower class as the class of the poor, and the middle class is in between.

According to a new report from the nonpartisan Pew Research Center,

> In the U.S., for example, 26 [percent] of Americans were classified as lower income, 59 [percent] as middle income and 15 [percent] as upper income. In Germany, those numbers were: 18 [percent] (low), 72 [percent] (middle) and 10 [percent] (upper). In Denmark, the difference was even more striking: 14 percent, 80 percent, and 7 percent, respectively...

> ...In the nearly 20 years from 1991 to 2010, the portion of American adults living in middle-class households fell from 62

[percent] to 59 [percent]...Besides the U.S., the nations with declining percentages of middle class adults were Denmark, Finland, Germany, Italy, Luxembourg, Norway and Spain. Those with growing middle classes were France, Ireland, the Netherlands and the U.K. Germany saw the steepest decline, falling from 79 [percent] in 1991 to 72 [percent] in 2010. Ireland reported the greatest rise in that same period, from 60 [percent] to 69 [percent]. (Daugherty 2019).

In addition to the tendency of the relative reduction of middle class members, the financial gains of middle-income Americans remained "modest compared with those of higher-income households, causing the income disparity between the groups to grow." (Kochhar 2018).

In the U.S. there is also "a list of five classes: upper class, upper-middle class, middle class, working class and lower class." (Newport 2018). According to the Gallup Public Opinion Survey in April 2018, "most Americans...put themselves into the 'middle' (40 [percent]) or 'working' (31 [percent]) class. Another 11 [percent] identified as 'lower' class, 15 [percent] as 'upper-middle' and 2 [percent] as 'upper.'" (Ibid.).

In contemporary capitalism, the middle class has been given special social significance. "The capitalist class is trying to win the middle classes over to its side by giving them various material privileges." (A Handbook 1980: 325). The middle class is believed to be the traditional engine of economic growth and social stability of capitalist society and that middle-class prosperity "has made America the most hopeful and dynamic country on earth and it is a foundation of strong democracy." (Traub & McGhe 2013).

The cornerstone of Joe Biden's 2020 campaign to be U.S. president is his economic plan: "Save the Middle Class to Save America."

In recent history—in which the "fruits" of globalization and neoliberalism are reaped by the rich and the richest—a special theory about the social stratification of society has been proposed, in which the world is "divided into only two classes: the 'losers of globalization' and those at the top, who grab 'everything, and whatever is left' for themselves" (Nad 2019). Such a view of the class division of society is especially present in European countries that were transformed from a socialist to a capitalist society.

The class stratification of society can also be viewed from the perspective of the ownership relations of the means of production in the process of creating new values, goods, and services intended for the market exchange (i.e., from the perspective of relations formed between labor and capital). By this criterion, there are three basic social groups or classes in contemporary liberal capitalism: the exploitative (capitalist, bourgeois) class, the exploited (working, middle) class, and the non-exploitative and unexploited class, which consists of members of society who are not exploited by anyone outside of it and do not exploit anyone. These social classes are the subjects of the following considerations.

THE EXPLOITATIVE CLASS

Social class represents that "the basic power relation in a capitalist society is the capitalist class." (Zweig 2004). It consists of the owners of capital, the capitalist-employer. The capitalist-employer, in order to perform their business ventures hire other workers, buy their labor force, and use it in the process of creating products and services, in addition to engaging their means of production (capital) and investing in their living labor, thus constantly exploiting workers and thereby increasing their personal wealth.

The American economist Michael Zweig believes that the representatives of the capitalist class are ….those most senior executives who direct and control the corporations that employ the private-sector working class. These are the 'captains of industry' and finance, CEOs, chief financial officers, chief operating officers, members of boards of directors, those whose decisions dominate the workplace and the economy, and whose economic power often translates into dominant power in the realms of politics, culture, the media, and even religion. Capitalists comprise about 2 percent of the U.S. labor force (Ibid.).

Workers under capitalism have always been forced to offer and sell their labor force to capitalist employers as a commodity because this was the only way for them to obtain the financial means necessary for their mere existence. In this respect, they depend on capitalist-employers because workers are not the owners of the means of production and because they do not have the special abilities and/or means necessary to engage in productive activity with their personal labor.

Given the fact that, in a market economy, the price of the goods supplied is often lower than the price of the goods demanded, the employer is able to buy the supplied labor force at a price lower than it is really worth. Thus begins the capitalist exploitation process of the wage worker, which materializes in the process of creating goods (products and services) and their realization about the market, acquisition, distribution, and the allocation of achieved revenues if the employer's company operates successfully. The wage (salary) paid by the employer to the hired worker is always lower than the actual value the worker has created by his living labor, i.e. than the newly created value.

The difference between wages and the newly created value produced by the labor force (surplus value) is appropriated by the employer in the form of profit. In this way, employers exploit their hired workers. The employer considers the appropriated surplus value as his earned income based on the ownership of capital (property), while he considers the wages paid to workers from his capital as his expense (worker income from wage labor).

The dominant social position of employers in appropriating total earned income is enabled by their monopoly of the means of production, which is maximally institutionally (legally) protected as well as extra-institutionally by the unquestionable authority of the capitalist state.

In addition to earning income based on their ownership of capital, capitalist employers can earn even more on the basis of their living labor.

Thus a new capitalism has been created, different from the classical capitalism, which had been based on the division of capital and labor embodied in different groups of people.

In the new capitalism, rich capitalists and rich workers are the same people. The fact that the rich now work contributes to the social acceptability of such an arrangement. Moreover, it is no longer easy for outsiders to determine which part of their income comes from the ownership of capital, and which from labor. While tenants were often ridiculed in the past for doing nothing but collecting rent, in the new capitalism regime, criticism directed at the top one percent is dulled by the fact that many members of this group are highly educated, work hard and have successful careers. Inequality is thus shrouded in a cloak of meritocracy. The inequality generated by the new capitalism is more difficult to problematize ideologically and probably politically, because there is no support for limiting them...(Milanović 2017: 152).

Of course, "wealthy capitalists" and "wealthy workers" could be said to be "the same persons" by the standard of living achieved by wealth gained. They are not, however, "the same persons" because of their position in the capitalist organization of social labor. Workers become rich thanks to their high-quality living labor and the high wage which capitalists pay them as hired workers. On the other hand, capitalists become rich because of their ownership of the means of production and the appropriation of unpaid part of the total living labor of workers who are exploited—and, of course, on the basis of capitalist's living labor, if the capitalist works. The fact that members of the capitalist classearn income from their living labor does not mean that their class status changes significantly because they do not become wage earners, since, as the owners of capital, they cannot exploit themselves. The "fact that the rich are working now" only points to the emergence of a new working energy and the enthusiasm of capital owners "in the new capitalism" and that Marx's view of capitalists as "non-workers" is not entirely correct.

It is true that not all owners of capital can easily be termed "non-workers," but they cannot be said to be workers who belong to the working class. The owners of capital and the capitalist class cannot be identified with hired workers and the working class because their material interests as social classes have always been opposed. This is why there is no foundation in reality for the claims of contemporary capitalist states "that the landscape of social class has changed almost out of recognition since the days when Marx himself was writing," that "we live in a social world where class is less and less important" or that "talk of class struggle is as archaic as talk of burning heretics at the stake. The revolutionary worker, like the wicked top-hatted capitalist, is a figment of the Marxist imagination" (Eagleton 2011: 160).

The relationship between the owners of capital and the owners of labor—capitalists and workers, the capitalist class and the working class—have never been, nor will ever be, harmonious because of their objectively different and opposing material interests. Viewed from the outside, these relations are more humane now than they were in the nineteenth century, but viewed from the inside, they have remained essentially unchanged. Capitalist employers have always been—and especially so nowadays—masters, and hired workers have always been servants of their masters. Capitalists still have in their hands not just economic power, but political power in both society and the state, which is why the capitalist class is also called the ruling class in the capitalist social order. Furthermore, the capitalist class is often called the upper class, bearing in mind its wealth, standard of living, and ownership of the means of production.

The wealth of capitalist class members differs within countries and between particular countries. The richest represent the oligarchic capitalist class, the so-called *super-class*.

> Oligarchic capitalist class privilege and power are taking the world in a similar direction almost everywhere. Political power backed by intensifying surveillance, policing and militarized violence is being used to attack the well-being of whole populations deemed expendable and disposable. We are

daily witnessing the systematic dehumanization of disposable people. ruthless oligarchic power is now being exercised through a totalitarian democracy directed to immediately disrupt, fragment and suppress any coherent anti-wealth political movement (such as Occupy). The arrogance and disdain with which the affluent now view those less fortunate than themselves, even when (particularly when) vying with each other behind closed doors to prove who can be the most charitable of them all, are notable facts of our present condition. The 'empathy gap' between the oligarchy and the rest is immense and increasing. The oligarchs mistake superior income for superior human worth and their economic success as evidence of their superior knowledge of the world (rather than their superior command over accounting tricks and legal niceties). They do not know how to listen to the plight of the world because they cannot and willfully will not confront their role in the construction of that plight. They do not and cannot see their own contradictions (Harvey 2014: 292).

THE EXPLOITED CLASS

The largest, most complex, and most contradictory social class in contemporary capitalist society is the exploited class (working class). Members of this social class are working people—the executants of various jobs from the simplest to the most complex; for example, from manual workers to the top managers in global corporations who are forced to sell their labor force, knowledge, and skills to capitalist employers. The wage level (income from wage labor) depends on the hierarchical position and the role of the hired employee and can range from very low to very high.

According to Zweig,

> the working class is made up of people who, when they go
> to work or when they act as citizens, have comparatively little
> power or authority. They are the people who do their jobs
> under more or less close supervision, who have little control
> over the pace or the content of their work, who aren't the boss
> of anyone. They are blue-collar people like construction and
> factory workers, and white-collar workers like bank tellers and
> writers of routine computer code. They work to produce and
> distribute goods, or in service industries or government
> agencies. They are skilled and unskilled, engaged in over five
> hundred different occupations tracked by the U.S. Department
> of Labor: agricultural laborers, baggage handlers, cashiers,
> flight attendants, home health care aides, machinists,
> secretaries, short order cooks, sound technicians, truck drivers.
> In the United States, working class people are by far the
> majority of the population. Over eighty-eight million people
> were in working class occupations in 2002, comprising 62
> percent of the labor force…(Zweig 2004).

In the economically most developed and wealthiest countries—but
not only in them—labor aristocracy (well-paid, rich workers), can be
found. The labor aristocracy are, however, still exploited by capitalist
employers in the same way as the poor workers. The wage that a hired
worker receives from an employer, whether high or low, does not
change the nature of capitalist wage relations. Even top managers in
many corporations who earn a high income based on their living labor
and are rich and even very rich, are in a wage position in relation to the
owner of the corporation if they are not simultaneously co-owners.

In political and sociological theory, members of the exploited social class (wage workers) are traditionally called the working class. Marx once called them proletarians because renting their labor force to capitalists was their only source of subsistence. Representatives of the exploited social class, the working class, exist in all social spheres where private employers dominate through their capital, not only in the sphere of material production in factories and production plants, but also in non-productive spheres of the state—in culture, art, education, health, and various service activities. For example, professors at private colleges are also wage workers because they are in a wage relationship with the owner or owners of a college.

Employees of the government—the administration, army, police, etc.—where the state has the role of their employer and their position is defined as a wage position also belong to the exploited social class.

The social division of labor has led to economic stratification and conflicting interests within the exploited working class, which makes it socially inhomogeneous. Members of this class with lower education, lower qualifications, lower wages, and generally lower standards of living are usually called the *lower class*. In the political vocabulary of the West, the lower working class is often referred to as the blue-collar class, which is associated with machine workers. On the other hand, highly educated members of the exploited social class, with high wages, high standards of living, and an appropriate status and reputation in society are called the *middle class* or the white-collar class, which originated in the nineteenth century.

It is true that the middle class is between the working class and the capitalist class according to earned income and standard of living, but by its actual class and political status, the middle class objectively belongs to the exploited class. Middle class is, in fact, the part of the exploited working class which has managed to achieve higher monthly and annual income thanks to its higher education, qualifications, working and intellectual abilities, and predispositions, thereby significantly improving its socioeconomic status. Its members are mostly employed in spheres outside of material production in the tertiary sector, but to a lesser extent also in direct production in better paid positions: engineers, managers, economists, lawyers, and others. Members of the middle class do not belong to the capitalist class because they do not own the means of production, are not owners or employers, and do not hire wage workers. Members of the middle class are, in fact, "workers of the middle class."

Many members of the middle class—although they are exploited workers—feel because they have stable employment, a high standard of living, and often live in considerable abundance that they are not exploited, nor do they consider themselves in a wage relationship to the owners of capital because such a thing would be contrary to their achieved status and reputation in society. "Money matters to people, but status matters more, and precisely because status is something you cannot buy. Status is related to identity as much as it is to income. It is also, unfortunately, a zero-sum game. The struggles over status are socially divisive, and they can resemble class warfare" (Menand 2016).

Within the middle class itself, depending on the wage rate and the achieved standard of living, there is a social stratification into upper and lower middle class. The upper middle class is closer to the capitalist class while the lower middle class is closer to the working class. The upper middle class is often referred to as the new class or the professional-managerial class, which considers itself neither capitalist nor the working class. The lower strata of the middle class, in periods of economic crisis, falls into the working class. Having a decreasing number of middle class members is a convincing sign that the socioeconomic situation in that society is deteriorating.

The ideologists and theorists of neoliberalism mainly address the issues of economic and social inequality outside the context of existing property relations and the contradictions between labor and capital. They especially emphasize the socioeconomic differences that exist within the working class and encourage conflicts between the lower and the middle class. These ideologists and theorists do so with the aim of relativizing the exploitative role of the capitalist class, trying to utterly obscure the essence of capitalist relations that have always been the harsh reality of capitalism. The owners of capital strive to present themselves to the world in every possible way as a social class that lives solely based on their work, skills, knowledge, commitment to the business success of their enterprise, and the maximization of their profits— not from exploiting someone else's labor, emphasizing that they are not at all responsible for building a wall between rich and poor or for the outbreak of economic crises in the world.

It is true that since Marx's time, major changes have occurred in the structure of society, primarily due to technical and technological improvements in the work process through the use of automated, robotic, and digitized machines, which, especially in recent times, largely abolish the positions of workers in direct production ("behind the machine"). Members of the working class are not, however, just "machine workers," but all those who are forced to sell their labor force to employers as a commodity, regardless of whether they perform productive or unproductive labor in their workplace. Thus understood, the working class still counts many members. According to the World Bank, there were 3.3 billion employees and working people in the world in 2016 (World Bank 2018). This data refutes Terry Eagleton's claim "that the landscape of social class has changed almost out of recognition since the days when Marx himself was writing" and that the working class "has disappeared almost without trace" (Eagleton 2011: 160).

In contemporary conditions, the technological revolution inevitably reduces the number of jobs of the exploited social class members because robots increasingly substitute their living labor. This revolution does not only displaces the labor of those with lower levels of education and qualifications, but also the work of members of the middle class with higher levels of education and qualifications in the same way as it happened with the mechanization of living labor of the nineteenth century working class.

The shrinkage of the working class is especially pronounced in former socialist countries, not because of the sudden robot applications in their process of production, but because of their uninventive transition to capitalism, when even some very successful state and socially owned enterprises were destroyed, intentionally or unintentionally. One gets the impression, which is probably wrong, that one of the main goals of this transition was to systematically reduce the number of members of the working class as much as possible in order to exterminate the political forces in these countries who could possibly rebel against the capitalist social order imposed on them after "the fall of communism." This has been partially achieved. Today's working class is largely de-subjectivized—not only in former socialist countries, but around the world—and it is no longer the subject of anti-capitalist and anti-exploitative actions as it was in Marx's time. Only in industrially underdeveloped countries does the working class resemble the proletariat of the nineteenth and early twentieth centuries (Markovic 2014).

The systemic reduction of the number of the working class members is a very good sign for neoliberal apologists because workers are slowly disappearing from the social scene, instead moving to areas outside the radius of the interests of capital—small, medium and large—either to the personal labor sector or the army of the unemployed (i.e. those seeking employment).

Despite all the changes that have taken and are taking place in the working class corps, this class still exists and has its place in the political scenes of contemporary capitalist states, including in the industrialized nations of the world, such as the U.S. This was confirmed by the U.S. presidential election held on November 8, 2016. In analyzing the reasons for the electoral victory of Donald Trump, an American businessman and the Republican presidential candidate, it is often stated that the American working class played a crucial role in electing him into office. A large contingent of the American working class voted for Trump because they were in an increasingly unenviable economic and social position due to the carelessness of the Democratic Party authorities.

During his eight-year term, former U.S. President Barack Obama often used the term "working class" in public speeches. When the financial and economic crisis broke out in the U.S. in 2007, one of his messages was that he would not allow the working class of Detroit, the center of the American automobile industry, to fall victim to the crisis. During the 2016 U.S. presidential campaigns, he said "Trump is not a friend of working class" (Rascoe & Oliphant 2016).

In contemporary political and sociological theory, the working class involves workers—the employees who are socially stratified at the bottom of the middle class, and whose income ranges between lower middle class earnings and those on the verge of poverty.

In the circles of apologists of neoliberal capitalism, the working class is not mentioned anymore, because it allegedly "disappeared" in the years after "the fall of communism" and almost ceased to exist. By that logic, it seems that only members of the "white-collar," (middle class and robots) contribute to the creation of products of social labor—not production workers.

The economic and social reality deny such claims, however. Production workers have always been a "traditional engine of economic growth" no less than the middle class, as it is perceived in the West, if not more so. After all, the majority of social gross product in the world, even in the most technologically advanced countries, is still more the result of the living labor of wage workers (members of the working class) than of the work of robots and other digitized production systems. Of course, there are factories around the world where this relation is different and is in favor of robotic labor, but robot labor is still far from prevalent.

Simply put, the technical and technological achievements and changes in the class structure of total social labor cannot conceal the obvious weaknesses of capitalist society, which is imperfect, deeply unjust, heartless, and inhumane. You can only survive in it if you are a capitalist or if you are a capitalist's servant— i.e., a slave of capital. Wage workers have been put in a position to suffer the capitalist exploitation unconditionally, keep silent, and not to revolt. In order to survive, it is better for workers to have any wage, any personal income, acquired under any inhumane conditions, than not to have it. Such production and social relations are a true reflection of capitalist morality, which can never be justified in any way and is the deepest contradiction of the contemporary neoliberal capitalist society. This society has become risky economically, socially, and politically, which fact that cannot be obscured by anything.

While in earlier capitalism there was a complete separation between capital and labor income, these two types of income are often intertwined in contemporary neoliberal capitalism. Not only do members of the capitalist class earn income from their labor and their ownership of property, but members of the exploited class also earn income from their labor for wage and partly from their ownership of capital. "People with [a] very high income from work (for example, managers of financial companies) save a good part of their income (or are paid with stock options), so they themselves also become the owners of significant capital. This way they simultaneously earn high income from both labor and capital" (Milanović 2017: 151).

The systemic possibility and economic practice that, in addition to wage income, members of the exploited social class also earn income on the basis of ownership of capital is undoubtedly one of the progressive changes in the organization and functioning of the contemporary capitalist economic system. This, of course, does not significantly change the essence of capital relationships inherent in capitalist society because wage workers, regardless of the fact that they earn an adequate income on the basis of capital ownership, remain dependent on their employer (the majority owner of the capital of a private company) and are still exploited by their employer.

THE NON-EXPLOITATIVE AND NON-EXPLOITED CLASS

In contemporary capitalism there is also the non-exploitative and non-exploited class, a separate social class fundamentally different from the capitalist and the working class.

This social class consists of working people who—with their personal labor and personally owned resources—perform their respective jobs in various production and service activities, create material goods, products, and services, sell them on the market, earn income if they are successful, and live on their earned income after paying their taxes and other obligations to the state and society.

Regardless of the fact that they personally own the means of production, they do not belong to the capitalist class because they do not exploit others, and do not belong to the traditional working class because no one exploits them. They are "their own bosses"—employers and executants of work at the same time.

Depending on their financial performance in their businesses, their attained standard of living, and established reputation in society, employees in the personal work sector, especially in the West, are classified as the middle class—either as upper middle or lower middle class, but not as the working or the capitalist class.

21.

FACTOCRACY AND CORPORATOCRACY

In the political history of government and governance, the rule has always been that the actual political power in a society is in the hands of individuals, social groups, and strata who rule over most of the available capital. Today, about 80 percent of the existing global capital—i.e., foreign direct investment—is in the immediate possession of global corporations, which is why the actual economic and political power is concentrated in the hands of corporations, albeit not formal official power, which is gained through elections. The economic power of some global corporations is greater than the economic power of many individual states. The private ownership monopoly of capital is the source of the power of global corporations.

The owners of global corporations and their control apparatuses have become the most important part of the *capitalist superclass* that controls the real, albeit not formal, levers of economic power and political influence around the world, in all states, including the U.S., the most powerful superpower. To describe their role in the contemporary world, the term *factocracy* was coined, which means having real, but not formal power.

Recognizing the growing local and global real power and influence of global corporations, their owners, and their executive administrations, governments and larger political parties of many states strive to have close partnerships with members of the corporate nomenclature in their countries and around the world. This connection of classical state power and corporate power—the association of state and capital—is called *corporatocracy* in contemporary political theory. The established relationship between the state and corporate leaders in society are not fixed, but change objectively according to the logic imposed by neoliberalism.

Increasing not only the factual but also formal influence, power, and authority in society, while simultaneously reducing the functions of the state is a global trend in the contemporary capitalist world. The executives of global corporations are increasingly being placed in positions of responsibility in state government systems, being elected ministers in the government, and becoming ambassadors. For example, the U.S. President Trump, at the beginning of his term, nominated Rex Tillerson, the former head of the U.S. oil corporation ExxonMobil, to be the secretary of state.

The personnel composition of parliaments in contemporary capitalist states reflects the relationship between labor and capital. Workers, the working class, and working people are inadequately represented in parliaments around the world. Parliaments have become, more or less, representative bodies of the rich and not the poor, despite the disproportionate number of the poor versus the rich in individual countries around the world. The capitalist superclass, i.e. the owners of corporate capital, has a decisive influence on the decision-making process in parliaments. Decisions made in governments or parliaments of contemporary states are, as a rule, in the interest of big capital, fashioned after the urban myth of American business: what is good for General Motors is good for the state. These are the two sides of contemporary neoliberal capitalist society, in which the rule of law passed by the legislators of the capitalist class (parliamentarians, representatives, congressmen, senators) must be obeyed by all members—that is, laws must be enforced without question.

22.

PLUTOCRACY: COMMUNIST WAY OF LIFE

Concentration of wealth leads naturally to concentration of power, which in turn translates to legislation favoring the interests of the rich and powerful and thereby increasing even further the concentration of power and wealth.

Noam Chomsky

At the present time, the dictatorship of capital is at work. The power of the capitalist class is absolute. It is superior to all other social classes and strata, sovereignly ruling throughout Europe and the world through its right-leaning political parties, which are inextricably linked to capital and its economic power. It does not matter how far some of these parties are to the left or right of the political center. The power of the capitalist class has become practically unchangeable.

In almost all "free and fair elections" organized by the government of the capitalist class "in the name of the people and the state," it is known in advance that they will surely be won by candidates of political parties representing its authentic interests—those on the right or those that gravitate toward the center, like many contemporary social-democratic parties do.

Although the political system retains its democratic form, since the freedom of speech and the freedom of association are protected and the elections are free, the system increasingly resembles a plutocracy. In Marxist terminology, it is a 'dictatorship of the proprietary classes,' although from the outside the system formally resembles democracy. As Marx concludes in *The Manifesto of the Communist Party*, the contemporary state is "but a committee for managing the common affairs of the whole bourgeoisie.

Indeed, this discrepancy between ideology and reality will not be a surprise for connoisseurs of political history. Rome grew inconspicuously into an autocratic empire, hiding behind the mask of a republic embodied in the senate. Eastern Europe was ruled by a bureaucratic class, while economic and political power was allegedly in the hands of the people. Today, every dictator claims to respect the will of the people – that is, to defend democracy (Milanović 2017: 161).

According to the French philosopher Alain Badiou,

....in our Western countries the rule is fairly simple: once in power, you can change some small details, but there is no question of changing the capitalist basis of society. Do you know of any 'democratic' country that is not in fact, and above all, dominated by an extremely stable capitalism? Elections are but a façade for preserving the dominant order (Badiou 2017).

Therefore, elections in capitalist countries—while officially declared "free and democratic"—in reality have proven to be an instrument of the permanent preservation of the capitalist social order and the eternal power of the capitalist class. Democracies in these countries has been reduced to the mere right of citizens to vote every four or five years, often in irregular conditions, and the final election results are largely foreseeable and allow, at best, only cosmetic changes to this order and the government, but do not substantially change anything. If by any chance there was the possibility for making significant changes in the capitalist order in free and democratic elections, the capitalist class would immediately abolish such elections, using "scientific arguments" to make their case that existing forms of electoral democracy are not the best democratic solution and that new electoral mechanisms must be found, without delay, that would be "more free" and "more democratic" than existing ones. The ultimate goal of this approach is clear: to preserve the capitalist order and the dictatorship of the capitalist class at all costs and not allow anyone to question its inviolable and untouchable power in society.

The capitalist social order, regardless of its manifestations, is constructed exclusively to protect the interests of the ruling capitalist class. This social order was created by the capitalist class, which defends it fanatically and with all available means, not only using its powerful armed forces, but also powerful media propaganda that speaks about capitalism as the best and eternal social order. It is so suggestive that exploited masses around the world are beginning to believe in the "benevolence" of the neoliberal capitalist order; that neoliberal capitalism somehow protects their economic and social interests because it allows them to find employment and receive an appropriate compensation, regardless of the fact that their pay is always lower than the invested quality and quantity of their living labor. In fact, through its propaganda, the ruling capitalist class very successfully conceals the essence of neoliberal capitalism's system of exploiting other people's labor, which enables the capitalist class to constantly and inappropriately get rich.

The ideologues of neoliberalism particularly emphasize that contemporary capitalism is a social order in which everyone has equal opportunities—including every worker and all working people, who are free citizens par excellence, with guaranteed right to vote in free elections where they freely and equally decide on the future of their country and their destiny in it. The contemporary capitalist reality, however, is quite different. While the capitalist class emphasizes the importance of free elections and the right of every individual citizen to directly influence the development of policy in their country, it wants to conceal the exploitative nature of its social order and to silence the right of every employed worker to participate in the distribution of income resulting from their overall labor—not only of the paid part of their work, but also unpaid labor appropriated by the owners of capital.

Big words such as democracy, human rights, and freedom have lost their original meaning under the constant pressure of the dictatorship of capital, withering away like flowers. Objectively, "there has never been more talk about rights and freedoms, but fewer and fewer realized rights and freedoms" than is the case today (Stević Gojkov 2016: 66).

This present time will be remembered in human history as the most ruthless dictatorship of the capitalist class and the cruelest exploitation of everyone in society who directly depends on the power and temper of capital—those who are forced to sell their labor force, and even themselves, as commodities to the owners of capital, the employers. Such a situation cannot be justified by anything, especially not by the suggestive propaganda of the rich and those they employ that spouts about achieved democratic developments, acquired human rights and freedoms, and the practically realized rule of law. The reality is quite different.

> The rich distance themselves from the rest of society—they live in elite parts of cities, which are protected by private guards and bodyguards instead of ordinary police. Instead of public parks, swimming pools and other sports facilities, they have

their own or visit luxury private clubs. Their children are not being sent to public, but to private elite schools and universities. They do not receive treatments in public hospitals, but in private clinics. They do not travel by public transport in overcrowded buses and subways, etc. In a word, being rich means having enough money not to mix with those who are not (Dušanić 2016: 36–37).

Analyzing the current situation in the U.S., the American political theorist Patrick J. Deneen says,

Today, some 70 percent of Americans believe that their country is moving in the wrong direction, and half the county thinks its best days are behind it. Most believe that their children will be less prosperous and have fewer opportunities than previous generation… It is evident to all that the political system is broken and social fabric is fraying…Wealthy Americans continue to gravitate to gated enclaves in and around select cities, while growing number of Christians compare our time to that of the late Roman Empire and ponder a fundamental withdrawal from wider American society into updated forms of Benedictine monastic communities. The signs of the times suggest that much is wrong with America…(Deneen 2018: 2).

All of the essential functions of contemporary capitalist states are subordinated primarily or exclusively to the interests of the rich— that is, to the interests of large capital.

Concentration of wealth leads naturally to concentration of power, transforming in laws [favoring] interests of the rich and powerful, enabling further concentration of power and wealth. Various political measures, such as fiscal policy, deregulation and rules of corporate management are designed in a way that they increase the concentration of wealth and power. This is what we see in neoliberalism era. This is a vicious circle in constant progress. The state is here to ensure safety and support interests of the privileged and powerful sectors in society, while the rest of population remains left to the mercy of brutal reality of capitalism. Socialism for the rich, capitalism for the poor (Chomsky 2017: 155).

For the richest in society it can be said that they live, not in socialism, but in real communism because they have everything they need and more, while the poor are carrying the heavy burden of the capitalist order, drowning in poverty and barely managing to survive.

The representatives of the contemporary American political elite resonate differently. In his speech at the World Economic Forum on January 18, 2017, Joe Biden, the then-outgoing U.S. vice president, stated that "imperative is an urgent defense of the international liberal order," and that the "United States of America and Europe have to fight for the defense of the values that brought us where we are today" (Chan 2017).

Insisting on defending the existing "international liberal order" means enabling the further widening and deepening of the gap between the rich and the poor in the world. The world of the rich, despite the altruism of rare individuals, is not ready to voluntarily give up even the smallest part of its wealth in favor of the poor because doing so would be contrary to the spirit of the capitalist social system and its bourgeois morality. That is why capitalism is permanently in a crisis that, to a greater or lesser extent, pushes it toward its own destruction. Some thinkers predict its inevitable end (Harvey 2014; Peović Vuković 2017).

All in all, what is now officially called capitalist democracy— that is, forms of governing imposed by the power of the ruling capitalist class, camouflaged by a democratic façade—is nothing but a *democratorship*, the negation of the true rule of the people (democracy). Democratorship is also any form of "exporting democracy" to other countries and imposing democracy on other nations against their wishes, interests, and needs, which is characteristic of the global behavior of the leading actors of contemporary liberal capitalism.

23.

DEMOCRACY EXPORT AND TRANSITIONAL COLONIALISM

Convinced of the effectiveness and power of the capitalist social order, the capitalist class has declared this order to be unquestionable, irreplaceable, and eternal because democracy, human rights, and freedoms "have reached their zenith" under it. Guided by this knowledge, leading capitalist countries have generously offered—and are still offering—their "democratic system" to all countries in the world with a "democratic deficit," declaring it an omnipotent medicine, a panacea, that is able to successfully solve all economic, political, social and other problems these countries face. Countries that have embraced the doctrine of neoliberal capitalism have been "selling" it using marketing methods and imposed it by force on states that were "misfits" and "renegades" that resisted the "values and benefits" of neoliberalism.

The "export of democracy" policy has become an integral part of the official foreign policy of the U.S., the most powerful capitalist country in the West and in the world. For example, spreading democracy to the Near East and elsewhere is an integral part of the official American foreign policy strategy, and is known as the Bush Doctrine, named after U.S. President George W. Bush.

Asserting a new and aggressive American unilateralism, the Bush Doctrine has embraced the motto 'We will build to suit ourselves,' because it perceives the United States to be 'the dominant power in the world, more dominant than any since Rome. Accordingly, America is in a position to reshape norms, alter expectations and create new realities...by unapologetic and implacable demonstrations of will' /Krauthammer, 2001/" (Kegley Jr. and Wittkopf 2004: 549).

The Bush doctrine was formulated after the terrorist attack of Al Qaeda on September 11, 2001 on selected targets in the U.S.: the twin towers of the World Trade Center in New York City, which were symbols of American financial power, and the Pentagon building in Washington D.C., the symbol of American military power. The Bush Doctrine was elaborated on in the National Security Council document "National Security Strategy of the United States of America", published on September 20, 2002 (Ibid).

In his inaugural speech on January 20, 2005, George W. Bush, following Woodrow Wilson's ideals of "democracy and freedom for all," said

> There is only one force of history that can break the reign of hatred and resentment, and expose the pretensions of tyrants, and reward the hopes of the decent and tolerant, and that is the force of human freedom.
>
> ...The survival of liberty in our land increasingly depends on the success of liberty in other lands. The best hope for peace in our world is the expansion of freedom in all the world.
>
> America's vital interests and our deepest beliefs are now one...
>
> So it is the policy of the United States to seek and support the growth of democratic movements and institutions in every

nation and culture, with the ultimate goal of ending tyranny in our world (Bush 2001–2008: 273–374).

According to Joyce P. Kaufman, an American professor and specialist in international relations and foreign policy,

> Bush is often equated with Wilson in the zeal with which he pursued the ideals of promoting democracy and pursuing a foreign policy based on values. However, Bush did not learn all the lessons of history, specifically, that values such as 'democracy' and 'freedom' cannot be imposed. For example, after becoming president in 1913, Wilson boasted 'that he could transform Latin America, if not the rest of the world, into constitutional democracies in America's image'…

> Clearly, Bush's foreign policy embodies some of the idealism of Wilson with the imperialism of McKinley or Theodore Roosevelt…(Kaufman 2010: 151).

Regardless of the changes taking place in the twenty first century on a global scale, the U.S. is making every effort to maintain its leading position in the world and to continue to "lead the world," believing that "the globalized world can have only one hegemon" (Bacevich 2002: 219–220 and 244). This is why the American administration, the American elite, and historians "have often argued over the issue of 'American exceptionalism,' the idea that the United States is somehow subject to rules and trends distinct from those prevailing in other advanced countries" (Jenkins 2017: xii).

During Hillary Clinton's presidential campaign as the candidate for the Democratic Party, Clinton seems to have most precisely defined the essence of American exceptionalism:

The United States is an exceptional nation. I believe we are still Lincoln's last, best hope of Earth. We're still Reagan's shining city on a hill. We're still Robert Kennedy's great, unselfish, compassionate country.

And it's not just that we have the greatest military or that our economy is larger than any on Earth. It's also the strength of our values, the strength of the American people. Everyone who works harder, dreams bigger and never, ever stops trying to make our country and the world a better place. And part of what makes America an exceptional nation, is that we are also an indispensable nation.

...People all over the world look to us and follow our lead....We are so lucky to be Americans. It is an extraordinary blessing. It's why so many people, from so many places, want to be Americans too. But it's also a serious responsibility. The decisions we make and the actions we take, even the actions we don't take, affect millions even billions of lives.

...When we say America is exceptional, it doesn't mean that people from other places don't feel deep national pride, just like we do. It means that we recognize America's unique and unparalleled ability to be a force for peace and progress, a champion for freedom and opportunity. Our power comes with a responsibility to lead, humbly, thoughtfully, and with a fierce commitment to our values.

... American leadership means standing with our allies because our network of allies is part of what makes us exceptional" (Clinton 2016).

The main goal of "American exceptionalism" has always been to draw the world's attention to the real supremacy of "American values" and to create a raison d'être for the inevitability of the "American nation" and its duty to distribute justice around the world. Following such a political philosophy, the U.S. has gone from being the "world's hope" into the "world's policeman."

According to its technology of political imposition, the contemporary "export of democracy," (i.e. the imposition of capitalism everywhere, at all costs) is irresistibly reminiscent to the "export of socialism" by Stalin and other authoritarian leaders of the USSR.

With an intensive campaign, comprehensive logistical support, and material assistance from the centers of global neoliberal politics, the ruling authoritarian and undemocratic regimes in European socialist countries were systematically undermined, eventually overthrown, and replaced by pro-Western and pro-market governments. Fortunately, these regimes were liquidated without major casualties or bloodshed. The main tools for "exporting democracy" to these countries have been incitement and organization of "colored" revolutions, such as: the 2000 "Bulldozer revolution" in Serbia, the 2003 "Rose Revolution" in Georgia, the 2005 "Tulip Revolution" in Kyrgyzstan, and the 2014 "Orange Revolution" in Ukraine. For example, John McCain, the late American senator, flew to Ukraine in mid-December of 2013 and incited mass protests ("Orange Revolution"), hand in hand with the leader of the Ukrainian ultranationalist party "Freedom," and fueled Russophobia in Maidan, the central square of Kiev.

Of course, all the "colored revolutions" were successfully launched and implemented primarily thanks to the mass support of citizens who were very dissatisfied with the standard of living in their socialist countries. None of these anti-socialist revolutions have been able to bring anything new, something never seen before, instead simply renewing capitalist values, nationalism, and religion in former socialist countries, which had already existed before they became socialist. This is why it can be said that the "colored revolutions" were conservative and uninventive, unlike the earlier socialist and communist revolutions, which offered something new, original, and different in trying to build a just society. They did not succeed but did leave instructive historical experience behind.

Bearers of neoliberal policy have also resorted to plotting coups d'états as well as carrying out direct military interventions. For example, the NATO bombing of the FRY in 1999 was an armed confrontation with Yugoslavia's socialist regime because it was the only remaining socialist country in the already "democratized" Eastern and Southeastern Europe. Strobe Talbot, an American foreign policy analyst, believes that the resistance of Milosevic's Yugoslavia to "widespread trends of political and economic reforms—not the situation with Kosovo Albanians –is in fact what explains best the NATO action against FRYU" (Talbott 2005).

Similar to the "colored" revolutions, leading Western countries were also intensively engaged in the business of "exporting democracy" to several Arab countries in Northern Africa and the Near East, and thus democracy was being "exported" during the "Arab Spring"—that is, democracy was aggressively imposed on numerous sovereign states. The first citizen protests, induced from the outside, began in Tunisia on December 18, 2010 and in Egypt in early 2011, followed by Libya, Bahrain, Syria, Yemen, Algeria, Iraq, Jordan, Morocco, and Oman. The "export of democracy" and the imposition of aggressive neoliberal capitalist policies were supported by the use of Western military force (NATO armed forces). After the intervention of this Western military alliance, complete chaos ensued, resulting in famine and total instability in Iraq, Afghanistan, Libya, Syria, Yemen, and several other

African countries, from which millions of people sought refuge in Europe. This is how the migrant crisis arose as a huge European and global problem, which now seems almost unsolvable.

The real economic interests of leading capitalist states have always been the driving forces behind the geopolitical strategy of "exporting democracy." During the transition period from socialism to capitalism in former socialist countries, especially in the smaller and the weaker ones, major capitalist states established complete political and economic control over them, used and are still using them as a source of cheap labor and raw materials, and occupied their domestic markets. This is a new form of colonialism—transitional colonialism, a product of the "export of democracy" that has been systematically enforced by the economically and politically most powerful capitalist states.

Every "export of democracy" to other countries has always led to the negation of the very essence of democracy and the transformation of states into democratorships, thus causing outbreaks of internal conflicts and local wars with unintended consequences.

The policy of "exporting democracy" has greatly contributed to the emergence of the Islamis State of Iraq and Syria (ISIS), also known as the Islamic State of Iraq and Levant (ISIL), the cruelest terrorist organization of our era. Hundreds of thousands of people from countries affected by civil and religious war—especially those exposed to ISIS terror—have left or are leaving their homes in Syria, Iraq, Afghanistan, Pakistan, Libya, Somalia, and other countries and fleeing mainly to the more developed countries of the EU, and to a much lesser extent to countries in the Western Hemisphere—the U.S., Canada, Brazil, etc.

The migrant crisis has grown into a burning problem for Europe and the world. It shows what the policy of "exporting democracy" and the hegemony of the great powers has brought and where will it lead.

As the newly elected 45th president of the U.S., Trump stated that the U.S. would avoid interventions in foreign conflicts in the future and that it would stop changing foreign regimes. "Instead of this, our focus will be the triumph over the terrorism and the destruction of ISIS" (Siddiqui 2016).

24.

ANTI-GLOBALISM AND ANTI-CAPITALISM

The contemporary capitalist order, characterized by neoliberalism and globalization, "became notorious because of salary reductions and making industrial workers obsolete in developed countries" (*Samuelson* 2017).

Members of the oppressed, exploited, and marginalized social strata rebel against the neoliberal capitalist order and its bureaucratic nomenclature, the imperialist "export of democracy," the enormous alienation of labor from capital and the capitalist exploitation, and against the world domination of capital and the cruel dictatorship of the capitalist class. It is a particular kind of *political resistance*, known in political theory and practice as *anti-globalism* and *anti-capitalism*.

The most common form of political resistance of oppressed social strata against globalism and capitalism are protests (demonstrations). In all the capitals of Europe and the world, the number of protests grow every year since the global financial and economic crisis of 2007-2008, which means that the crisis continues and that the world has not yet come out of it. Extreme social inequality, mass unemployment, the high indebtedness of many states, and slow economic growth remain the main reasons for the protests of the oppressed and disenfranchised social strata.

Anti-globalist and anti-capitalist protests often manifest themselves as political resistance against the dominance of transnational financial and trade capital and against global economic, political, military, and other institutions. Hence at almost every session of the IMF, the World Bank, the World Trade Organization (WTO), the World Economic Summit—the summit of the world's most developed countries (the G7 and G20 summits)—, NATO, the World Social Summit, and other global organizations face mass demonstrations of anti-globalists, which are at times very fierce, and often sparking brutal reactions from local police in the name of protecting global interests and maintaining established global values.

One of the leading centers of the anti-globalization movement is the World Social Forum (WSF), based in Porto Alegre, Brazil, which has an extensive network around the globe and fights for global justice and solidarity.

In 1998, a network of globalization critics was formed in France as a non-governmental organization, known as the Association for the Taxation of Financial Transactions and Civic Action (ATTAC), which has about 90,000 members worldwide and operates in fifty countries with the slogan, "For a solidary world economy, and against neoliberal globalization."

According to Alain Touraine, a French sociologist,

> ...at the turn of the new century, anti-capitalist movements came to dominate an important section of public opinion, resulting in a capacity for massive mobilization of discontented wage-earners and consumers. Thus, we are witnessing the formation of an important movement of opposition to globalization—a movement which soon chose to change its name, in order to make it clearer that its aim was to construct a different kind of world organization/alter-globalization" (Touraine 2007: 21).

Anti-globalists consider neoliberal capitalism a form of contemporary imperialism. They believe that the concept of sustainable development is a neoliberal fraud, free trade cannot solve the problems of poverty and unemployment, and that economic development must be aligned with the social needs of the world.

25.

1968 STUDENT MOVEMENT

Be realistic, demand the impossible!
Legacy of 1968: The Slogan of Paris Students

Students in the West demonstrated their discontent with the capitalist social order in 1968 by organizing a student movement and general rebellion against the power and dominance of capital and the increasingly pronounced social differentiation in society. The "guru" of the student movement not only in the West, but also globally, was the German philosopher Herbert Marcuse. He described the capitalist society of the time as a comprehensive system of repression that stifled dialogue and absorbed opposition.

The student movement of 1968, in its essence, expressed the aspirations of the student masses in the West and around the world for a better, more just society. The students advocated for radical changes in such a captive society, affirming leftist, socialist, communist, and social democrat ideas, which Marcuse shaped into neo-Marxism. Unlike Marx, he did not place hope in the working class, but in students and other marginalized social groups such as ethnic minorities, women, and poor countries. He believed that the working class "which [had] the characteristics of a mid-[nineteenth] century English industrial worker" no longer presented a threat to capitalist order because capitalism is included in their system of production and is not protected from contamination by particularist interests (Marcuse 1978: 60).

Massive student protests in Belgrade in 1968 were part of the global revolutionary student movement and the birth of a global new left. The iconic slogan of that movement "Be realistic, demand the impossible," has not, even after fifty years, lost any of its relevance. Under the slogan "Down with the Red Bourgeoisie," Belgrade, Serbian, and Yugoslav students demanded the introduction of "more communism" into the existing socialist and self-managed social order. The social and economic reforms carried out by Yugoslav leadership, especially those of 1965, have contributed to the affirmation of market laws and freer action and led to a reduction in administrative and non-market forms of economic activities. Such development of socialism in Yugoslavia was, however, assessed by some communist centers of power, especially in Moscow and Beijing, as a "right turn" away from the established communist direction. As a result, Yugoslav state and party leadership were often accused of revisionism and restoring capitalism in Yugoslavia. In accordance with "more communism," Belgrade students demanded that the University of Belgrade change its name to the Red University "Karl Marx."

Student protests in Belgrade were suspended after a television address by President Tito on June 9, 1968. Tito said he supported most of the student demands, emphasizing that while "there were some irregularities," "no one is irreplaceable, not even [him]" and that he was "happy to have such youth who had proved to be mature." Students interpreted his speech as an acceptance of their demands, so demonstrations turned into events filled with songs and cheers for Tito. After the student demonstrations, the energetic implementation of the economic and social reforms of 1965 were abandoned, and most of the student demands have never been met.

Students have not won anywhere in the world. A valuable historical experience has, however, remained in the aftermath of the 1968 student movement as inspiration for new, future leftist visions and achievements. In the years and decades since the 1968 student movement, instead of "more communism," which was one of the demands of Belgrade students in socialist Yugoslavia, the world stage has been dominated by the undivided power of capital in the forms of Thatcherism and Reaganism (i.e. neoliberalism), bringing "more capitalism" everywhere in the world, especially in former socialist countries. Capital was constantly pushing the pendulum of the historical development of society to the right, and did so very intensely, quickly, and as far as it could after the "fall of communism" in the 1990s.

Almost fifty years after the student protests of 1968 in Serbia and its capital Belgrade, peaceful protests of students and citizens erupted in the spring of 2017. The 2017 protest movement was called the "anti-dictatorship protest," because of alleged election fraud and potential vote theft in the presidential election, which was held on April 3, 2017, and won by Aleksandar Vučić in the first round. In essence, however, these protests were an open rebellion against the grim economic and social situation in the country—the widening and deepening of the gap between the rich and the poor in society. In this respect, in their own way, they were reminiscent of the 1968 Belgrade student protests.

It can be said that the common thread of the student protests in Belgrade of 1968 and 2017 was leftism. After almost three decades, a hammer and a sickle returned to the streets of Belgrade. In the 1968 student protests, however, leftism was very clearly articulated, not "dumb" (unarticulated) as in the 2017 student protests. In fact, the demands of the Serbian left were not heard well at the 2017 protests because of uncivilized ad hominem messages and hysterical cries against the newly-elected President Aleksandar Vučić ("Boo, Vučić") were incomparably louder, which trivialized the very meaning of the protest. It was also noticeable that students protested mostly because of elections they largely did not participate in with a number of opposition leaders for whom the election results did not work out in their favor, some of which were of anti-leftist orientation. These protests were politically utterly unsuccessful.

26.

WRECK OF THE OLD LEFT

The notion of the left is ambiguous and inoperative.

Todor Kulić

In the years after the fall of the Berlin Wall and the collapse of socialist regimes, the world scene has been sovereignly ruled by the political right of all colors and shades. All political parties of leftist ideological orientation were pushed into an extremely defensive political position and practically politically marginalized with the exception of, to some extent, social democrats, who tend to sit on "two chairs." "Because the working-class movement had been so battered and bloodied, and the political left so robustly rolled back" (Eagleton 2011: 6) in the capitalist West, the earlier endemic fear of socialism and communism has disappeared—especially the fear of Eurocommunism ("socialism with a human face") which was propagated by several Western European communist parties in the 1970s and 1980s. The hatred of the capitalist elite, however, toward socialism and communism has remained unchanged; perhaps even increased.

The global historical and social changes in the 1990s have caught the left of the world—especially in Europe—unprepared for the challenges that these changes have brought with them. The collapse of the Soviet bloc was a real shock for the left because it did not expect the dynamics of social change to occur on a global scale. The left has been gripped by ideological action and organizational disorientation, and was thus politically bruised. The left has also been socially marginalized because of its own conformism and submissiveness before the crumbs that remain for the leaders of the left after the large meals of the bourgeoisie.

In the intellectual and ideological circles of the victorious right-wing—the political articulators of the interests of big capital—there has been widespread speculation that the political parties of the left (workers' parties, communists, socialists and social democrats) are no longer needed by anyone, not even workers and working people in general, because the historical changes made in the 1990s guaranteed every possible human right and freedom worthy of a human being. The class winners of the 1990s historical changes are deeply convinced that socialist and communist ideas were successfully buried for all time and that they would never rise again from the ruins of socialism. Shifty left-wing intellectuals believed that time had forever overtaken the left and all its political parties, regardless of their differences.

The left has faced the problem of political and ideological turncoats in its own ranks, in the most serious form. Even some "virtuous communists" have begun to renounce Marx and Marxism, declaring publicly that they were never communists or Marxists. All of a sudden, they have become virtuous believers. For example, in the newly created states in former Yugoslavia, Marxist literature was expelled from home libraries—works by Marx and Engels, Lenin, Tito, Kardelj, and other Soviet and Yugoslav Marxist theorists—and thrown into dumpsters. Works of Marxist literature have been swiftly removed from the windows of all state and other bookstores.

The predictions and expectations of capitalist circles and the political right about the end of the political left have not come true historically, however. Left-wing political parties have not disappeared from the political scene, despite the fact that many converts appeared in their ranks. In very difficult political conditions, they somehow managed to survive the disappearance of socialism by significantly adapting to the era of absolute rule of capital. They stopped disputing the basics of capitalism loudly and started to tacitly reconcile with imposed neoliberal values, and even to secretly admire them. The capitalist exploitation of workers no longer bothers them much and they do not publicly oppose the enormous social differences in their countries.

In the general political atmosphere successfully created by neoliberalism, the traditional political parties of the left in the West and the world are tired, worn out, and ideologically still wandering. Their leaders were overtaken by time in every aspect, and the very word "socialism" has almost completely lost its meaning. Leftist parties are no longer relevant political factors in almost any European country.

> There is still no organized left in Europe that would turn anti-capitalism into a hegemonic consciousness. Resistance is scattered and decentered. That is why multi-party elections are still basically a one-horse race. And the plural neoliberal public is not a mind filter, but a power filter. Although the accumulation of risk is becoming more and more obvious, there is no accumulation of social rebellion (Kuljić 2002: 480).

All traditional left-wing political parties that were labeled as socialist, social democratic, or democratic have lost many important features of the true left and cannot cope with the neoliberal capitalist political spectrum dominated by right-wing parties—i.e., the parties of capital. Their leftism has faded, and trust in them is at the lowest level. Knowingly or unknowingly, they betrayed the authentic interests of exploited and impoverished workers, whose trade union rights and basic human rights are increasingly less protected.

The situation that has been created in society makes it difficult to notice the real differences between the political parties of the traditional left and the classic right and determine the extent of their divide. Left-wing parties without particular ideological demands or obstacles can successfully cooperate with right-wing parties and become an appendage of right-wing governments. It is no longer strange for members of the left to "party-hop" into the parties of the right in order to obtain state power and material privileges.

It occasionally happens that some right-wing parties, because of their electoral needs and victories, are greater protectors of the interests of impoverished workers and other social strata than the traditional parties of the left ideological spectrum, which are politically and ideologically disoriented. Thus, thanks to the votes of the poorest workers and other strata of society, candidates from the right win elections very easily.

For instance, the "declining living standards for many ordinary Americans and the demographic shifts that threaten the majority status of white Americans helped to create the pool of angry voters that elected Mr. Trump" to the U.S. presidency in November 2016 (Rachman 2017). Trump is "the far right in many ways...The left must remind people what that man really is..." (Béja 2017). Bernie Sanders, a U.S. senator from Vermont, believes that Trump won because he managed to take advantage of

> ...the anger of a declining middle class that is sick and tired of establishment economics, establishment politics and the establishment media. People are tired of working longer hours for lower wages, of seeing decent paying jobs go to China and other low-wage countries, of billionaires not paying any federal income taxes and of not being able to afford a college education

for their kids—all while the very rich become much richer (*Sanders Statement* 2016).

The traditional parties of the left, especially social democrats and socialists, have accepted the postulates of Thatcherism and Reganism uncritically, adapted to neoliberalism, accepted the growing social inequality in society, and forgot about class struggle and the principles of social solidarity.

The left in Serbia is in a particularly deep political crisis because it abandoned its leftist tradition. The two largest nominally left-wing political parties, the Socialist Party of Serbia and the Democratic Party, and several smaller socialist and social democratic parties have practically turned their backs on workers and the working class. These parties do not represent their interests loudly and convincingly, have succumbed to contemporary wild neoliberal capitalism, and are far from representing the true modern anti-liberal and anti-capitalist left. For them, their raison d'état to be in power at all costs became far more important than the class struggle against the capitalist exploitation of working people.

All over the world, social democratic parties "flaunt" and manipulate the middle class, considering it the most capable social force when it comes to the nonviolent transformation of neoliberal capitalism into new socialism, which usually means a civil society of social justice.

> These parties believe they are the bearers of a 'great historical compromise of labor and capital.' That is mostly just an illusion in the current historical moment, especially in post-real-socialist societies. They are also in a serious crisis, which has been going on for a long time and its end is not yet in sight. The European left

has, in general, experienced a collapse like never before in the time after World War II (Vidojević 2015: 359).

In the late nineteenth and early twentieth centuries, social democracy truly advocated for changing the capitalist order in order to seek a compromise between labor and capital and fought for the realization of basic worker rights—its orientation was, therefore, truly leftist. Current social democracy is a big class disappointment. Its overall contribution to changing the contemporary neoliberal capitalist social order is a "big round zero." The relationship between labor and capital remains exploitative and wage-earning. In its current neoliberal form, capitalism is even more exploitative than it has ever been before. "Therefore, it can be said that the social democratic party today is primarily recognized as a party of government and peripheral social changes, and not as a key party that can initiate fundamental changes in the system, which oppose primitive and cruel capitalism" (Ibid.: 371).

Of all the leftists, the capitalist class is the most tolerant of the "social democrats," because their criticism of the capitalist social order is the mildest and most acceptable compared to "socialists" and "communists." Therefore, it is no exaggeration to say that social democracy is, in fact, "capital-left."

In order to preserve its social order, the capitalist class very skillfully manipulates the middle class, often proclaiming it the pillar and the engine of this order, instead of itself.

Today, socialists are not very different from social democrats. They also turned their backs on realizing the authentic interests of all the social strata that depend on capital and the economic and political power of capitalists (working and middle class). Socialist and social democrat parties have found a compromise with right-wing parties in their division of power, but between labor and capital. In the conditions of such a political positioning of social democrats and socialists, it is unrealistic to expect any significant changes to the essence of capitalist production relations.

This is why old-fashioned social-democrat and socialist parties throughout Europe, and especially in the Balkans, are rightly said to have turned into a "repair shop for the torn shoes of capitalism." They can think whatever they want about themselves and can call themselves the political left, but their pro-capitalist actions are evident. Leftist liberals are along the same political lines; despite advocating respect for human rights and freedoms, leftist liberals do not see that without the abolition of capitalist exploitation and wage labor and the elementary material equality in society, it is not possible to prevent violations of basic human rights and freedoms by the legal order itself, no matter how perfect it is.

27.

NEW LEFTIST MOVEMENTS AND INITIATIVES

Even before the global financial and economic crisis of 2007 and 2008—and especially afterwards when it became clear to exploited workers and the impoverished masses that the good life promised by the bourgeoisie in the 1990s would not happen—a new democratic left of the twenty-first century started to emerge, and new left-wing political parties, associations, and movements were founded. The new democratic left, although still in its infancy without a consistent conceptual and ideological platform and fragile in every respect, is expanding its ranks with new supporters, especially among the younger generation, and is already present and active in the European and global political arena.

The new left opposes neoliberal capitalism, the exploitation of workers and all working strata in society, the unbearable social differences between the rich and the poor, the unlimited power of capital, the monopoly of political parties intrinsically linked to capital, and the economic and political dictatorship of the capitalist class and global superclass. It advocates for a new and economically more balanced relations between workers and owners of capital and balancing the interests of labor and capital while also protecting the authentic interests of workers and all other working strata in society who live exclusively from their living labor and sell their labor as a commodity because they are forced to do so.

In the 2015 Greek parliamentary elections, the Coalition of the Radical Left in Greece, abbreviated SIRIZA (Greek: Συνασπισμός Ριζοσπαστικής Αριστεράς), won 149 of 300 parliamentary seats and formed a majority government led by Prime Minister Alexis Tsipras. Since then, SIRIZA has broken into the social-liberal and the left wing. In the early Greek parliamentary held on July 7, 2019, the ruling left-wing SIRIZA, led by Tsipras, was overwhelmingly defeated by the New Democracy, the Greek conservative opposition led by Kyriakos Mitsotakis.

The Spanish left-wing political party Podemos ("We Can") was created in early 2014 by Pablo Iglesias, who remains its leader. Podemos fights against social inequality, unemployment, and the economic woes in Spain following the European debt crisis of 2007 and 2008. In the elections for the national parliament held on December 20, 2015, Podemos won 21 percent of the vote and became the third largest party in the parliament, holding 69 out of 350 seats.

From the position of the new left, Podemos presented itself to Spain and the world more as a "party of system blockade" than a "party of hope," which opened new democratic horizons for Spanish society (Panović 2016).

In the United Kingdom (UK), "the Labour party sunk to the level of filthy fight for leadership, because mainstream and Blairist parliamentarists launched a coup against [the] radically left leader, Jeremy Corbyn, elected by its membership. It seems probable Corbyn will survive this political battle, thanks to his energetic counter-attack and the election system he inherited from Ed Milliband" (Galbraith 2016).

Jeremy Corbyn considers himself a follower of Marx and a democratic socialist. Under his leadership, more new members joined the Labor Party than under the neoliberal socialist Tony Blair

(Unkovski Korica 2016: 3). In the early parliamentary elections in Great Britain held on December 12, 2019, the Labour Party suffered a historic defeat to the Conservative Party, which won the absolute majority of seats in Parliament, resulting in Corbyn resigning as the leader of Labour in March 2020. According to Greek leftist Janis Varoufakis, the defeat of Jeremy Corbyn's Labour Party in the UK "threatened the radical left's momentum" (Varoufakis 2019).

The first round of presidential elections in France held on April 23, 2017 showed that its "left wing is alive," "it is not true the leftism is dead" and that "left wing is truly active when it is truly left" (Martelli 2017).

The presidential candidate of the radical left, Jean-Luc Jean-Luc Mélenchon ran under the banner of the party La France insoumise (FI), which translates to unbowed France or unsubmissive France. Mélenchon won 19.58 percent of the vote and thus opened "a new chapter in the history of French left…In [the] days before the elections, [the] left wing was mainly non-existent, while the right was loud and convinced it can triumph once again. The result was far more complex than they expected" (Ibid.). Mélenchon achieved "an impressive result…He succeeded [in organizing] a fresh start for the left, pulling it out of sociological and structural ghetto, so it doesn't represent only educated urban members of the middle class, but a wider national basis around the whole country…" (Ventura 2017). The recent political rise of the left in France is, one might say, a kind of barometer of the situation in the "left hemisphere" of Europe and around the world.

In 2015, due to the ideological and political differences within the Democratic Party—the leading political party in Serbia after the regime overthrow of Slobodan Milosević—political actors of left ideological orientation founded a new left-wing political party led by Borko Stefanović called the Serbian Left, joining forces with a small number of Serbian radical leftists. The Serbian Left participated independently in the parliamentary elections held on April 24, 2016, but won only 0.94 percent of the vote, thus remaining below the threshold needed to enter parliament.

The Serbian Left was one of the founders of the Alliance for Serbia (Serbian: Savez za Srbiju, SZS), a comprehensive coalition of different opposition political parties in Serbia, created in September of 2018 on the initiative of Dragan Djilas, the former mayor of Belgrade and the former president of the Democratic Party.

At the November 2018 panel of the Alliance for Serbia in Kruševac, Borko Stefanović was physically attacked. This attack was the main reason why peaceful street protests (called Stop to Bloody Shirts) began, which subsequently grew into peaceful street protests (One of Five Million) organized throughout Serbia. In 2018 and 2019 in Belgrade alone, 53 such protests were held every Saturday and persistently demanded systemic changes and the resignation of the current government led by Aleksandar Vučić.

On April 19, 2019, Dragan Djilas, one of the leaders of the Alliance for Serbia, founded the Party of Freedom and Justice (Serbian: Stranka slobode i pravde, SSP), a center-left political party, which virtually merged with the Serbian Left.

In Serbia, for a long time, there has been the idea of forming a truly left-wing political party with a democratic socialist orientation to fill the space between the social democratic parties and the classic communist left, which has been vacant since the establishment of the multi-party political system in 1990. The realization of this idea now seems likely. The well-known Serbian sociologist Jovo Bakić announced the establishment of such a political party, scheduled for December 22, 2019 (the Day of Yugoslav People's Army, which was a national holiday in Yugoslava), but postponed until the end of January

2020 or later. This new left-wing political party would unite the Social Democratic Union (Serbian: Socijaldemokratska unija, SDU), the Left Summit of Serbia (Serbian: Levi samit Srbije), and the Democracy in Europe Movement 2025, a pan-European, cross-border movement of democrats (DiEM 25), bringing together the supporters of Janis Varufakis in Serbia. Most likely, a new left-wing party in Serbia will be called the Workers' Party (Vlaović 2019).

The political future of a new left-wing political party in Serbia is not easy to predict. The existing "political market" of the ideas of true left orientation, not just classical communist thought, currently does not have the sufficient political support of the electorate in Serbia, which is why political parties of the left ideological spectrum currently have no significant political significance or influence on the state. The main battle for the affection of the Serbian electorate is taking place in the "right hemisphere" of the political spectrum. Furthermore, the basic ideological matrix of all right-wing political parties is the same or very similar. Their mutual competition is not conceptual and ideological in nature, but is exclusively a political battle for power for its own sake, and is always of the right political orientation.

For political parties of the left—not only in Serbia, but in general—to get out of the long-term crisis in which they found themselves, the following three conditions have to be met.

First, the importance of class consciousness needs to be affirmed in the political organization and actions of the parties of the "left hemisphere" of society, starting from the classic Marxist approaches to this issue. Without such consciousness, political actions to improve the class position of workers will not be successful. The capitalist class and its "right hemisphere" parties hold the reins of power firmly in their hands because the "left hemisphere" parties underestimate the importance of class consciousness and abandoned every possible form of class struggle. This is why Marx's works and classical Marxist literature on class consciousness and class struggle must be studied again and properly evaluated.

Second, there has to be the possibility of creating new left-wing parties as authentic as possible with new democratic socialist visions that are capable of confronting political parties of the right on equal footing and with political knowledge and skills. Old, traditional left-wing parties find it very difficult to adapt to new times, needs, and requirements.

Third, new party leaders are needed who able to formulate and promote true democratic values and new socialist ideas of a broad political spectrum, such as, for example, the introduction of self-management in enterprises and local communities and at higher levels of social organization and society.

If these conditions are not met, it is illusory to fantasize about the collapse and end of capital or to have a vision of a new possible democratic society of social justice, equality, and of comprehensive social and labor rights without exploitation or living at the expense of other people's labor.

The problem of the new left, especially of communist and socialist orientation, and characteristic of the traditional left, was and remains *fractionism*—belonging to different ideological formations, such as Marxists, anarchists, Trotskyists, Leninists, Stalinists, Maoists, Titoists, moderate, and extreme leftists. In Russia alone, there are fifty communist fractions today in various shades of red. Fractionism and factions constantly degrade the political power of the parties of the left and diminish their ability to change existing capitalist society into a new socialism—more precisely, to *feasible socialism*, which is a new conceptual definition of socialism coined in the modern sociological and political school of thought in the West.

The left could be relevant to the contemporary European and global political scene only if it offered its own specific solutions to the increasingly difficult developmental, economic, political, and social challenges facing humanity today, such as the global coordination of sustainable development, the widening and deepening gap between the rich and the poor, neocolonialism, the crisis of the capitalist order, the migrant crisis, and environmental and demographic challenges.

The new left's strategic point of political struggle must be must be Marx's discovery that the surplus of value in capitalism stems from the capitalist exploitation of the unpaid portion of workers; total living labor, which is appropriate for the given social reality, notwithstanding all internal stratifications, frictions, and divisions.

Leftist ideas and political resistance to growing social inequality resulting from the exploitation of workers are also present in the U.S., the main patron of world capitalism and current neoliberal views. Bernie Sanders, the aforementioned U.S. senator who publicly describes himself as a "democratic socialist," is particularly noteworthy. His leftist ideas about "American socialism" during his 2016 primary campaign to be the Democratic presidential nominee won him the sympathies of the majority of the younger generation of Americans, the middle class, and the socially most vulnerable. "After decades of being dismissed as a radical movement, socialism in America is back in the spotlight" (Nilaya 2015).

During a tumultuous campaign in which Sanders challenged Hillary Clinton's candidacy, Sanders' leftist ideas about "American socialism" and

> ...his rhetoric [has] rattled the American public, because any socialism, even [a] moderate one, is utterly demonized and excluded from this country's policy in early 40s. Therefore,

Sanders represents the return of socialism in political discourse, after more than half of a century of hibernation. This is where he proves to be important—he opened a space for a new, growing left (Wolff 2016).

Hillary Clinton was "surely not a leftist" (Béja 2017) and was supported by the owners and loyal servants of big capital—mostly members of the American superclass—as well as members of the D.C. elite, the financial circles of Wall Street, and leading media groups in the country. In the end, despite the fact that Sanders was a more convincing candidate, Democratic Party leadership, under the influence and pressure of the interests of big capital, nominated Clinton for U.S. president. Clinton was ultimately defeated by the Republican candidate, the billionaire Donald J. Trump. "Bernie Sanders bravely tried to create left populism, but Clinton and Obama destroyed him during unfair pre-elections of the Democratic Party" (West 2017).

Today, *urban democratic movements* and *civic democratic initiatives* are becoming increasingly politically important worldwide. They have become a kind of megatrend.

It became obvious that international investments and other business interests are getting advantage[s] in decisions regarding how the city will be shaped.

When people actually see the connection between seemingly separated issues—for example, forcing mega-projects, closing social [centers] for the poor, [the] lack of care for schools—thousands of people happen to go out on the streets in rebellion towards the way our cities are governed.

Many movements rose in cities, out of the need to re-evaluate the fact they succumbed to profit making, while citizens watch their environment getting less and less liveable.

I don't want to say that before the era of neoliberalism everything was just perfect, but certain important changes made people go out on the streets (Meyer 2016.).

The Occupy Wall Street protest movement began on September 17, 2011 in Zuccotti Park, located near New York City's Financial District in downtown Manhattan. The Occupy movement declared that it was opposed to social and economic inequality in American society, the greed of corporate-financial capital, and the widespread corruption of political elites and the undue influence of corporations on the government. The slogan of the protesters was "We are the 99%," referring to the income and wealth inequality between the richest 1 percent and the rest of the U.S. population. On November 15, 2011, the protesters were expelled from Zuccotti Park after vigorous police intervention.

Although the Occupy Wall Street movement failed to change the state of affairs in American society, the ideas and political warnings of the movement remain very relevant, especially among the young and socially disadvantaged American population. Commenting on the emergence of the Occupy Wall Street movement, Noam Chomsky, a preeminent American intellectual, says

> ...the Occupy movement has helped rebuild class solidarity and communities of mutual support on a level unseen since the time of the Great Depression. The Occupy movement spontaneously created something that doesn't really exist in the country: communities of mutual support, cooperation, open spaces for discussion...just people doing things and helping each other. That's very much missing" (Chomsky 2012).

In 2014, following the example of the Occupy Wall Street movement, the Movement for the Occupation of Cinemas was created in Serbia, inspired by the famous Belgrade cinema Zvezda, which had undergone wild privatization and left to decay. The occupation of this cultural institution failed because the political bureaucratic apparatus was stronger than the democratic force of the movement. Several local movements and initiatives were similarly launched in Serbia. Twelve of these organizations founded the Civic Front on April 13, 2019, an umbrella association of local movements from all over Serbia: "Do not let Belgrade d(r)own," The United Movement of Free Tenants from Niš, the Local Front(s) from Kraljevo, Valjevo, and Vlasotince, "Go hard!" from Mladenovac, "Critical Mass" from Kula, the Local Alternative from Vrbas, the movement "Loud and clear" from Požarevac, the Initiative for Požega, Civic Turnaround from Zrenjanin and "Only local" from Bečej.

Thanks to the actions of new left political parties and new democratic movements and initiatives, socialist and even communist ideas are no longer frightening to Western capitalist societies three decades after the demise of socialist countries, and they are no longer "allergic" to the word "socialism." "Socialism" has become quite familiar in everyday political vocabulary in the West, perhaps even excessively used, although to the same extent in former socialist countries. In any case, being a "socialist" is something completely normal today, and even being "communist" is no longer a political disaster.

It can be argued that without an educated, strong, and well-organized new political left, society cannot find a way out of the maze of deep political contradictions and permanent economic crises that shake the modern capitalist world. It is not at all about starting a new ideological struggle between right and left, but solely about the need for the sustainable survival and general progress of society. The condition for achieving such far-reaching goals is the constant advocacy and fight for true democracy, real economic and political rights, human freedoms, and more just relationships in the product distribution of social labor that is free of any form of exploitation of other people's labor.

28.

SUSTAINED AND PROGRESSIVE CAPITALISM

*Capitalism depends on the reproduction
and intensification of exploitation work.*

Herbert Marcuse

In contemporary academic and ideological circles of the political right and in certain social democratic layers of the world's political left, the dominant belief is that the existing capitalist social order is simply God-given.

There are several well understood advantages inherent in capitalism that make it superior to any other system for organizing economic activity. It has proven to be far more efficient in the allocation of resources and the matching of supply with demand, far more effective at wealth creation, and far more conducive to high levels of freedom and political self-governance. At the most basic level, however, capitalism has become the world's economic ideology of choice primarily because it demonstrably unlocks a higher fraction of the human potential with ubiquitous organic incentives that reward hard work, ingenuity and innovation (Gore & Blood 2010).

Despite receiving generous praise, modern capitalism has also been the subject of harsh criticism. Some claim that neoliberal capitalism is obsessed with short-term thinking, achieving instant results in every business venture and investment, that it does not take enough care of people, society, and the planet, and that such an unsustainable situation causes market turmoil, deepenng the gap between the rich and the poor while delaying solving acute climate problems. *The Manifesto for Sustainable Capitalism*, formulated and published by Al Gore and David Blood, states that

> We are once again facing one of those rare turning points in history when dangerous challenges and limitless opportunities cry out for clear, long-term thinking. The disruptive threats now facing the planet are extraordinary: climate change, water scarcity, poverty, disease, growing income inequality, urbanization, massive economic volatility and more...
>
> Before the crisis and since, we and others have called for a more responsible form of capitalism, what we call sustainable capitalism: a framework that seeks to maximize long-term economic value by reforming markets to address real needs while integrating environmental, social and governance (ESG) metrics throughout the decision-making process (Gore & Blood 2011).

The ideologists and theorists of capitalism are, like successful employers, firmly convinced that capitalism is historically affirmed, its ideological foundations are unparalleled and untouchable, and that it can only be further improved and perfected, but its essence cannot be significantly changed. For example, Germany's minister of finance, Wolfgang Schäuble, believes that the liberal world order "is still the best of all the possible worlds, for ethical, political and economic reasons. And we want that order to progress or at least not to regress" (Radičević 2017: 2).

According to the German historian Jürgen Kocka,

> ...capitalism lives off its socially-owned, cultural, and political embedding, as much as it simultaneously threatens and corrodes these moorings. It can be influenced by political means and those of civil society *when* and *if* these are strong and decisive enough.

> Seen from this perspective, one could say that, every era, every region, and every civilization gets capitalism it deserves. Currently, considered alternatives *to* capitalism are hard to identify. But *within* capitalism, very different variant and alternatives can be observed, and even more of them can be imagined. It is *their* development that matters. The reform of capitalism is a permanent task. In this, the critique of capitalism plays a central role (Kocka 2016: 169).

> Unlike capitalism, socialism has never been "able to learn," which is its irreparable disadvantage.

French economist Thomas Piketty believes that

> ....there is always an alternative, there are always different ways to organize capitalism, economy, society. When we look at fiscal history, the history of the social state and the distribution of wealth, we conclude that there are many possible solutions. It is wrong to believe that there is only one way. There is no ideal model; each country must find its own solutions, its own institutions.

> ...If we want to regulate capitalism, we need to have confidence in democracy, to organize fiscal, social, financial institutions that will control the multinational enterprises and the financial sector (Piketty 2015: 14).

According to Joseph Stiglitz, a Nobel laureate in economics, in the race to succeed neoliberalism there are

> ...at least three major political alternatives: far-right nationalism, center-left reformism, and the progressive left (with the center-right representing the neoliberal failure). And yet, with the exception of the progressive left, these alternatives remain beholden to some form of the ideology that has (or should have) expired.

> The center-left, for example, represents neoliberalism with a human face. Its goal is to bring the policies of former U.S. President Bill Clinton and former British Prime Minister Tony Blair into the twenty-first century, making only slight revisions to the prevailing modes of financialization and globalization. Meanwhile, the nationalist right disowns globalization, blaming migrants and foreigners for all of today's problems...

> By contrast, the third camp advocates what [Stiglitz calls] *progressive capitalism*, which prescribes a radically different economic agenda, based on four priorities. The first is to restore the balance between markets, the state, and civil society...

> The second priority is to recognize that the "wealth of nations" is the result of *scientific inquiry*—learning about the world around us—and social organization that allows large groups of people to work together for the common good. Markets still have a crucial role to play in facilitating social cooperation, but they serve this purpose only if they are governed by the rule of law and subject to democratic checks. Otherwise, individuals can get rich by exploiting others, extracting

wealth through rent-seeking rather than creating wealth through genuine ingenuity. Many of today's wealthy took the exploitation route to get where they are. They have been well served by Trump's policies, which have encouraged rent-seeking while destroying the underlying sources of wealth creation. Progressive capitalism seeks to do precisely the opposite.

This brings us to the third priority: addressing the growing problem of concentrated *market power*...The rise in corporate market power, combined with the decline in workers' bargaining power, goes a long way toward explaining why inequality is so high and growth so tepid. Unless government takes a more active role than neoliberalism prescribes, these problems will likely become much worse, owing to advances in robotization and artificial intelligence.

The fourth key item on the progressive agenda is to sever the link between economic power and political influence. Economic power and political influence are mutually reinforcing and self-perpetuating, especially where, as in the U.S., wealthy individuals and corporations may spend without limit in elections. As the U.S. moves ever closer to a fundamentally undemocratic system of "one dollar, one vote," the system of checks and balances so necessary for democracy likely cannot hold: nothing will be able to constrain the power of the wealthy. This is not just a moral and political problem: economies with less inequality actually *perform better*. Progressive-capitalist reforms thus have to begin by curtailing the influence of money in politics and reducing wealth inequality.

...The alternatives offered by nationalists and neoliberals would guarantee more stagnation, inequality, environmental degradation, and political acrimony, potentially leading to outcomes we do not even want to imagine.

Progressive capitalism is not an oxymoron. Rather, it is the most viable and vibrant alternative to an ideology that has clearly failed" (Stiglitz 2019/30 May).

Undoubtedly, capitalism as a system can be improved, perfected, ironed out, and regulated in order to make it a better and more sustainable system than its current neoliberal form through a combination of appropriate economic and social measures. Numerous practical solutions are at hand that can mitigate the effects of unemployment, exploitation, and poverty, while also reducing present social tensions and contradictions inherent in contemporary neoliberal capitalism. Such solutions include unconditional monthly unemployment benefits, increasing the real minimum wage, subsidized or free housing for the poorest, subsidizing prices of basic groceries, health insurance for all, "free" education for children from socially disadvantaged families, longer and subsidized vacations, stricter requirements for terminating employment, increasing severance pay in the event of job loss, introducing a 35-hour working week, duration limits for occasional and temporary employments, and better hygiene and technical protection at work. All of this is, of course, modest, but certainly better than the current situation.

All of these suggested and similar measures, no matter how significant in the socioeconomic sense, do not, however, call into question the very nature of capitalist production relations—i.e., the antagonistic relationship between labor and capital and workers and employers, which have been the central economic, political, and social problem of the capitalist world.

29.

IS LIBERAL CAPITALISM SUSTAINABLE?

*The bourgeoisie, wherever it has got the upper hand,
has put an end to all...
and has left remaining no other nexus between man
and man than naked self-interest,
than callous "cash payment."*

Karl Marx and Friedrich Engels

Neoliberalism has undermined democracy for 40 years.

Joseph E Stiglitz

We must end neoliberalism, or neoliberalism will end us.

Fred Guerin

*The problem we live in is that this system
is not only not working, it's breaking down*

Richard D. Wolff

The world has gone mad and the system is broken.

Raymond Ray Dalio

Capitalism is, by its internal systemic structure, the generator of cyclical economic crises and the widening gap between the rich and the poor. "Liberalism and market capitalism perpetuate titanic and

246

permanent forms of inequality that might have made dukes and earls of old blush…" (Deneen 2018: 140). These are the incurable diseases of contemporary capitalism, viewed through the prism of its historical development to date.

All previous "enhancements" and intrasystem "reforms" of capitalism have not changed the basic nature of capitalist production relations. Capitalism today remains as it has always been: a social order dominated by the monopoly of private property, the separation of labor and capital, and the exploitation of wage workers and working people who are forced to sell their labor force to the employers, the owners of capital. In this respect, even the most developed concepts of state welfare, such as the Nordic model, have not fundamentally changed anything in capitalism.

Speaking of "the accumulating catastrophe as evidence" and "the ruins" created by liberal capitalism, Deneen warns, "To call for the cures of liberalism's ills by applying more liberal measures is tantamount to throwing gas on a raging fire. It will only deepen our political, social, economic, and moral crisis" (Ibid.: 25). He believes that

> …the greatest current threat to liberalism lies not outside and beyond liberalism but within it.…Among the greatest challenges facing humanity is the ability to survive progress…The triumphant march of liberalism has succeeded in at once drawing down the social and natural resources that liberalism did not create and cannot replenish, but which sustained liberalism even as its advance eroded its own unacknowledged foundation…While we have been slow to realize that the odds were in favor of the house, the damning evidence arising from liberalism's very success affirms that only

blinkered ideology can conceal liberalism's unsustainability (Ibid.: 28–31).

Branko Milanović, a Serbian-American economist, opines that

....growing income inequality still threatens the ideological domination of capitalism, showing its ugly side: an exclusive focus on material goods, an ideology in which the winner gets everything, and disregard for the non-monetary motivation. But since there is no significant ideological alternative and there are no powerful political parties or groups advocating alternatives, the capitalist ideology seems invincible. Of course, no one guarantees that this will be true in twenty or fifty years, because emergence of some new ideologies is possible, but today, that is the reality.

Is democratic capitalism sustainable? That is quite another matter. First, it should be noted that these two words (democracy and capitalism) have not historically always gone together. Capitalism existed without democracy, not only in Franco's Spain, Pinochet's Chile and Mobutu's Congo, but also in Germany, France and Japan, and even in the United States at the time when black people were excluded from politics, or in Britain, with its restricted access. It does not take much imagination to imagine a possible split between capitalism and democracy. Inequality could play an important role in this separation, which it already plays, by giving the rich immeasurably greater political power than the members of the middle class and the poor. The rich dictate the political agenda, fund candidates who protect their interests, and make sure only laws that suit them are passed... American political scientist

Larry Bartels found that U.S. senators are five to six times more likely to respond to the needs of the rich than to the needs of the middle class. Moreover, Bartels concludes: 'There is no clear evidence that the views of low-income voters have any influence on how senators vote.' Not only has the middle class been decimated but... democracy itself has been compromised...

...Democratically elected representatives almost exclusively respond to the needs and demands of the rich. Money has never played a more important role in American politics, and the Supreme Court's decision to grant the rights of individuals to corporations "opened the door, legally and formally, to an unprecedented increase in the influence of money on political decision-making.

Since promoting current globalization processes is in the interest of the rich, who benefit greatly from these processes...and the middle class and the poor could formally jeopardize those interests, the rich have focused on suppressing democracy (although this is not exactly how the goal has been defined for some of the applied measures). Suppression takes place in two parallel ways: 1) suppressing the voice of the poor, and 2) building something that [Milanović calls] false consciousness among members of the lower middle classes and the poor (Milanović 2017: 156–157 and 161).

It is unhistorical to think that capitalism is an eternal social order and marks the peak of the civilizational development of society or that there is nowhere further to go. The owners of capital and the capitalist class must be aware of this fact, as should many ideologues and apologists of the capitalist order, inside of which they live a privileged and good life. Slave owners and feudal lords were also once convinced that their social systems were the best and would last forever, which did not happen. By the same historical logic, a similar fate will befall the capitalist social order sooner or later. Capitalism is therefore not the end of human history, nor civilization.

The signs of the looming downfall of the capitalist order can be seen in the increasingly pronounced discontent of a huge number of exploited working and impoverished masses in all four corners of the world. The words of Eric Hobsbawm, one of the greatest historians of the second half of the twentieth century, also testify to this social paralysis. In May 2009, in an interview with the German weekly news magazine *Stern*, Hobsbawm said that in capitalism today, we are all on Titanic and we will eventually run into an iceberg (Kuljić 2012).

In this context, the following warning from Joseph Stiglitz has a special meaning:

> The neoliberal experiment—lower taxes on the rich, deregulation of labor and product markets, financialization, and globalization—has been a spectacular failure. Growth is lower than it was in the quarter-century after World War II, and most of it has accrued to the very top of the income scale. After decades of *stagnant* or even falling incomes for those below them, neoliberalism must be pronounced dead and buried (Stiglitz 2019).

The latest public opinion polls in Germany show that its citizens are increasingly critical of the capitalist system.

> According to a study conducted by the *YouGov* agency and the statistical portal *Statista*, only 16 [percent] of Germans polled have a positive view of capitalism, despite the fact that Germany has become the strongest economy in Europe and

one of the largest in the world, based on the capitalist economic model.

In the country of origin of Karl Marx and Friedrich Engels, only three percent of people have an extremely positive views of capitalism, 27 percent have no positive or negative views, while as much as 57 percent of respondents see it in a bad light (40 percent view it somewhat negatively, and 12 percent very negatively)…

When the researchers asked respondents to tell them their understanding of capitalism, as much as 60 percent of them saw capitalism as a system in which the rich become even richer and the poor even poorer (Radičević 2017: 2).

Alain Badiou advocates a world with more equality and fewer social differences, i.e. a more just social order. He believes that "capitalism gives power to a handful of people on the basis of means of production and wealth. It's a sick world. Pathologies should be exterminated or cured, and capitalism has become a disease of humanity. It is not a normal condition. In today's world, it may be, but only because communism has, so far, proved to be unsustainable" (Badiou 2014).

Dismantling "socialist totalitarianism" has had negative repercussions on the functioning of the neoliberal capitalist system itself, which seems to have been more energetic, economically more vital and successful, and even more generous to the socially disadvantaged in the years before the fall of the Berlin Wall than afterwards. Why?

During the Cold War, the West sought to prove to the world that the capitalist economic and political system is incomparably better than the socialist system on a global, national, and local level, constantly being compared to and competing with socialism wherever and whenever possible. The competitive spirit of capitalism was its "fuel" before the collapse of socialism. This competition was compounded by its fear of leftist parties becoming stronger and the emergence of communist parties in Italy, France, Spain, Greece, etc. The threat of revolutionary events in those countries and their possible spread to other capitalist countries in the world, resulted in capitalism creating a very powerful anti-socialist propaganda machine which persistently proclaimed that the capitalism the best social order and socialism the worst.

After the end of European socialism in the 1990s, capitalism suddenly lost the competitive spirit of the Cold War because it no longer had an ideological opponent on the world stage to compete with in order to prove that capitalism was more desirable. Immediately after the collapse of the USSR, Russia turned to the development of capitalism. The People's Republic of China, because of its market orientation and property pluralism, is not considered a socialist country by anyone in the West, regardless of the fact that it is still governed by their communist party.

30.

JAPANESE MODEL OF FIXING CAPITALISM

It can be said that the traditional Japanese business philosophy *kaizen*—coined from the words kai (change) and zen (good)— is continuously improving and maintaining capitalism. The worker is at the heart of this philosophy.

> The company accepts and treats the worker as a family member, [and] takes care of him and his family. Any even remotely large company has a special department that takes maximum care of a 'married' worker's family. The core of this business philosophy is the rule that...[a] motivated and satisfied worker is one of the most important prerequisites, if not the most important, for success of the company (Jović 2017: 74 –77).

Given that in the kaizen system the employer takes comprehensive care of the workers and their families, Japanese workers do not feel the burden of capital on their backs, even though their companies are privately owned in the hands of their employers. They do not consider themselves wage workers or exploited, but instead as an inseparable part of the "business family." Thanks to its kaizen system, Japan has, for a long time, been resolving antagonisms between labor representatives and representatives of capital more successfully than many other capitalist countries in the West who are solely obsessed with profit at all costs.

The kaizen system has also been the key to the business successes of the largest Japanese companies and the economic and technological achievements of Japan in the second half of the twentieth and the beginning of the twenty-first centuries. Thanks to its dynamic development, Japan often qualifies as a "global economic miracle." It has become the fourth economic power in the world, after China, the U.S., and India, with a GDP of 5.4 trillion U.S. dollars in 2017, despite not having significant natural resources, which is why it has been forced to import almost all basic raw materials and intermediate goods (World Factbook 2019).

Most Japanese employers are convinced that without genuine caring for employees and their families and their maximum work motivation and commitment to the companies in which they work, it is not possible to achieve desired business successes or economic and general social progress. However, in the era of globalization, Japanese corporations are increasingly influenced by American and global neoliberalism, which suppresses the traditional kaizen business philosophy and makes the economic and social position of workers in the corporation more insecure and uncertain.

Nevertheless, the achievements of the Japanese kaizen business philosophy, which in some respects resembles Yugoslavia's socialist self-management, could be helpful in tracing a possible way out of the maze of contemporary neoliberal capitalism.

31.

NOT ALL WAS BAD IN SOCIALISM!

The permanent crisis in which the capitalist social system has found itself has prompted not only the need to read Marx's *Capital*, but the need to critically evaluate the overall achievements of former socialist constructions, and the historical experience and heritage of an entire generation without interfering with daily politics and readily available ideology that is loyal to the capital and capitalist class. The goal of is to find systemic solutions for the social organization of labor that will be better and more functional than existing neoliberal capitalism.

In assessing the value of socialism, one should keep in mind the fact that the start of the socialist construction in the countries of Eastern Europe took place in extremely unfavorable global social circumstances. Their economic recovery after the enormous material devastation caused by World War II was far slower than Western European countries. One of the crucial reasons for this situation was political in nature. The USSR and Eastern European countries did not accept the U.S. offer to participate in the European Recovery Program, known as the Marshall Plan and named after U.S. Secretary of State George Marshall. Under this plan, which took effect in early 1948, the U.S. provided 15 billion dollars in economic assistance to Western European countries by 1952. At that time, an ounce of gold (about 30.1 grams) was worth 35 dollars, and as of September 14, 2020, is worth 1,956,72 U.S. dollars (Goldprice 2020).

The USSR, in whose ideological and political orbit all socialist countries were in at the time, condemned the Marshall Plan.

> The essence of the vague, particularly convoluted formulations of the 'Marshall Plan' is to create a bloc of states that would be linked by obligations to the U.S., and to give American loans as a reward for European states to give up their economic, and subsequently their political independence. While the [Truman]] Doctrine played the card of terrorist intimidation of those countries, the 'Marshall Plan' [is] about feeling their economic strength, trying to seduce those countries, and then binding them with dollar 'aid' (Zhdanov 1947: 30–32).

Thanks primarily to the Marshall Plan, and not so much to the capitalist system itself, the countries of Western Europe managed right from the start to make faster economic progress than the socialist countries of Eastern Europe and China, which was declared a socialist country only after its adoption of the Marshall Plan in 1949. With huge capital investments in the economic recovery and accelerated development of West Germany, the U.S. wanted to demonstrate the advantages of the capitalist system over the Soviet socialist system, which ruled East Germany and had slower economic development compared to capitalist West Germany.

Not everything in socialist countries was as grim as depicted by the surly critics of socialism from the West, however.

> The so-called socialist system had its achievements, too. China and the Soviet Union dragged their citizens out of economic backwardness into the modern industrial world, at however horrific a human cost; and the cost was so steep partly because of the hostility of the capitalist West. That hostility

also forced the Soviet Union into an arms race which crippled its arthritic economy even further, and finally pressed it to the point of collapse. In the meantime, however, it managed along with its satellites to achieve cheap housing, fuel, transport and culture, full employment and impressive social services for half the citizens of Europe, as well as an incomparably greater degree of equality and (in the end) material well-being than those nations had previously enjoyed. Communist East Germany could boast of one of the finest [childcare] systems in the world. The Soviet Union played a heroic role in combating the evil of fascism, as well as in helping to topple colonialist powers. It also fostered the kind of solidarity among its citizens that Western nations seem able to muster only when they are killing the natives of other lands. All this, to be sure, is no substitute for freedom, democracy and vegetables in the shop, but neither is it to be ignored" (Eagleton 2011: 13–14).

One should also not lose sight of the fact that in the seventy years between the 1920s and 1990s, from time to time in some important domains and businesses, the USSR was more successful than the U.S,--that is, the Soviets managed to be technologically ahead of the Americans. For example, the USSR launched the first space satellite before the U.S., sent the first man into space, built the first nuclear power plant, and produced the most powerful rocket engine in history. Such achievements in and of themselves speak volumes about socialism as a social order. The frontal underestimation of socialism and all socialist achievements, which is a long-standing norm in the capitalist West, is a great systemic and historical error, as is their public uncritical overestimation.

The vast majority of people, not only in the post-communist world but also in the capitalist West, feel the need for higher forms of solidarity and equality, and they want to enjoy some economic and social benefits that existed in former socialist countries. These are primarily free education, free health care, free kindergartens and nursing homes, longer paid maternity leave, paid vacation and similar social benefits, which were all common practices in former socialist countries. To finance these needs, the state collected the necessary funds from all employees, and thus their real salaries were objectively lower, especially when compared to salaries in the West. So, even in socialism, nothing was free, as is mistakenly believed.

Ensuring a high degree of social solidarity is the best way to mitigate the consequences of the existing system of capitalist exploitation, which has been capturing workers' creativity and energy to work more and better and heartlessly turning a free man into a wage worker. This is, however, inconsistent with the capitalist system. That is why the abolition of the capitalist exploitation is imposed as a historical necessity.

In a new non-capitalist and non-exploitative free and democratic society, there should be no objective circumstances for the establishment of a "dictatorship" of those social strata who were exploited and disenfranchised in capitalism, i.e. "the dictatorships of the proletariat and the precariat."

32.

JUST SOCIETY: UTOPIA OR REALITY?

If humanity ever strived for justice,
it would have already achieved it.

William Hazlitt

A just society is not egalitarian but it is an equitable society.

John Rawls

The complexity of the question of justice "has perennially aroused the avid interest of man ever since he began pondering the riddles of the universe" (Gow 2014).

The oppressed, disenfranchised, exploited, and poor people who have suffered while doing hard work in slave-like conditions constantly strive to overcome injustice and oppression in society, and struggle to live in a just society or one that is as just as possible. In achieving these aspirations, they fight against oppressors and exploiters in all possible ways, including uprisings, rebellions, and revolutions. The historu of their struggle is as long as the history of the society itself, which is endless.

Justice, fairness, and truthfulness are at the heart of the prophecies, testaments, and counsels of God's messengers, prophets, apostles, and philosophers—from the Jewish prophets Abraham and Moses, the Persian philosopher and prophet Zoroaster, the Chinese philosopher Confucius, and the Greek sages and philosophers Socrates, Plato, and

259

Aristotle, to Jesus Christ, the son of God and creator of Christianity, and the Prophet Muhammad, the creator of the Islamic religion, as well as many subsequent religious and philosophical thinkers and sages.

The oldest and most significant sacred texts, such as Judaism's Old Testament, Torah, and the Talmud, Christianity's New Testament, Islam's Qur'an, Buddhism's Pāli Canon, Zoroastrianism's Avesta, Sikhism's Adi Granth, Baha'i's Most Holy Book, and many other books of faith pay due attention to the issues of truth, philanthropy, kindness, care for neighbors, justice, and the essence of a just society in the broadest sense.

In the scriptures of the Old Testament, the covenant made between God and the Jewish people through Moses required all people of the Jewish religion to respect the Ten Commandments of love and justice.

Jesus Christ believed in the equality of all people and in freeing slaves. He despised rich, greedy, arrogant, and selfish people. He hated the wealth of the Roman slave-owning aristocracy and believed that their wealth should belong to all people. Slaves and the lowest strata of the slave-owning society—the urban poor and the oppressed—saw the true meaning of life in the teachings of Christ, and it became their faith. They began to experience Christ as the messiah, that is, their savior and just teacher.

The Qur'an—the holy book considered to be the source of Islam and Islam's basic religious, moral, civil, and criminal law—records the commandments received from *Allah* (the Arabic word for God) by his Prophet Muhammad, a poor man who patched his own clothes, but also a strong military leader. Many of these commandments involve divine and human justice, the Islamic concept of "justice and a just society," the struggle "against oppression and injustice" and the battle "between justice and injustice on an individual, as well as social plan" (Nasr 2014).

The elimination of extreme poverty and extreme wealth is among the twelve principles written in the Most Holy Book.

Many thoughts of the Chinese philosopher Confucius about philanthropy, conscientiousness, consideration for others, and mutual trust, as well as those summarized in his famous quotes such as: "If you want to raise yourself up, help others raise up," "Never do to others what you would not like them to do to you," "The superior man understands what is right; the inferior man understands what will sell" are timely and applicable in a present burdened with pronounced social injustices and social inequalities.

The Persian prophet and thinker Zoroaster, whose teachings can be summarized in the maxim "Good thoughts, good words, good deeds," was very engaged in defending the rights of cattlemen and peasants who were repeatedly suffering as victims of pillaging.

The works of ancient Greek philosophers such as Socrates, Plato and Aristotle are a reservoir of valuable knowledge about law, justice, fairness, and righteousness, and are an inspiration to many scientists. Aristotle, who was Plato's student, who in turn was a student of Socrates, discussed justice as the first virtue and created "a system that had a great influence on subsequent ethical thought. In Aristotle's *Nicomachean Ethics*, he starts with the premise that there are two forms of justice: universal and particular.

The principle of universal justice requires that laws, in accordance with the common good, be obeyed and fellow citizens be treated as equals. It is commutative (or corrective) justice.

Particular justice occurs in the relationship between the individual and the community and between individuals. A citizen should participate in the total amount of goods (not only material, but also goods such as honor, reputation, and power) in proportion to their contribution to society. This is distributive justice.

According to the principle of universal justice, one who acts in line with the law is just, and according to the principle of particular justice, a just person is one who does a good deed for someone believing that it will suit or benefit the other person. In some cases, these two meanings can be contradictory, because the same deed can be unjust as per the first interpretation while simultaneously being the opposite according to the other.

In the *Nicomachean Ethics*, Aristotle emphasizes the need to confront the relationship of equity to justice and the equitable to the just, saying that "on examination they appear to be neither absolutely the same nor generically different." According to Aristotle, "the equitable and the just are...one and the same...What creates the problem is that the equitable is just, but not the legally just but a correction of legal justice." (Aristotle 2014).

How close are we to the realization of the idea of a just society? To what extent are contemporary capitalist countries truly just societies?

Throughout the long history of the development of society, production relationships and social formations have changed from slavery, feudalism, to contemporary capitalism, but the nature of exploitation itself has not changed. Slave owners oppressed the slaves in ancient history. The feudal lords oppressed serfs in the Middle Ages. Since the beginning of the New Ages in the fifteenth century, capitalists have oppressed wage workers.

A just society represents centuries-old unfulfilled human aspiration. So far, no one has been able to create a society without economic and other inequalities. Man's aspiration for a better, happier, and more just life has never been a utopia, however, but has always been a real-life goal worth fighting for. The contemporary capitalist social order in which we live, willingly or unwillingly, is an unjust society. The economic and other inequalities created by this order have become socially and politically unsustainable and socially unacceptable, especially in former socialist countries, where tycoons and controversial businessmen—the newly formed capitalist class—have become rich beyond all measure.

Economic and others social inequalities have become the main cause of all current problems on a global, macroeconomic, microeconomic, national, and local level. That is a fact, just as it is a fact that today's society is more just and more humane than it was hundreds of years ago.

In the charter of the UN and other relevant international documents, there is not a single word that would give owners of capital, the employers, the right to exploit and oppress wage workers in order to become rich at the expense of others.

The realization of a just society is an ideal for which the exploited and oppressed strata of society must constantly fight and ultimately win, no matter how long their struggle will last. Therefore, a just society is not a utopia, but a possible and foreseeable reality. Any success achieved for this goal, even the smallest, would be a historical step toward a desirable new society that is more just and more responsible than the existing capitalist society.

33.

IS THE EUROPEAN UNION A JUST SOCIETY?

The crises of neoliberalism are also shaking the vision of the future of EU.

Todor Kulić

Yugoslavia is a laboratory for future European challenges.

Roland Dumas

For a long time, the EU has faced the problem of inequality between rich and poor member states, especially after its enlargement campaign early in the twenty first century. Eleven former Eastern European socialist countries were admitted as full members of the EU: the Czech Republic, Estonia, Hungary, Latvia, Lithuania, Poland, Slovenia, and Slovakia in 2004, Romania and Bulgaria in 2007, and Croatia in 2013, although it was known in advance that almost all of them did not meet the prescribed conditions and admission criteria for entry. At the time of the accession of Poland, Hungary, the Czech Republic, and Slovakia to the EU, the GDP per capita countries was 40 percent to 60 percent lower than France, and the differences in wage levels were even larger (Ocić 2017: 65).

The differences in the level of economic development between newly admitted EU member states and its "old" members have remained essentially unchanged, and may have increased. Member states of the EU in the east and south are poorer and underdeveloped and increasingly lagging behind EU member states in the north and west of Europe, which are rich and developed. The of economic relations in the EU is a source of political extremism and a cause of constant political friction.

The differences between these countries in GDP per capita remain drastic. In 2017, the GDP per capita in Bulgaria was estimated to be five times lower than the GDP of Luxembourg: 21,800 USD versus 105,000 USD (World Factbook II 2019).

The economic situation and relationship in the EU have been further worsened by the global economic and financial crisis of 2007 and 2008. The EU suddenly faced the unsolvable problem of regional harmonization in its expanded economic space. Almost all eastern and southern EU member states are drowning in debt, especially Greece and a final solution to their debt crisis is not yet in sight. The "belt-tightening policy" persistently being pushed by international financial institutions—led by the IMF—has so far failed to resolve the debt crisis within the EU. Creditors, as a rule, put debtors in an extremely difficult economic, political, and social positions. The imposed conditions for rescheduling external debts and the price of repayment are usually extremely burdensome and financially exploitative and extortionary.

Current policies of neoliberal capitalism—social policy in particular—have become the Achilles' heel of the EU.

> The development of social policy has never reached the full agreement of EU countries, some of which had a tradition of broad social policy, while others (like Britain in Thatcher's time and later) feared that their neoliberal policy, which included restrictions or eliminations of different social benefits...

Discontent with the neoliberal economic policies promoted by the EU—which have led to the rise of inequality in Europe, along with the weakening of the middle class—has reopened the question of the significance of social policy in the context of further reforms of the EU. In this framework, there are particularly large differences between the employment rates in the member states, that is, the unemployment rate. While FR Germany, for example, has an unemployment rate of around 4.5 [percent] (in 2016), in Spain, it is around 20 [percent] (Lopandić 2017: 87–88).

In December 2017, around eighteen million people in the EU were out of work (Eurostat 2018). Every fourth citizen of the EU—118 million people today—are poor or at risk of poverty (Županić 2016).

Technologically, the EU is behind the United States and advanced East Asian economies, especially China and Japan, and faces the problem of competitiveness. The prices of EU goods, products, and services on the world market are higher than the main global competitors due to high production costs.

Member states of the EU pursue autonomous economic policies, especially their individual fiscal policies. The EU does not have its own finance minister, only the ministers of its member states. With the exception of foreign affairs and security, there are no other important ministries in the EU. For example, there is no minister of defense and no chief of general staff.

Some EU member states increasingly emphasize the issues of national sovereignty and identity, believing that they transferred more of their sovereign rights to the EU than they should have, and that those rights should be restored as soon as possible. They do not delegate their most professional and capable personnel to the executive bodies of the EU.

In addition to the extremely complex procedure of approaching and joining the EU, best represented by its policy of opening and closing famous chapters, the frequent changes in EU regulations make the European path more difficult for candidate countries. For many of them, the EU has become a "moving target" to which they adapt "on the fly," to a greater or lesser speed, with more or less success.

Euroscepticism, i.e. distrust in the EU, is on the rise, both in EU member states and in countries that aspire to quickly become full members. Insufficient internal economic and political unity, as well as the ever-present Euroscepticism among the citizens of Europe, undermine faith in the future of the EU.

François Hollande, the former president of France, in an interview for six European dailies, warned that the EU is at a turning point. Hollande stated that European awakening implies a clear choice of the form of organization. A Europe of 28 countries cannot remain united but must become a *multi-speed EU*. According to Hollande, "For a long time, this idea of a differentiated Europe, with different speeds and distinct paces to progress, has provoked a lot of resistance. But today this idea is necessary. Otherwise Europe explodes." One country cannot hinder others. Hollande especially warned Poland and Hungary that the EU is not a marketplace, but a system of values. The EU cannot go back to a loose community of strong nation states gathered around a single market and defense, as demanded by the governments of those states (Maurice 2017).

Why is the EU in crisis? Because it is exclusively a product of the interests of the European bourgeois, capitalist class; it uncritically accepted the neoliberal ideology of Thatcherism and Reganism; neglected the development of its system of social justice and solidarity in society; and systematically distanced itself from the interests of the working class and all the working strata of European society. The European social, economic, and political scene is dominated by the command of big capital. The political, bureaucratic, and intellectual elites of the European capitalist class effectively govern the EU. The European Commission (the government of the EU), has become the executive committee of representatives for European capital— primarily the owners of its global corporations. The broadest social policies are pushed to the social periphery. The uncritical acceptance and practice of neoliberalism, and production relationships based on the separation of labor and capital are at the root of the current EU crisis.

The interests of the European capitalist class and its workers—that is, the working class and all the working strata of European society— are conflicted to the core. It is a classic class conflict that the European bourgeois elite persistently covers up by talking about European values— such as respect for human rights, human dignity, freedom, democracy, equality, and the rule of law—while marginalizing the burning contradictions between labor and capital, along with the economic and social differences between the rich and the poor in the EU.

Therefore, as long as workers and other working strata in the EU are exploited in order for the rich to get even richer and the poor even poorer, every story about human rights and European values remains empty talk. Social inequalities and capitalist exploitation have been and remain the central economic, political, and social problems of the EU and its member states, though not the only ones, of course.

British intellectual Martin Jacques believes that Brexit is "primarily a working-class revolt" (Jacques 2016).

268

The real remedy for solving the acute problems of the EU is the institutionalization of production relations, which would be based on the true democratic integration of labor and capital in every European company—not on the economic and political domination of capital over labor, which is now widespread. The EU has a future only as a just society. That is why far-reaching reforms are necessary, and not only in the countries that aspire to promptly become full members.

The best chance candidate countries have for joining the EU is to wholeheartedly follow, pursue, and implement the policies of neoliberal capitalism, which are infinitely loyal to the global centers of capital power. Serbia is one of those countries.

Pope Francis warns that "the heart of the European political project could only be man himself, and the first element of European vitality must be solidarity" (Pope 2017).

At the heart of current and all future reforms of the EU must be its citizens, their authentic interests, and the interests of employees in companies—not just the selfish interests of capitalists, or, as Marx once disparagingly called them, non-workers. Achieving a balanced relationship between labor and capital is a condition of any economic progress and social stability. "The fight against class stratification, class injustice and discrimination is the way to establish true social justice and solidarity" (Manifesto No. 3, 2013).

Without a specific and comprehensive program for realizing the ideas of social justice and solidarity and without the liberation of every wage worker who is dependent on and exploited by the owners of capital, it is not possible to reach economic and political cohesion within the EU. This is what all Europeans, the EU, and Europe need today and will need tomorrow. "If neoliberal Europe fails to transform, it will most likely fall apart. The left must be ready for that and have a plan B" (Mesec 2017).

The possible collapse of the EU could very quickly mean that European nations would face new uncertainties and fears of conflicts that cost them dearly in the past. That is why preserving the EU is a top priority, which is something its leadership especially insists on. Jean-Claude Juncker, the former president of the European Commission, stated in a conversation with U.S. Vice President Michael Pence during Pence's official visit to Brussels in February 2017, that he "clearly made the warning that Washington should not encourage other countries to imitate Brexit" and said to Pence,

> Do not call on others to exit as well, because if the [EU] breaks up into pieces, you will have a new war in [the] Western Balkans. The only possibility for this part of Europe that has suffered a lot...is to at least lean on [the] European perspective. If we leave them alone, Bosnia and Herzegovina, Republic of Srpska [one of the two entities of Bosnia and Herzegovina], Macedonia, Albania, all these countries, we will have war again" (Barber 2017).

Indeed, nothing in this world is more important than living in peace and freedom. It is precisely the pursuit of lasting peace that is at the heart of the idea of the ever-closer unification of the European peoples and states. The guarantee of lasting peace in Europe and the world is dependent on the transformation of the EU into a society of social justice and solidarity—a just society that is non-capitalist, democratic and free. The EU becoming a legally viable state union of European nations, capable of effectively suppressing possible "centrifugal forces," and implementing a single economic policy is of paramount importance for the stability and prosperity of the European continent.

34.

CIVIL SOCIETY OF SOCIAL JUSTICE

We need to stop thinking through a capitalist prism.

Slavoj Žižek

The contemporary neoliberal world order, as already mentioned, rests on two main pillars. First, the absolute monopoly of the means of production by private owners, and second, the unlimited exploitation of the workforce by the same owner. These foundational elements are the most significant limitations, burdens, and dangers of the neoliberalism. In the long run, this system cannot achieve a desired state of social or political stability. The current separation of capital from labor and the very nature of social justice and equality are mutually exclusive.

Without radical changes to the neoliberal system one cannot expect social justice or desirable social equality. Social inequalities due to the unequal distribution of capital and income, driven by the capitalist system and combined with the cyclical emergence of latent and volatile economic crises, have become socially unmanageable and unsustainable. These inequalities are the product of the neoliberal system and not a consequence of deviations from its fundamental principles (Deneen 2018: 149).

Is there an alternative to the contemporary capitalist system? If there is,

What is a feasible alternative? The simple logical answer is: 'discard neoliberalism.' The introduction of the alternative model would start from doing just that. It would be sensible to start from seeking resolutions to problems that neoliberal governments have failed to tackle in practice: why [and] how has inequality grown for the last few decades? Why have good jobs disappeared? Why have median wages stagnated for more than four decades in the U.S. and since the 1970s in the UK? Why is housing unaffordable in England now? How has the debt regime at both sovereign and household levels surfaced in the U.S. [and the] UK and, regarding sovereign debt, in the Eurozone and Japan? Why is the U.S. stock market performing so well? Those phenomena are neither accidents nor totally unrelated incidents. Neoliberal deregulation policy has unleashed greed in the financial sector, causing the 2008 financial crisis (Yokoyama 2017).

Neoliberal power lost the momentum of the nineties due to the economic crisis of 2007 and 2008. While this crisis was not as profound as the one in the 1930s, it has seriously shaken the neoliberal system. As a result, various system alternatives started emerging. The ideas of anti-capitalism, antiexploitation, stronger social justice, a just (or at least more just) society, and similar topics have been discussed freely without the fear of prosecution or a vicious response from the bourgeoisie. Some believe that a possible alternative to the current system is a synthesis of the best of capitalism and the best of socialism, thereby creating a new order. This new system would be as economically efficient as capitalism, but like socialism, be socially just and secure by giving society free healthcare, free education, and other social safety nets. "Historical experience during revolutions and coups unequivocally shows: socialism without the best of liberalism becomes a dictatorship of political power; liberalism without the best of socialism turns into a dictatorship of profit. These dictatorships, if strengthened, by their internal logic, lead to totalitarianism" (Vidojević 2016).

This system would be neither capitalist nor socialist. It would not follow contemporary neoliberal ideologies. It would also not follow the Stalinist socialist system or the more liberal Yugoslav self-management order, although the Yugoslav model is considered in some scientific circles as civilizational invention and the hope for humanity because those types of socialism disappeared from the world due to their systemic and structural shortcomings.

This new order would be organized according to the needs of humankind with equal opportunities for all. The system would be humanitarian and socially just, democratic, and free. This new society would be more technologically advanced than it is today. The vertical of this new, genuinely democratic system would be based on human dignity, honoring of its identity, and valuing labor in real terms. There would be true equality between all types of ownership without private, public, or state monopolies. There would be self-management and the direct integration of labor and capital. There would be no exploitation of labor and there would be no extreme wealth or extreme poverty. In this real democratic society, there would not be the resentful state care for its citizens, allowing humankind's true solidarity to rise to its fullest potential. Now, saying it is easy, doing it is hard, but the reality is that the world's future is without capitalism. In that new world, society will be free from capitalist exploitation, and people will truly be free—not the superficial freedom seen today. Such a society is not an unattainable uptopia as those who follow capitalist ideology would have us believe. Rather, it is realistic and achievable, no matter how lofty it may seem.

Those who refuse to imagine the wonderous possibilities of a truly liberal, post-capitalist, technologically advanced society "are bound to fall prey to the absurdity pointed out by...Slavoj Žižek: a greater readiness to fathom the end of the world than to imagine life after capitalism" (Varoufakis 2019).

After the fall of the Belin wall in 1989, the West was euphoric and triumphalist. Socialism was demonized and made a thing of the past. Neoliberal capitalism was promoted as the best social system, "the end of history," and the final solution without an alternative. Now, however, democratic, liberal (market) socialism has become a legitimate alternative discussed as a likely future (Mesec 2017). Around the world today, Marx and his ideas—along with actual lessons on practical and theoretical planes that emerged from the "socialist construct" of the last century—are subject to serious study and discussion. Socialism is no longer taboo. There are open discussions about it not only in Western Europe, but in the U.S., the heart of modern neoliberal capitalism. "When numerous Americans talk about socialism these days, they in fact refer to the aversion towards capitalism and [the] *status quo*, which has disappointed them gravely" (Wolff 2016).

Indeed, time and patience are necessary to achieve the birth of a new socialist idea. This idea can be realized through the development of critical thinking and the mobilization of citizens focused on constructing a socially just and responsible society. There is undeniably a lack of novel, original socialist ideas applicable to the present, however. While there are many left-leaning thinkers who reaffirm and interpret pre-existing socialist or social-democratic ideas, intellectuals who offer new theoretical perspectives and ways to change the current state of the society are rare. There is a lack of practical and applicable solutions and mechanisms that could replace the current neoliberal capitalist system economically, politically, and socially. Those are the fundamental problems in designing, establishing, and constructing a just society.

It is not important to give a name to such a system. The new left already calls it *socialism of the twenty-first century* and believes that this system is the ambition of the widest strata of society around the world. Such a qualification of a new social system is naturally received with a great deal of skepticism and opposition from the right. The name itself should not overshadow its economic, political, and social quintessence. Such a system must be truly non-capitalist, socially just, democratic, and free and must not be dogmatic, authoritarian, or exploitative. Such a society could be called a *self-managed democratic society* or the *third path of social development in the twenty-first century*—not to be mistaken with Tony Blair's social democratic ideas offered by ideologists and theorists.[3]

Naturally, the ideologists and political elites of neoliberal capitalism, the so-called neo-liberocracy, will energetically oppose any new non-capitalist or neo-socialist system. Led by selfish material interests and capitalist logic, these neo-liberocrats will continue with their agitprop to convince the world that the current neoliberal capitalist society is not exploitative because everyone lives exclusively from their labor and knowledge and that neoliberal society is a just society. Ultimately, their argument is that Marx's theories and constructs are nothing more than fairytales.

---

[3] For a more detailed definition of Blair's third path, see *Third Way-Renewal of Social-Democracy"* by Anthony Giddens and "Instead of an Introduction, or Searching for the Third Way" by Sreten Vujović

35.

MARKET: AN ACHIEVEMENT OF CIVILIZATION, NOT THE PRODUCT OF CAPITALISM

Underlying most arguments against the free market is a lack of belief in freedom itself.
The market gives people what the people want instead of what other people think they ought to want.

Milton Friedman

The market is one of the greatest achievements of civilization and is over six thousand years old. The two oldest ancient peoples, the Sumerians and the Akkadians, inhabited ancient Mesopotamia and their first state organizations, city-states, formed a market between the fifth and third millennium BCE. The Sumerians and Akkadians sold and purchased (exchanged) various goods they produced. They were engaged in agriculture, farming, fruit growing, and cattle breeding. They made pottery and used bronze, making knives, swords, saws, axes, hammers, and nails. Various statues, gates, furniture, buildings and weapons have been found by archaeologists. They used leather and glue, and made bags, shoes, and beer. They used irrigation systems to build canals and dams. Sumerians and Akkadians made bricks and built large houses with multiple floors. They invented the potter's wheel, which they later used in order to make a regular wheel. Vehicles with wheels appeared around 3500 BCE. They knew and used mathematics, arithmetic, and geometry and were very interested in astronomy. Based on their observations of the stars, they made the first calendar that divided the year into 12 months. Sumerians and Akkadians were the creators of the *hexadecimal numerical system*—the division of a circle into 360 equal parts (degrees), division of a degree into 60 equal parts (arc minutes), division of an arc minute into 60 equal parts (arc seconds), division of an hour into 60 minutes, and the division of a minute into 60 seconds.

In major museums in the U.S. and around the world, one can find an excellent cross-section of Sumerian material culture—the pillars and bricks used to build temples and courtyards, weapons and tools, pots and vases, harps and lyres, jewelry and ornaments. Sumerian clay tablets still exist in the literally tens of thousands and inform us about the social and administrative organization of the ancient Sumerians, their literature, religion, philosophy, and ethics. "And all this because the Sumerians were one of the very few peoples who not only probably invented a system of writing, but also developed it into a vital and effective instrument of communications" (Kramer 1981: xx–xxi)

As for the Babylonian Empire, formed between the third and second millennium BCE on the foundations of the Sumerian and Akkadian empires and their rivalry, "the favorable geographical position of Babylon contributed to a rather significant development of trade...Trade agreements on agricultural products were made in special squares, where the prices of goods were determined..." (Avdijev 2009: 62).

There is archaeological evidence that in the world's oldest civilizations—Sumerian, Akkadian, and Babylonian—the market operated regularly and that goods were exchanged using money, meaning that there was a real commodity-money exchange. In short, in the world's oldest civilizations, authentic commodity production and the market exchange of commodities, products, and services existed and were developed.

The market is the product of the social organization of labor, not social formation. It is neither slave-owning, feudal, capitalist, nor socialist, but simply is the market. The identification of market and commodity production with capitalism has no historical foundation because capitalism did not invent market or commodity production. The social organization of labor existed long before the capitalist social order was created. The market has always been and remains only the market. Any possible attributes ascribed to it do not change its social nature. This also applies to commodity production: its character does not change even if it is termed "capitalist." That is why the apologists of capitalism should stop emphasizing the market and equating capitalism with the market—and vice versa—and stop recommending the market to other countries, especially former socialist countries, as an original capitalist cure for all diseases their economies and societies suffer from.

The market, as an invention of the civilizational process of socially organizing labor rather than an invention of capitalism, never determines the true nature of social relations in a given social order, but always determines the nature of relationships among people established by the disposal of production factors and the results of labor. For instance, the position of the worker in contemporary neoliberal capitalism is not a wage position because of the free market, including the "labor market." Instead, it is exclusively because of capitalist production relations and the monopoly of private property rights to capital that turns a free worker into a wage worker. The fundamental contradictions and problems of contemporary neoliberal capitalism do not belong to the market, but to the systemic separation of labor and capital, the unbearable exploitation of workers, the working strata in society, and their alienated labor.

The German historian Jürgen Kocka believes that the term "capitalism" should be replaced with "market economy."

> Capitalism is a controversial concept. Many scholars avoid it. To them it seems too polemical, since it emerged as a term of critique and was used that way for decades. The term is defined in different ways, and frequently not defined at all. It encompasses a great deal, and it is hard to delineate. Would it not be better to dispense with the concept and, say, talk about a 'market economy?' (Kocka 2016: 1).

The market is not a perfect economic mechanism of social distribution because it does not operate according to "God's justice," instead operating according to its own laws. It does not recognize in advance to any commodity producer (economic entity) the individual operating costs of producing any given commodity. A commodity producer whose individual operating costs are lower than the conditioned market average of operating costs for a commodity achieves a positive business result on the market. And vice versa: a commodity producer whose individual operating costs are higher than the conditioned market average of operating costs for a commodity achieves a negative business result on the market. Provided that the market is truly free, without restrictions on supply and demand (i.e. monopoly and monopsony, oligopoly and oligopsony) and that this free competition functions without any restrictions, it is ultimately the most objective measure of the quantity and quality of everyone's work and work results.

The market objectively measures and evaluates not only the success of the business, but the reach of a country's economic policy and the effectiveness of domestic and foreign policy and diplomacy. For example, a state cannot boast the success of its foreign policy and be proud of its diplomatic service's efficiency while constantly having a deficit in its balance of trade and balance of payments in foreign economic relations. Or, a state with a high unemployment rate, difficult living conditions, a decreasing total population, and whose young and educated people migrate abroad in large numbers cannot boast that its domestic policy is good.

The market simply cannot be excluded from the general social organization of labor; it cannot be compensated by anything in an economically successful way. "There is no market if its allocative, distributive and selective functions are denied" (T. Ž. Nikolić 1989: 23). The laws of the market are relentless, almost like the laws of nature, and manifest themselves in a similar way. Just like the blind forces of nature, the blind forces of the market are spontaneous, anarchic, and unpredictable. The problem with the market is that it often does not perform any of its functions (allocative, distributive, selective, and informative) in an ideal way, but in a destructive way. Depending on time and space, the market evaluates the behavior of each actor on the economic scene after the fact and not before the event. The cyclical movement of economic activity is immanent in the nature of the market, which creates numerous economic problems, such as periodic economic crises, economic stagnations and recessions, rotations of inflation, and unemployment or stagflation (situations of stagnation and inflation). The market alone is not able to revive economic activity when the economy is in a depression phase.

Wherever there is a problem with general public goods (defense, protection of the natural environment, science, culture, art, etc.), regardless of whether the goods are free to use or not or generally available to all consumers or not, doing business according to market principles does not always give satisfactory results. For example,

> nearly every advance in science, technology, and mathematics emerged from people working together at universities supported by government funding. Creativity and innovation come from many places. Companies produce influential innovations, but so do other institutions that operate outside the confines of the profit motive, competitive markets, and the bottom line (Ashoff 2016).

The development of the public goods sector in a society cannot be successful either if it is isolated from the market and its mechanisms, however. For example, the market must have an adequate influence on art production. Art cannot depend only on the influence of state representatives in cultural institutions, and even less on party representatives and political activists. That is why art production is increasingly striving to enter and have its value and reach assessed on the market and to free cultural activity as much as possible from the bureaucratic constraints that hinder and stifle artistic creation.

The market does not always successfully perform its allocative function by revealing the most rational ways to invest funds, especially where large and long-term investments are needed, or by identifying where there are great risks: the constructions of large ports, bridges, tunnels, and roads. Modern markets are more imperfect than perfect. Free market competition is aggressively suppressed by oligopolistic and monopolistic trends of market regulation, dimensioning, and the structuring of supply and demand. Consumers often do not have in advance all the necessary information about the pros and cons of consumer goods offered on the market, but rather learn this information after a delay.

36.

HARMONIZATION OF ECONOMIC FUNCTIONS OF THE MARKET AND STATE

In addition to the market, economic planning, the social orientation of the economy, and the role of the state are all necessary to correct the market when and where it is needed in all social organizations of economic life. Spontaneous market developments always have a negative national and global impact on the economy. Companies must protect themselves from occasional market disruptions the same way they protect themselves from natural disasters such as floods as much as objectively possible in their given conditions. "The existence of a free market does not of course eliminate the need for government. On the contrary, government is essential both as a forum for determining the 'rules of game' and as an umpire to interpret and enforce the rules decided on" (Friedman 2002: 14).

For example, protecting nature or vaccinating children cannot be left to the market, but these and similar functions must be performed by the state. It is not realistic to expect something like that from global corporations because they are preoccupied with making a profit and conquering new markets.

In some situations because of general interest, certain types of commodities must be produced that are not demanded directly by the market. When this occurs, the state can influence the level of supply and demand on the market through commodity interventions or price policy. The state cannot, however, abolish the law of supply and demand, market logic, market competition, or the aspiration of market actors to be better than others and achieve the highest possible income and profit, whether that actor is an individual, a company, or a state.

State action in organizing the economic life of a society only becomes a problem when the those in power start imagining that they can be better than the market in performing the economic functions that objectively only belong to the market. Any disregard for the market pushes society into subjectivism and voluntarism and can ultimately lead to some form of totalitarianism.

> The concept of the market, which is often imagined as a self-optimizing mechanism it is a mistake to interfere with, but which in fact, left to itself, continually increases inequality. Another concept, closely related, is meritocracy, which is often imagined as a guarantor of social mobility but which, Piketty argues, serves mainly to make economic winners feel virtuous (Menand 2016).

That is why an economic system is needed in which the economic functions of the state and the market will harmonize, permeate, and complement each other instead of opposing each other. Ultimately, this shows the wisdom of governing a state and society. The price of overestimating or underestimating the economic role of the state or the market must always be paid dearly. Former socialist countries in the Eastern Bloc constantly faced a variety of economic problems because of their disrespect of objective market laws. For example, keeping food prices low through administrative measures for a long period of time to protect living standards always led to shortages. Likewise, the proclamation of full employment as a strategic objective of socialism led to economic inefficiency because, for example, work performed by one worker, as per market-recognized standards, was instead done by two or more workers. In such conditions, workers were not motivated to work hard and were not afraid of being fired because there was no one else to step in for the idlers.

Organizing contemporary economic life requires that the limitations of the authentic economic functions of the market and state be defined as precisely as possible, as well as where they intersect and intertwine. Regardless of their mutual contradiction, the market and the state can be used rationally in the economic and technological progress of society, leading the way in development instead of market and state forces working against each other. Any absolutization of economic functions into either only the market or the state and the polarization of the economic organization of society inevitably leads to economic and social crisis. In order to suppress market disruptions and any party or bureaucratic subjectivism and voluntarism, the modern state does not renounce making plans, instead studiously preparing and adopting short-, medium-, and long-term plans, which inform how the state directs the actions of foreign and domestic investors, creditors, and responsible state authorities. Through this process, the state realizes planned development objectives within their planning period.

Global neoliberal policies implemented over the last three to four decades have disrupted the balance of relations between the state and the market, weakening the state and strengthening the market.

> Since Reagan, the market has been declared a sanctuary, at the expense of the state. The state has become a problem. When this caused a crisis, after eight years of Bush Jr.'s rule, it became clear that a market without…law grows into…law without a market: tax cuts, increased military spending, neglecting infrastructure, banks with papers instead of the money, dangerous mortgage roulette… (Fuentes 2009).

A JUST SOCIETY: THE WORLD AFTER NEOLIBERALISM

The global financial and economic crisis of 2007 and 2008 raised the issue of the place and role of the market and the state and their mutual relations in organizing economic life at the local, national, and global level.

> The doctrine 'market is the best regulator' has been shown to be false. Everyone wanted minimal state regulation and they did damage suffered by the entire world...We should not forget that the key economic categories in the United States have been created with the help of the state—the Internet, medicine, and many others. They have later turn[ed] to private financiers, but the state is their catalyst. In the future, it must be resolved how to find a balance between the market and the state, and...discussions on this issue are going in a positive direction (Stiglitz 2009).

Tom Piketty, a French economist, pays special attention to the role of the market and the role of the state.

> The possibility of greater state intervention in the economy raises very different issues today than it did in the 1930s, for a simple reason: the influence of the state is much greater now than it was then, indeed, in many ways greater than it has ever been. That is why today's crisis is both an indictment of the markets and a challenge to the role of government. Of course, the role of government has been constantly challenged since the 1970s, and the challenges will never end...Some are outspoken in favor of an even greater role for the state, as if it no longer played any role at all, while still others call for the state to be dismantled at once, especially in the country where it is least present, the United States. There, groups affiliated with the Tea Party call for abolishing the Federal Reserve and

returning to the gold standard. In Europe, the verbal clashes between 'lazy Greeks' and 'Nazi Germans' can be even more vitriolic. None of this helps to solve the real problems at hand. Both the antimarket and anti-state camps are partly correct: new instruments are needed to regain control over a financial capitalism that has run amok, and at the same time the tax and transfer systems that are the heart of the modern social state are in constant need of reform and modernization, because they have achieved a level of complexity that makes them difficult to understand and threatens to undermine their social and economic efficacy (Piketty 2014: 473– 474).

In search of a balance between market and state functions, the problem is that there are no previously established theoretical models and recommended formulas for a precise and timely dosing of necessary market freedom and purposeful state intervention in economic situations with the result that in practice, there would be neither too little nor too much market or state. Extreme situations frequently happen in real life because of an exaggerated emphasis on the role of the market or the role of the state. For example, in the late twentieth and early twenty first century, the use of the market and its forces was exaggerated in the organization of economic life, which led to local and global economic and financial crises.

These crises should not, however, be blamed on the market as an economic mechanism, but on the neoliberal macroeconomic and global economic policies pursued by the most developed countries in the world. The market mechanism is similar to a medicine—it can be used correctly or incorrectly and cause desired or undesired effects.

37.

LABOR MARKET AND
THE RIGHT TO WORK

After the "fall of communism," the free market—which includes the market of commodities capital and labor—was declared the alpha and omega of global development, and the corpus of human rights and freedoms declared the quintessence of true democracy. Ideologists and theorists of neoliberal capitalism have promised and persistently persuaded people that the free market, especially the free labor market as the third component of the market mechanism, would be able to effectively guarantee the right to work, especially given that the number of unemployed, able-bodied people is constantly increasing around the world.

Three decades after the "the fall of communism," it has become evident that their predictions did not come true. Unemployment as a failure to exercise the right to work has become a burning economic and social problem, not only in the countries that have gone through or are still going through the transition from socialism to capitalism, but also in many industrially and technologically developed countries. It has now become clear everywhere and to almost everyone that the right to work as a fundamental human right cannot be successfully exercised through the neoliberal ode to the miraculous powers of the "invisible hand" of the free market and free labor market. It has been confirmed through practice that the labor market, no matter how significant role in any market economy is and no matter how organized, is not able to solve the problem of unemployment in society in a desirable and right way.

Creating necessary new jobs is possible only with new investments in sustainable economic development in an economically rational way and is why the labor market cannot be a substitute for the role that investors, especially private ones, play in society to solve the problem of unemployment. Without the creation of new jobs, the fate of exercising the right to work is uncertain. It is the material basis of all other rights and the quality of life of each individual depends on how that right is exercised. For an unemployed person who is able to work and looking for employment, exercising the right to work is more important than any other human right. That is why the right to work is considered a fundamental human right.

Naturally, investors closely monitor situation of workers in and relationships to the labor market, regardless of the fact that their final decision on the allocation of their investments, i.e. capital, is made in accordance with the requirements of the domestic or foreign commodity market. The higher unemployment is, the bigger the reserve army of labor, as Marx said, and in turn, the lower the price of labor will be (i.e. the acceptable wage)—and that, as a rule, attracts investors. The lower per capita income is in a country, the lower personal income is, and the higher the education level of wage workers is, all of which results in foreign capital being more economically motivated to enter with an appropriate legal certainty in business. Such situations are a real mecca for return on invested capital at high profit rates and for earning high profits at the expense of low paid wage workers. This is an example of the exploitation of workers in contemporary conditions of globalized circulation of capital.

The labor market is also very important for evaluating the quality of "commodities" it offers, differentiating simple from complex work, and differentiating skilled from unskilled labor, because not all workers are equally diligent, capable, or qualified. Capitalism hires diligent, capable, and qualified workers for the lowest possible wages. This is in the nature of capital, and the "game" of capital and labor is determined precisely by the labor market.

The use of the term "labor market" is questionable from a theoretical standpoint, however. In a market, in addition to commodities and capital, there are also specific workers and working people who offer their workforce of an appropriate quality to their employers. Labor cannot be mechanically separated from workers so it can then appear on the market on its own, in some specific form. De facto, the labor market is an abstract category, invented by economists of a particular orientation. This science, because of the need to theoretically generalize economic phenomena, is often forced to use theoretical abstractions in its scientific method, even when it comes to the everyday life of specific people.

The labor force is only an assumption of the future quantity and quality of workers' living labor and is only of interest to the capitalist employer. The workers' living labor is exclusively a production category, not a market category. As a purposeful activity, living human labor, in cooperation with the other two factors of production—the means of labor and objects of labor— creates new values and new goods, which then take on a commodity character on the market. Labor is a measure of the value of a commodity, although not always a measure of its price, which is ultimately determined by supply and demand in the market.

Workers and working people, as free people, as citizens (*citoyens*), are not being forced by anyone from the outside to appear on the market, where they are free to offer their labor skills and where employers are free to hire and pay them like any other factor of production that can be bought and sold on the market. Of course, in this market process, employers, the owners of capital, who seek and buy labor of a certain quality, always do better than the workers who offer and sell their labor.

Workers are forced to offer their working skills and abilities on the market and sell them to the owners of capital at a price (wage), because that is the only way they and their families can survive in the conditions and relations of neoliberal capitalism since the means of production (capital) are in the hands of employers and do not belong to workers and working people. Employers treat workers on the market like any other commodity—raw materials, means of labor, etc.—offered on the market. They hire suitable workers at a price that is dependent on the quality of their working skills, which employers need to perform their current and future jobs, and for a certain period of time.

Unlike slave owners who bought slaves for an indefinite period of time, capitalists buy workers' labor force for a definite period of time, which is why this segment of the market is called the workforce market or labor market. That is the civilizational difference between capitalism and slavery. The capitalist class has granted workers an amount of "freedom" that suits its exploitative interests while workers have failed to win the freedom that would suit their interests. The character and logic of the production relationship established between "slave and master" (Hegel) are the essence of every exploitative society.

The goal of launching the terms "labor market" and "right to work" into the social orbit was to conceal and obscure the wage position of the workers and their systematic exploitation by contemporary neoliberal capitalism, and to bypass and avoid the use of the term *workforce market* because it does not fit into the proclaimed neoliberal capitalist value system of "human rights and freedoms." The "labor market" is, in fact, a euphemism for the "worker market."

38.

PROPERTY MONISM: MONOPOLY OF SINGLE FORM OF OWNERSHIP

Property has always determined the form of economic organization of a society, the nature of production relations, and the character of its socioeconomic and political system. In all previous social formations, one form of ownership has prevailed—*property monism.*

It is believed that in original social communities, common property (collective property) dominated, which included everything the community owned and belonged to every member of the community.

The dominant form of property in capitalism is the private property of the means of production and exchange. It is "the heart of capitalism, its absolute condition of existence" (Badiou 2017). Private property was also the dominant form of property in social formations before capitalism, in feudalism and slavery, and has always been considered a sacred right. In capitalism, it is particularly sacralized and absolutized, and granted a monopoly status in society. The capitalist state watches over it, protects and maintains it through all available legal, economic, and other means, including the use of force. The titular of private property rights is the owner of capital, the capitalist employer.

In recent economic history, especially after the Great Depression and World War II, *state property* acquired the right of citizens. Faced with economic crisis and war destruction, capitalist states, especially those where left-wing political parties came to power, implemented nationalization measures of key economic sectors, such as energy, mining, metallurgy, and transport, and nationalized property was declared state property. Depending on the power relationship of the left and right political forces in a capitalist society, state property would gain or lose its importance. The political right, unlike the left, has always identified state property with state socialism and sought to remove it from capitalism, which was largely achieved with the transition to the era of neoliberalism. In some capitalist countries, such as Brazil, during its military dictatorship of 1964-1985, state property had an extremely privileged status in society. State property has never acquired a dominant position in capitalism, however.

Apart from state property, one of the forms of property in capitalism is *cooperative property*. There are cooperatives in capitalism—for example, in agriculture, crafts, and service industries. Cooperative property is jointly owned by cooperative members, but also has a secondary social role similar to state property.

Capital also includes *personal property*. Personal property includes goods for personal consumption that determine the standard of living of their owners, and the means of production, used by their owner for self-employment and to combine in their personal work to perform a given activity.

In administrative-centralist state socialism, found in the USSR and socialist countries in its orbit, including Yugoslavia in the first years after World War II, the dominant form of ownership was state property.

In the self-governing socioeconomic system of Yugoslavia, the dominant form of ownership was *social property*, understood as a "system of relations between people, not relations between man and things," which by constitutional order guaranteed a monopoly position relative to other possible forms of property.

In the era of neoliberalism, all former European socialist states, partly the People's Republic of China, and even some capitalist countries with a strong state sector, such as Brazil, unhesitatingly accepted the policy of privatizing state (social) enterprises—that is, transforming state property into private property as the dominant, absolute form of ownership out of the competition of other possible forms of ownership.

39.

PROPERTY PLURALISM: EQUALITY OF ALL FORMS OF OWNERSHIP

The monopoly of any particular form of ownership in the social organization of labor effectively negates democracy and freedom. The essence of true democracy is pluralism in every form, even in ownership. Therefore, in a new socially just society, all historically recognized and possible forms of property would exist under equal conditions: private, state, social, and personal property, along with their derivatives: collective, cooperative, corporate, *waqf*, etc[4]. In other words, property pluralism would be the backbone of a new democratic social order and a just society. The relationships between different forms of ownership would be competitive because none alone guarantees the efficient use of factors of production automatically or in advance, nor their efficient allocation. No company is successful or unsuccessful because of its form of ownership. Instead of the form of ownership itself, it is much more important how the active factors of production are managed in a company.

No private company is *a priori* more successful than a state-owned, socially owned, or personally owned company. It is possible for a state-owned company to be more successful than any private company and possible for a socially owned company, as they existed under socialist self-management, to be more economically efficient than a private or a

---

[4] A waqf is an Islamic endowment of property to be held in trust and used for a charitable or religious purpose.

state-owned company. An employee-owned corporation or cooperative organization can offer better products and services at a more reasonable price than any other private, state, or social company on the market.

In the market economy, how a company is organized and its management style is infinitely more important than the form of ownership. Company management can be successful or unsuccessful in private, state-owned, or socially owned enterprises and worker performance can be good in any company, regardless of the type of ownership of the company.

Market competition between companies of different ownership forms where one can prove to be better than others would help drive sustainable development of the economy and society more successfully than the competition between companies of one form of ownership. All companies would strive to adequately manage available resources in order to achieve the best business results on the market, and contribute to the increase of social product and wealth. Property pluralism is better suited to the market organization of social labor and the nature of the market instead of property monism. In a truly democratic and free society, the economic rationality of a form of ownership would be assessed and determined only by the market and based on its relations to the commodities produced in different forms of ownership— not by someone's ideology and the centers of political and economic power in a society.

Historically, the social status of certain forms of ownership has always been constitutionally determined in accordance with the ideological and political interests of the holders of political power in a society. For example, private property was given monopoly status in capitalist societies while in socialist societies, monopoly status was given to state and social property. The capitalist class and state have protected private property, treating it as a "sacred right" and "sanctuary" that must not be questioned by any means. The socialist states of the Eastern Bloc and socialist Yugoslavia had a similar relationship to state property under self-management.

In a new society, no one would have the right to discriminate between companies of different ownership types. In every state in such a society, the successful operation of a company and whether it generates business income on the market would be important—not whether it is private, state, social, collective, or personal property.

Likewise, all possible forms of property should be legally protected under equal conditions. Each form should be considered "sacred" and have the same treatment that private property now has in the contemporary capitalist world. This requires the systemically enabling the free competition of different ownership forms in creating and realizing market values.

PRIVATE OWNERSHIP

Why would *private ownership* of the means of production be necessary in a new society?

Private ownership encourages the entrepreneurial spirit of individual business entities and gives them maximal business and material motivation. Any suppression of private initiative, inherent in private property, would "produce" objectively negative economic and social consequences. Private property is not, however, in and of itself the most economically rational form of property. With poor management, any private company is doomed and will go bankrupt sooner or later, regardless of the fact that it is privately owned.

Private property is not even the most socially ideal form of ownership. In capitalism, the exploitation of workers hired by capitalist employers is immanent in private property, generating a class stratification of society into the rich and the poor, and those between them—the middle class. These are the main shortcomings of private property. Therefore, it should not be fetishized, absolutized, or sacralized, nor should private property ownership be attributed qualities that it objectively does not and cannot have.

Of course, the shortcomings of private property cannot be completely eliminated, but can be significantly mitigated and made somewhat more bearable. First of all, private property should be deprived of its current privileged, monopoly position, provided by the existing capitalist order, and systematically equated with other forms of property. Without the constant, immediate, and strong support of the ruling capitalist social class, private property would have no advantage over any other form of property.

On the other hand, it is necessary to open up the possibilities of different regulations for relationships between workers and capitalists that work toward the democratic integration of labor and capital. The legal and economic system must maximally encourage wage workers to purchase shares of the capitalist companies they work for and in that way directly participate not only in their ownership as "small capitalists," but also in the management and distribution of the company's profits. Without the systematic institutionalization of workers' active participation in the management of capitalist companies, it is not possible to start the social transformation of capitalist societies into just societies.

Furthermore, the progressive taxation of capitalist property and the institutionalization of a basic income for all citizens would significantly limit the influence of private property on the class stratification in society. Implementation of these and similar systemic measures would cause private property to increasingly look like personal property, and thus capitalist society would resemble a non-exploitative, just society.

STATE OWNERSHIP

Why is *state ownership* of the means of production necessary in a new democratic and just society?

Because state ownership with high-quality management can sustain economically efficient companies like privately-owned companies and—why not—more successful companies. Theoretically, no state-owned company can be a priori declared unsuccessful or successful. Workers in state-owned enterprises can do a good or poor job just like workers in private enterprises. It all depends on who manages a private or state-owned company, and how.

The state can be a successful entrepreneur only if the state-owned enterprise is truly state-owned, truly public, and managed adequately, following the strictest global business standards. The business success of any state-owned company, just like any private company, directly depends on the abilities of its management team.

State-owned companies become an economic and social problem when they are managed in a subjectivist and voluntarist manner and when they are managed by loyal, verified, and prominent political party activists and government cadres—which are universally unprofessional— regardless of the state organization's form in the country. At the same time, economic efficiency of state-owned companies is not a big issue because the state always covers business losses. This has always been the main problem of state-owned companies in former socialist countries.

State-owned enterprises are, rightly, subjected to the sharpest social criticism when they effectively become party enterprises and cease to be truly state-owned, when party affiliation becomes the dominant criterion when choosing enterprise management team instead of expertise and entrepreneurial knowledge, and when only loyal members of the ruling political party or parties can become employees. State property then becomes *political party property*, and a state-owned enterprise becomes a *political party company*. This practice is possible primarily because state property is not as systematically and constitutionally protected as it should be, and therefore state-owned enterprises can easily become the prey of political parties in power. State-owned enterprises can have a significant place in the market economy system, but only if they are free from any subjectivist and voluntarist influence from the outside and if they are led by competent professional managers selected on the basis of public competition, regardless of their citizenship, political. or religious affiliation, and not through the decisions of the executive bodies of the parties in power.

Moreover, there should be no ideological affiliation of the state property. It should be in no way associated with socialism, much less with the scientific body of work of Marx.

State property and enterprises of this form of ownership must exist in general interest social labor sectors where the market is not able to perform its economic functions in the best possible way, such as infrastructure and certain social activities like health and education. Of course, state-owned enterprises can also exist in any other sector of labor—production and non-production— when there are market and social reasons for them to exist.

Lately, the capitalist West has been changing its outlook on state ownership. For example, the former opposition leader of the British Labor Party, Jeremy Corbyn, advocated for the nationalization of certain key economic sectors in Great Britain, such as energy and railways.

SOCIAL OWNERSHIP

Why would social ownership of the means of production as a "system of relations between people, and not the relations between man and things" exist in a new democratic and just society?

In the former Yugoslav system of socialist self-management based on social ownership, there were dozens and even hundreds of successful, and even very successful social enterprises, that were well-known and recognized in domestic and foreign markets. These enterprises were certainly more successful than many of the most successful private enterprises in Serbia and other states currently in the territory of Yugoslavia today. Social property should therefore be brought back to life exclusively for economic— not for any ideological—reasons, despite the fact that the bearers of politics and the government of neoliberalism have officially anathematized it. Today, without any doubt, the economic situation in Serbia and other former Yugoslav republics would be incomparably better if successful social enterprises were preserved and if self-management had been supported as a form of socialist privatization. Furthermore, a number of unsuccessful socially owned enterprises could have been saved from bankruptcy if the state helped them install better management, including bringing in capable managers from abroad, and if it had provided enterprises with appropriate financial support and bank loans with longer repayment periods and lower interest rates.

In any case, the administrative liquidation of socially owned enterprises and their self-managed bodies (workers' council, board of directors, working people's assembly, workers' control) is contrary to the essence of democracy, freedom, and the market valuation of everyone's work in society. If a social enterprise is able to operate successfully, why would anyone prevent it from operating and force it to transform into a private enterprise because of the ideological dogmas of neoliberal capitalism?

In the conditions and relations of socially owning the means of production, it is significantly more possible than any other form of ownership to increase common goods, which become increasingly important in the future and belong under equal conditions to all citizens of a given social community. Such goods are, in fact, real public, social goods—not state goods, which are created under other property regimes and primarily meant to satisfy the particular interests of the nomenclature of the political party in power and the owners of capital. Social ownership and the common goods inherent to it enable societies to reach a non-capitalist, non-exploitative, truly just society in the fastest and shortest way. In that sense, Marx's conception of social property has distinct scientific and practical value. In any case, discrediting social property, which is a tendency of neoliberal apologists, is a great civilizational mistake because the influence common, social goods on the form the future organization of society and the economy will take is objectively inevitable.

The creation of common goods implies the need to rely as much as possible on the resources, knowledge, and work energy of all able-bodied citizens—especially young people, including their voluntary work, such as youth work actions, in economic and social development. Relying solely or predominantly on the inflow of foreign capital (direct foreign investments) and the transfer of domestic economic resources and capacities to foreign partners as a part of concessions and strategic partnerships are not guarantees of the successful progress of a country, especially in the absence of a long-term economic development strategy.

No one invests their own capital in another country in order to bring happiness to it, but to gain returns on their investments and make as much profit as possible. Historically, all countries that managed to develop economically and technologically to the maximum achieved that primarily by relying on their own resources, the working energy of their own people, and their willingness to sacrifice what was necessary to development, and not by relying on the capital of others. Even West Germany and Japan were able to rise after suffering great destruction in World War II, primarily thanks to work heroism, the voluntary work actions of their people, especially their youth, and not solely because of the economic assistance received from the U.S. through the Marshall Plan and direct investments.

COMMON OWNERSHIP OF ASSOCIATED WORKERS

Why would the common property of freely associated individual workers as a separate derivate of social property be necessary in a new society?

Because this derivative form of social property already exists in economic and social practice. For example, the auto transport company Jugoprevoz Kruševac AD from Kruševac, Serbia, is a worker corporation. All means of their production are truly common—i.e., the collective property of its freely associated individual workers. This company was once a successful self-managed social enterprise, but was brought to the brink of ruin due to the negligence of Serbian society and the proclaimed policy of privatization at all costs, resulting in its old, worn out, and technically defective buses, neglected bus station, high business losses, decimated labor collective, and workers without salaries who were apathetic and disoriented. Nobody wanted to buy the company in such a condition, regardless of the fact that it was being sold for practically nothing.

Being in this hopeless situation, the workers who were "left in the lurch" and remained loyal to Jugoprevoz Kruševac AD until the end and did not abandon it even in their hardest times, tried to save it from final collapse and inevitable liquidation, taking their destiny into their own hands to cope with the economic difficulties and personal hardships. Eventually, the workers succeeded. Thanks to the understanding and support of the local self-managed bodies of Kruševac, the workers were granted a bank loan and with the funds obtained, they bought the entire property of the company. The property of the company, which had been socially owned until then, became the private property of the individual workers employed in it in proportion to the amount of their participation in the purchase of the property. In this way, the socially owned enterprise was transformed into a joint-stock company, and the private property of the individual workers-shareholders became collective property. For several years, the worker-shareholders gave up part of their earned wages and lived on minimal wages in order to provide the funds necessary for the technical and technological modernization of the company. The worker-shareholders have directly selected and still select a team of managers who they believe will successfully manage the company.

At the general meeting of shareholders held on June 29, 2016, Jugoprevoz Kruševac AD had a total of 76,138 ordinary shares with voting rights. It was decided at this meeting that the entire amount of their net profit, which amounted to 55,666,033 dinars at the end of the 2015 business year, should be directed

> to retained earnings. Such a distribution is appropriate considering the available financial capabilities and needs of the Company, whereby funds in the form of retained earnings are

kept for investment purposes in accordance with the needs of the Company, and at the same time, there is a possibility that, if the conditions are met for the payment of interim dividends, the responsible authority of the Company will make a decision on its payment" (Jugoprevoz 2016).

Today, Jugoprevoz from Kruševac is an exemplary work collective and successful worker corporation that is impeccably organized technologically. It operates successfully in intercity, international, and city transport, thanks to its capable management. It regularly fulfills its obligations to the state and pays salaries to workers who believe in an even better future. Workers are happy with their new ownership status in the corporation. Nobody is exploited by anyone. The employees feel that the entire property of Jugoprevoz is truly their own, inalienable from them, and not "everyone's and nobody's," the way the property of socially owned enterprises was often wrongly treated under Yugoslav self-managed socialism.

The situation in the Serbian economy would be incomparably better today if in the process of transforming property relations in society, the state financially supported workers to purchase the property of socially-owned enterprises, instead of generously supporting tycoons and newly formed capitalists (Komazec 2008: 52-53).

Cooperative property also rests on the logic that the collective property of freely associated individual workers is a special form of social property on which different organizational forms of cooperatives are based. According to the economic relations it establishes and reproduces, cooperative property is the joint property of individual cooperative members united in a given cooperative.

PERSONAL (INDIVIDUAL) OWNERSHIP

Why is personal ownership of the means of production necessary in a new society?

Because a regular increase of the relative share of personal labor in the total social labor has been demonstrated. The digital economy, based on new information technologies, provides new opportunities for the development of this sector of labor. Self-employment and personal labor with funds owned by citizens, the so-called personal labor sector, is already starting to become a megatrend in the world economy, if that is not already the case. Many professional and capable people in the world and in Serbia want to be "their own boss," a "one-person company" or a "one-man company," instead of working for someone else—a capitalist employer or the state. They do not want to be exploited or to exploit anyone. Such micro-companies reaffirm their success on the market on a daily basis while also competing with companies of other forms of ownership.

A "one-person company" can grow into a private company by employing one or more workers—when "his own boss" becomes the employer, i.e., "someone else's boss." The means of production then pass from being personal property and personal labor to private property; "his own labor" become private capital, and the holder of personal labor ("his own boss") becomes a capitalist employer and begins to exploit his first and each subsequent employee to appropriate the unpaid part of their total living labor, which is the logic of the capitalist mode of production. This is when personal property transforms into private property, establishing the capitalist production relationship.

The independent performance of various production and service activities that involves the personal labor and personal property of citizens is the best possible illustration of the foundations and relationships a just society should be based on in order to truly be a social organization of labor that excludes the exploitation of other people's labor generated by the means of production monopoly of private property.

Furthermore, the economic logic of business prevalent in the personal labor sector is the starting point for organizing joint forms of labor and resources in many sectors of economic activity, from agriculture and industry to service activities, in which no one exploits and everyone earns income in proportion to their invested funds and invested living labor.

The systemic treatment of personal labor that uses the personal property of citizens must be identical to the treatment of labor in any other form of property. Personal property must be equal to private, state, and social property and production relationships reproduced in the personal labor sector must be transparent and socially controlled.

PARTNERSHIP BETWEEN NOMINAL OWNERSHIPS

In the conditions of property pluralism, the holders of different forms of ownership are guided by their aspiration to achieve the best economic results, can mutually establish special relations of property partnership instead of participating in classic market competition with each other.

In contemporary economic practice, there is already a public-private partnership. The state, as the holder of state-owned property, and a private entrepreneur, as the holder of private property rights, jointly participate with their capital and managerial knowledge in the implementation of relevant investment projects in infrastructure and other sectors.

40.

INFLUENCE OF OWNERSHIP ON THE POLITICAL ORGANIZATION OF SOCIETY

In the United States, the political system is a very marginal affair.
There are two parties, so-called, but they're really
factions of the same party,
the Business Party. Both represent some range of
business interests.

Noam Chomsky

The political organization of every society has always directly depended on its dominant form of ownership. As a byproduct of property monism—the monopoly of one form of property— there is always a political organization of society in which power is concentrated in the hands of one political party, or several ideologically and politically related parties, and materially tied to the same form of property. This is *political monism.*

Political parties and movements characteristic of the political right of society have emerged on the foundations of the monopoly of private property. All are intrinsically tied to private property and the reproduction of capitalist production relationships, regardless of their minor or major ideological differences on domestic and/or foreign policy issues. For every political party of the right, however, the preservation of the very being of private property, the pillar of the capitalist order, is more important than any of its particular interests.

In former socialist countries, the monopoly of state (social) property enabled the existence of one-party political systems and the political monopoly of their communist, worker, or socialist parties. For example, a one-party political system exists currently in China, and one could say that it works successfully as measured by its indisputable economic achievements. The political party monopoly of the Communist Party of China is based primarily on the dominance of state property in the organization of Chinese society, but also on the effective state-party control of private property. The Communist Party of China does not allow private property to be spotlighted in political parties or organizations. Official representatives of the Chinese communist establishment are always actively present on the management boards of private Chinese corporations and companies and are in charge of implementing party policies. Chinese private entrepreneurs (capitalists) can have state support and be successful in business only if they strictly adhere to the political program of the Communist Party and its up-to-date directives. Any deviation from the established party program is severely punished.

Property and political monisms are characterized by authoritarian and autocratic rule. In societies and countries with this form of political power, "free and fair elections" are a mere formality because the winners are known in advance. In China, the winners are always candidates of the Communist Party, and in contemporary capitalist countries the winners will most often be candidates of right-leaning political parties whose basic ideological matrices are the same, derived from the monopoly of private property (property monism). It is simply not possible to have real, functional political pluralism under the conditions of property monism. The political parties of the left, who oppose property monism, are nothing but decor through which the right-leaning parties show the "democracy" of their established system of government, which is essentially one-party system.

Unlike property monism, property pluralism opens the door for new non-capitalist, non-exploitative, non-authoritarian, and non-autocratic political and economic entities to enter the social scene and establish their status and real power in society through non-private forms of owning the means of production.

Property pluralism implies genuine *political pluralism*, a form of political organization where there are several diverse political parties materially linked to different forms of ownership and power is concentrated in the hands of the political parties that win the most votes in free and fair elections and thereby win the trust of citizens who go to the polls. Property and political pluralism enable the development of true democracy, true freedoms, and human rights. Citizens forced to sell their labor to be wage workers cannot claim to be free. Their mere existence is in the hands of capitalist employers; they directly materially depend on them and are therefore subjects to a neoliberal capitalist system.

It is a historical necessity to open up all possibilities and areas for the systemic institutionalization of all feasible forms of non-private, non-capitalist property, including contemporary systems of participation (self-management) in the world and the mandatory participation of workers in the profit distribution of capitalist enterprises. This is the material basis and guarantee of the more successful positioning and activities of left-wing parties in political systems. Without radical changes to and the ultimate abolition of the neoliberal capitalist system, political parties of the true left will stay on the margins of society and have no real influence.

Abandoning every form of property monopoly and abolishing the monopoly of private property would allow for the creation of true *political pluralism in society*, dethroning the existing economic and political power of the capitalist class, which is so blinded by its selfish interests that it does not see that many people are struggling in poverty, begging in the streets, searching through dumpsters for food, and starving.

Political parties, movements, and initiatives characteristic of the left can survive and have adequate political influence only when non-capitalist forms of property (state, social, common, and personal) are systematically equated with private property. Otherwise, they are doomed to failure—or, at best, vegetating.

41.

WHAT IS A WORKER CORPORATION?

In a new non-capitalist democratic society, worker corporations would exist in addition to private, state, and social enterprises as a specific form of social enterprise, created by joining the labor and resources of its freely associated individual workers.

Economic relations in a worker corporation would be based on the principle of shareholding.

> But it cannot be a simple copy of capitalist joint-stock companies. A solution could also be sought in the model of shares which are locked within the collective, which are acquired exclusively on the basis of work and in accordance with the work contribution, and their owner loses them upon termination of employment, with appropriate modalities of compensation. That way, the employment relationship would become a property relationship, and the ownership of the company would be indivisible common, collective property.

> On that basis, the workers, as co-owners, would participate in the management, in accordance with the value of their shares, including decisions about disposal of the newly created value. This could be a way to constitute a new true self-management in production and other activities of economic entities. This would open up the perspective of a new economic freedom for each individual (Manifesto No. 2, 2013).

The capital of the worker corporation would be entirely common—the collective property of freely associated individual workers and as such, would have specific, nominal holders known by their first and last name. Such property would in fact be the only or the only possible realistic form of social property. The material foundation of this social property would be the labor contribution of an individually associated worker based on their living work and personal funds invested in the worker corporation.

The social status and stability of economic relations in a worker corporation would be normatively regulated by appropriate systemic legislation. This would enable the free transformation of a worker corporation into a private company when someone becomes the majority owner of capital by purchasing the shares of individual workers, and vice versa, in accordance with pre-determined conditions and established procedures. It would thus be possible for a private company to become a worker corporation if employees were to become the majority owners of its capital.

The specific content of material relations between individually associated workers would be regulated by an agreement on the establishment of a worker corporation, so each worker always knows which part of the jointly owned capital belongs to them, including an appropriate share in achieved revenue, and their personal consequences in the event of operating losses.

If it is in the interest of individually associated workers, the agreement on establishing a worker corporation could also establish a mechanism to prevent the emergence of a predominant owner of the joint capital, therefore preventing it from becoming a traditional private enterprise.

Worker corporations would be a market-oriented economic entity in the same way private or state-owned enterprises are. After all, why can't a worker corporation, in which all workers individually own a portion of joint capital, operate efficiently with its high-quality management apparatus and make a profit on the market like any other private or state-owned enterprise?

Goods (products and services) created by the workers in their own worker corporations are truly their own and as such have a special significance in this day and age of the increasing alienation of workers from their products and selfishness generated by the monopoly of private property. Such common goods, in the way they are created and used, are associated with communism, but not with "that communism whose centenary we celebrate [the October Revolution], but communism as a collective interest in common goods" (Latour 2017: 20).

A worker corporation would, in fact, be a true workers' self-managed enterprise in the hands of the freely associated workers, who manage their own economic, labor, and other relationships without the tutelage of the state or private owner. Such an enterprise is not a utopia, but a possible business and democratic framework of the social organization of labor in this era.

The establishment of worker corporations and workers' self-managed companies should be maximally encouraged by all available financial, banking, fiscal, and monetary resources, as well as managerial cadres. This is not, however, what happened in the ownership transformation of the Poljoprivredna korporacija Beograd (PKB), the Belgrade Agricultural Corporation, which was predominantly under state ownership. Instead of being transformed into a mega worker corporation, it was quickly privatized during the summer of 2018. It would have been an incomparably better solution, socially and economically, if the state had financially helped the workers of PKB buy its assets and choose their management according to global standards. The property of PKB would have become the common property of its employees, who would have then been materially motivated to economically succeed because they were working exclusively in their own interest, and not in the interest of a capitalist employer.

42

EXAMPLES OF WORKERS' SELF-MANAGEMENT IN THE WORLD

Regardless of the fact that since the demolition of the Belin Wall, the word "socialism" has become largely "vulgarized and politicized" in political discourse, socialism has still managed to survive. Today,

> there are significant elements of something like authentic socialism in the Western world, notably worker-owned (and sometimes managed) enterprises, cooperatives with real participation, and much else…they can be thought of in Bakunin's terms, as creating institutions of a more free and just society (Chomsky–Polychroniou 2017: 108–109).

Worker participation in decision-making and the participation of people in decisions that affect their lives occurs "as a means to democratize society or as a means to preserve its democratic character" (Adizes 1975: xvii). In many capitalist enterprises, in addition to enabling workers to participate in the ownership of their capital, there are also special worker advisory bodies. For example, workers' councils directly participate to an extent in the management and business operations with their proposals.

In order to reduce strike outbreaks in enterprises, the French president Charles de Gaulle once introduced a system of participation that legitimized the obligatory agreements between workers and employers and the participation of workers in the profits of the enterprise. Participation as a system was also legalized in Italy. In Germany, participation was first introduced in mining and heavy industry, and later became much more widely present (Vujačić 2019: 17). "The Israeli from the beginning of [the twentieth century has] experienced [community] organizations and [various] form of cooperation with the kibbutz and Moshe movements" (Adizes 1975: 3).

There has long been a practice that private enterprises, especially small and medium sized ones, are taken over by workers after going bankrupt. Workers renew the work process using personal funds and bank loans, becoming co-owners of the enterprise's assets and directly managing all business operations. In the U.S., Europe, and elsewhere, there are already enterprises directly managed by workers that operate successfully according to the principles of participation, (self-management).

The American Morning Star Company is successfully operating through the direct involvement of workers in its management. "No one at the company has a boss. Employees negotiate and set individual responsibilities with their fellow workers. Everyone can spend the privately held company's money without budgetary constraints. Nobody carries a title, and there are no promotions. Compensation at the largest tomato processor on the planet is peer-based" (Wartzman 2012).

One of the most innovative private chemical manufacturing enterprises in the U.S., W. L. Gore & Associates, Inc., founded in 1958 in Newark, Delaware by Wilbert and Genevieve Gore, operates on self-organizing principles and is privately owned. It has more than 10,500 employees (associates) worldwide who are also part-owners of the enterprise through their associate stock ownership plan. Gore & Associates has offices in more than 25 countries and manufacturing operations in the U.S., Germany, the UK, China, and Japan. It is well-known on the world market for its Gore-Tex fabrics. Today, its revenue is $3.7 billion. Evaluating its business successes, the company states that

> We believe Gore's success is a direct result of the values that are the foundation of our company's culture. This culture is built on a deeply held belief in Associates and in the innate drive of each person to reach his or her full potential. We are collectively committed to fostering a safe and healthy work environment where all Associates can develop their talents, enjoy their work, and responsibly direct their activities" (*The Gore* 2019).

The Grammy-winning Orpheus Chamber Orchestra, found in 1972 and based in Carnegie Hall in New York City, operates solely on self-management principles, without the orchestra chief (*Orpheus* 1972).

In order to relax tensions between labor and capital and motivate workers to be more attached to the corporation they work for, either employers, the owners of capital, leave direct management to the workers, or workers get involved in management or the corporation's ownership.

In the U.S., the Employee Stock Ownership Plan (ESOP) has been operating since 1974, and is being implemented in different ways. Employees can buy the company's shares directly or receive them from the company as a bonus; receive a shareholder pledge and participate in the distribution of profits; or become the owners through worker cooperatives in which everyone has an equal voice. Employees usually opt for ownership shares in the company, however. ESOP has been affirmed through practice and there are currently almost 7,000 ESOP plans in the U.S. (NECO 2018). The National Center for Employee

Ownership (NECO) estimates that about 28 million employees participate in employee ownership plans. Overall, employees now control about eight percent of companies' capital (Josephs 2018).

During the recession triggered by the economic and financial crisis of 2007 and 2008, "employee-owners were four times less likely to be laid off" than non-owner employees (NECO 2020).

The participation of workers in capitalist enterprises undeniable political and social significance, in addition to economic advantages. In practice, it firmly and unequivocally affirms that the capitalist order can be socially better and fairer than it currently is, but such social awareness, is, unfortunately, almost non-existent in post-transitional societies. In Serbia, for example, many capitalists who acquired their capital by taking it from self-managed workers are not only reluctant to allow workers to participate in the management of their enterprises, but avoid mentioning the word self-management, despite the fact that Serbia has a long tradition of self-management. Workers of the Gun Foundry (Topolivnica) in Serbia's Kragujevac and supporters of the Serbian socialist Svetozar Marković, who was an advocate for direct democracy and self-management, organized large worker and people's demonstrations from February 15-27 in 1876. These demonstrators developed a red flag of self-management on the streets of the city and fought for democratic and humanistic rights for the working class. There was also the newspaper called *Self-Management*. During socialist self-management in Yugoslavia, meetings called "The Red Flag of Self-Management" were held in Kragujevac every year where experiences with self-management were exchanged and solutions were sought for specific problems Yugoslav self-managers encountered in their daily work.

43.

WORKERS' PARTICIPATION IN SHARING EMPLOYERS' PROFIT

The capitalist social order can be changed and transformed into a just society only through abolishing the exploitation of wage workers and institutionalizing fairer relations, rights, and the obligations of capital owners and wage workers in distributing profits earned in capitalist enterprises.

The goods created by a capitalist enterprise intended for the market are always the result of labor and capital's reproductive cooperation, the two inseparable and interdependent factors of production. The capital of the owner cannot create a new value, product, or service without the cooperation of workers' living labor, their knowledge, and their skilled hands. Moreover, living labor, regardless of its quality, cannot create a new value without capital. Therefore, all products and services of every capitalist enterprise are always the joint work of the involved capital of the owner, the employer's personal labor, and the living labor of wage workers. Consequently, the profit which a capitalist enterprise makes by selling products and services on the market is always common, owned by both the owner of the capital and the workers. Thus, profit cannot belong entirely to the owners of capital, as is currently the case, but also belongs to the workers in proportion to their individual contributions to the total invested living labor.

The contribution of the worker to the achieved profit of the capitalist enterprise is always greater than his paid living labor—the wage determined and paid by the owner of capital. A worker's unpaid living labor is appropriated by the employer in the form of profit because of the employer's ownership rights of the means of production, as well as the employer's personal labor contribution if they directly participate in the management process.

Of course, the capitalist class will use all available means to preserve and defend its acquired right of private ownership of the means of production in order to continue easily appropriating profit gained through workers' unpaid living labor.

44.

CHARACTERISTICS OF PROFIT AND INCOME

The two most important economic indicators of success of every enterprise in a market economy, regardless of the form of ownership, are profit and income. The maximization of profit and income is the material basis of the development and progress of both an enterprise and society. The difference between profit and income is only in the theoretically different understandings of how certain factors of production contribute to the creation of new values.

The labor theory of value starts from the premise that only the workers' living labor creates new value, and that the means of production (means of labor and objects of labor) transfer only their value (transferred value) to a new product, the enterprise income thus represents the market recognition of expended newly added labor. In capitalism, this is formulated as the sum of paid wages and realized profit—the gain of the enterprise. Profit is, in fact, a monetary market expression of surplus value (the unpaid part of the total invested living labor of the worker), which is then appropriated by the employer, the owner of capital, by virtue of his ownership of capital.

The marginal theory of value, begins with the idea that all involved factors of production contribute to the creation of newly created value in proportion to their quality and quantity—not only workers' living labor. The enterprise then makes a profit when the costs of all of these factors are lower than the total income earned through its operations.

Regardless of these different theoretical approaches, the most important thing in the business of any enterprise is that it manages its available resources adequately, utilizing the material factors of production (capital) and living labor (labor force) rationally so in that way the enterprise can maximize profit and income acquired because of the success of their produced goods, products, and services on the market.

Measuring the business success of an enterprise in a market economy is a thread that connects and permeates profit and income, despite the fact that profit follows the logic of the capitalist cost of commodities (c + v), while income follows the logic of the real cost of goods

(c + v + m). Profit and income are not only microeconomic aggregates that measure the business success of an enterprise, but simultaneously authentically reflect the character of an enterprise's production relationships and the established laws of social distribution derived from the ownership of the means of production.

Viewed through the prism of production relations, profit is a sublimation of the separation of labor and capital and workers' alienation from the total results of their labor. Income, however, is a sublimation of labor and capital's integration under the control of workers and the direct connection of workers with the total results of their labor. In other words, profit is a socioeconomic expression of relationships based on private and state ownership, while income is an expression of relationships based on social and common property and personal labor through the personal ownership of the means of production.

Capitalism is not the way it is because of profit or because owners of capital are obsessed with constantly maximizing it, but because profit belongs exclusively to capitalists and partly to the state, but not to its original creators, the workers in production providing the material and creative basis of society.

45.

TAXATION OF THE RICH

You don't make the poor rich by making the rich poorer.

Winston Churchill

The proper way to tax the property and income of capital owners (the rich) is one of the most controversial issues in economic theory and practice. There are two main schools of thought on this problem: *utilitarianism* and *libertarianism*.

Utilitarianism is based

on the idea of the 'diminishing marginal utility of income,' which holds that the added happiness of an extra $100 of income is very high for the poor but very low or even negligible for a rich person. Thus, taxing $100 from a billionaire and giving $100 to a hungry and impoverished individual would only negligibly diminish the utility of the billionaire (if at all) but will markedly raise the utility of the hungry person. Since the utilitarian's goal is to maximize overall wellbeing in the society, typically thought of as the *sum* of the utilities of the members of society, the followers of utilitarianism will generally favor a tax-and-transfer scheme of income redistribution from rich to poor.

Economists have traditionally argued that such utilitarian redistribution comes at the cost of economic efficiency...The act of redistribution, for example, through taxes of the rich and transfer payments to the poor is alleged to cause distortions, inefficiencies, and waste, leading people to work less hard and to deploy capital in less productive ways... That such a view is far too pessimistic (Sachs 2015: 224).

Another school of thought is libertarianism.

According to it, the most important ethical rule is freedom. The meaning of life, as per libertarianism, is the freedom to choose one's own path. The greatest harm occurs when the state takes that freedom away from the individuals...

A libertarian rejects the utilitarian idea of redistribution through taxation. According to that opinion, taxing a billionaire to help a hungry individual means unjustifiably violating the freedom of that billionaire. A libertarian can encourage a billionaire to set aside a hundred dollars for charity, but will defend that billionaire's right to decide for himself whether to do so. Therefore, a libertarian considers most of the taxes to be an illegitimate interference with the freedom of taxpayers, with the exception of the necessary taxes, used for national defense and justice" (Ibid.: 210).

The political right worldwide consists of the capitalist class—the owners of capital, the rich—and believes that progressive taxation is a punishment for business success and that it calls into question the essence of the capitalist entrepreneurial spirit: the aspiration and effort to maximize profits. They also warn that without an increase in the profits of a capitalist enterprise, there would be no new investments, no new jobs, insufficient economic and income growth, and therefore a lack of sufficient funds available to meet the current and future needs of socially disadvantaged citizens, the poor and hungry. "It's an article of faith on the American right that low taxes are the key to economic success" (Krugman 2012: 119).

After the 1990s, leading capitalist countries took this arguments into account and opted to reduce the tax burden on the property and gross profit of capital owners, believing that such a tax policy would encourage faster economic recovery and the sustainable growth of their national economies. The opposite happened, however. The global financial and economic crisis of 2007 and 2008 broke out, primarily in the U.S. and Europe. Unemployment increased, economic activity declined, and therefore the overall social situation in the country deteriorated.

Paul Krugman, an American economist and Nobel laureate, points out that the economists Thomas Piketty and Emmanuel Saez

> have added a further argument: sharp cuts in taxes on high incomes, they suggest, have actually encouraged executives to push the envelope further, to engage in 'rent-seeking' at the expense of the rest of the workforce. Why? Because the personal payoff to a higher pretax income has risen, making executives more willing to risk condemnation and/or hurt morale by pursuing personal gain. As Piketty and Saez note, there is a fairly close negative correlation between top tax rates and the top [one] percent's share of income, both over time and across countries" (Krugman 2012: 45).

The Serbian economist Jovan B. Dušanić believes that "the tax cuts and the abandonment of progressive taxation is one of the 'neoliberal dogmas,'" that providing tax benefits to wealthy investors does not accelerate economic growth, but leads to "collecting less taxes, so instead of better, we have worse civil services" (Dušanić 2016: 36–37).

The empirical experience of Sweden refutes the argument of the rich that the progressive taxation of property and profit leads to divestments in the economy and society. This modern European state has made progress in every aspect thanks to their progressive taxation of the property and profit of the rich. The richest Swedes do, however, often move their capital to tax havens around the world, similar to the rich in other countries,

Economic growth at a local, national, and global level primarily depends on how owners of capital—employers—manage their available capital and whether they invest it in business projects that bring income or loss—not on the foundations of a given tax system. Investment and market failures, unprofitable ventures, and the failed management of invested factors of production are the main factors stunting economic growth, not the progressive taxation of the rich. Hypothetically speaking, even if progressive taxation of property and profit were abolished, the issues of faster economic growth and earning higher income would remain open.

The American economist Jeffrey Sachs believes that

> many kinds of redistribution to the poor are actually highly efficient investments in the health, skills, and productivity of the poor. These are high-return investments that the poor themselves would be eager to make if only they had the household income or borrowing capacity to make them! In this way, the utilitarian emphasis on redistribution can be doubly justified, not only as equitable but as also efficient, leading to high-return investments that otherwise would not be made because of the failure of market forces alone to provide adequate investment funds to the poor (Sachs 2014: 225).

The redistribution of income from the rich to the poor, that is, the progressive taxation of the property and profit of the owners of capital, cannot be considered a threat to personal freedom of capital owners. It is primarily a matter of returning at least a minimal part of the value taken away from the exploited and poor strata of society over the centuries of capitalist exploitation, starting from the original imperialist colonization of the world and the original accumulation of capital until now.

The development of the capitalist production of goods and services is inconceivable without actively relying on available general, common, social, and state goods—from infrastructural to cultural, among others. These goods are always the result of total social labor, and not the "labor contribution" of existing owners of capital through the exploitation of workers. An appropriate redistribution of income from the rich to the poor is nothing but the repayment of their debt to society, which uses these acquired funds to feed the hungry, clothe the naked, heal the sick, and educate the illiterate.

The necessity of progressive taxation of the rich is supported even by some of the world's most famous rich people. For example, Bill Gates, the founder and owner of Microsoft and the second richest man in the world, says that

> our system can be a lot more progressive (…richer people paying a higher share). A key element is making capital gains taxation more like ordinary income (some have suggested making them the same) and having an estate tax more like we had in the past (55 [percent] above $3.5 [million]). European countries collect…more taxes…through consumption taxes, but those are not progressive. If people want the government to do more it needs to be funded…I see us needing to improve

our education and health services. So yes, I have paid $10 [billon] but I should have had to pay more on my capital gains (Piper, 2019).

Why is Bill Gates a proponent of progressive taxation? Because he is deeply aware of the fact that the wealth he acquired and still acquires is not only the product of his undeniable creative abilities and management skills, but also a product of the unpaid and underpaid living labor of the workers he hired and still hires and the total social labor materialized in the educational, scientific, and technical-technological achievements of society.

According to Thomas Piketty,

a tax on capital would be a less violent and more efficient response to the eternal problem of private capital and its return. A progressive levy on individual wealth would reassert control over capitalism in the name of the general interest while relying on the forces of private property and competition. Each type of capital would be taxed in the same way, with no discrimination a priori, in keeping with the principle that investors are generally in a better position than the government to decide what to invest in…

To sum up: the capital tax is a new idea, which needs to be adapted to the globalized patrimonial capitalism of the twenty-first century (Piketty 2014: 371 and 373).

The problem of taxation and social inequality is particularly acute in former socialist countries. All of the former socialist countries in Eastern Europe that have undergone privatization, which has resulted in the growth of inequality, must re-establish greater public control over the mechanisms which deepen this inequality.

[Piketty insists] that the issue of progressive taxation on income and wealth is inseparable from their democratic transparency.

When we do not have a progressive tax, as is the case in Russia, it means that we do not have a public insight into income and property. This corresponds to the model of a society which is extremely oligarchic, in which a large part of national property is privatized under conditions that are often scandalous. Individuals have become rich overnight thanks to privatization at very low prices, and then, in many cases, left the country with assets, settled in Paris, London or elsewhere, and continued to take away income and dividends from their country while living abroad.

This model is disgusting and leads to the strengthening of nationalism. When we do not solve social problems within the country in a peaceful and rational manner, there is a tendency to try to get away with it by calling for hatred towards others, by laying the blame on foreign workers or other countries. All former communist countries must raise the question of what to do now that they no longer have public property, when they have privatized a large part of their economy. If we are content with privatizing everything and not setting up alternative institutions for inequality control, we are moving towards a society which is extremely unequal" (Piketty 2015: 14).

Despite all the controversy and criticism, justified or not, the progressive taxation of the rich on their capital and return on capital (profit) is the most reliable and efficient fiscal method of collecting the material resources necessary to lift billions of people out of poverty, extreme destitution, and social misery.

The present managing director of the IMF, Kristalina Georgieva, estimates that income and wealth inequality has become "one of the most complex and difficult challenges in the global economy" over the last decade. She suggests that governments needed to rethink their policies and consider progressive taxation. In her view, "progressive taxation is a key component of effective fiscal policy...Our research shows that marginal tax rates can be increased without sacrificing economic growth" (Taylor 2020).

The international non-profit organization Oxfam "urged governments to hike tax rates for corporations and the world's richest to tackle the growing wealth gap" (Oxfam 2020).

Taxing the rich is not so easy to achieve in reality, however.

Why? Because globalization makes it difficult to increase the income tax, which is the main generator of inequality, and without a coordinated action of the majority of countries – which today seems unthinkable – the probability of that happening is very small.

Simply put, capital is difficult to tax because it is extremely mobile, and countries that benefit from it have no reason to give up those benefits. Tax havens exist not only in miniature states, but also in large states such as the United States and the United Kingdom... Even the best paid workers are increasingly difficult to tax because they can easily move from one country to another: nothing prevents a top paid manager from running his/her business from Singapore or Hong Kong instead of London or New York (Milanović 2017: 175).

Existing tax havens are, without a doubt, among the weakest links in the global economic and democratic system and their eradication is an important condition for the non-market transfer of an income percentage of the rich to the poor. The highest bodies of the UN should abolish all tax havens in the world without delay. Preparing an appropriate decision to that end should be one of the priorities of the existing UN administrative team, led by the Secretary General, António Guterres.

46.

UNIVERSAL BASIC INCOME (UBI)

Universal basic income is a system in which all citizens receive a standard amount of money each month to cover basic expenses like food, rent, and clothes.

Definition of UBI

To the hungry people it doesn't matter if they starve into one-party or multiparty system.

Milovan Ilić Minimaks

At the start of the third decade of the twenty first century, poverty is the number one social, economic, and political problem of humanity at a local, national, and global level and is why the distribution of income and social wealth must change radically in favor of the socially vulnerable. Although the rich are not naturally willing to easily and voluntarily separate from their income and wealth, they must be aware that maintaining existing social inequalities in the world is no longer possible. Furthermore, the rich must be willing to share an appropriate portion of their income and wealth with the socially disadvantaged, the poor, and the poorest in society.

One of the ideas to address and rectify widespread poverty is the institutionalization of universal basic income (UBI). UBI is a "transfer provided by the state in a unique and uniform way, regularly and without conditions, to every adult member of society. It is the obligation of the state in a fixed amount, regardless of whether a person is wealthy or poor, lives alone or with others, is willing to work or not" (Ružica 2016).

In accordance with the idea of UBI, every member of society would be guaranteed an objectively acceptable standard of living above the established poverty line—i.e., basic living conditions worthy of a human in the twenty first century. The introduction of UBI would replace existing transfers, such as social benefits and allowances in the event of job loss or unemployment. Many countries are already allocating substantial budget funds for this purpose.

Having a guaranteed UBI would significantly improve the material position of socially vulnerable citizens, especially those with incomes below the poverty line, and this number is very large. While there are many unemployed people, there are also many employees whose salary is insufficient for a normal life. The number of unemployed people tends to increase because robotization and digitalization of work processes reduce the need for the existing and negates the need for a new labor force. A large number of young people in the world have no prospects for employment and are on the brink of poverty. Among the socially vulnerable are also persons who earn their income by performing various temporary, occasional, and overtime jobs, also known as the precariat, who are not able to cover basic living expenses through work alone. Pensioners, disabled people, and those without income—the homeless, beggars, and people forced to dumpster dive in order to survive—are also socially vulnerable.

Countries differ in their perspectives on a guaranteed UBI depending on their level of economic development. In poor, undeveloped, underdeveloped, and developing countries, UBI seems like a utopia because the total national income and per capita income are insufficient for its realization. However, some industrialized countries have already moved in the direction of making the idea of UBI a reality.

Finland is the first country in the world that has started testing a model of providing unconditional monthly allowance for all unemployed people. Based on a unique social experiment, as of January 1, 2017, two thousand randomly selected unemployed Finnish citizens receive a basic monthly allowance of 560 euros, unconditionally—they do not have to work, nor do they have to look for a job if they do not want to. They will not pay tax on that allowance, even if they find a job and earn income in addition to the allowance. The experiment is expected to last two years, with the possibility of extending it to several years. It is expected to reduce poverty and the number of non-production workers (clerks) and increase employment (Henley 2017).

Since the spring of 2017, Canada—the Ontario province, to be exact—has been conducting experiments that introduce universal basic income in three cities based on a previously scientifically prepared pilot program. Ontario makes up forty percent of Canada's economy and has more than 1.7 million people living on an income below the poverty line (20,676 dollars for individuals and 41,351 dollars for a family of four). Over the past fifteen years, through several waves of layoffs, the number of jobs in the automotive industry and other manufacturing sectors in Ontario were significantly reduced. In Canada's capital of Ottawa alone, four thousand jobs were cut during that period of time.

Due to this social situation, the Liberal Party, which is in power in Ontario, decided to implement a pilot program for UBI, expecting that it would, if done properly, give people the opportunity to learn about the possibilities of creating their own business, continuing their education, or developing professional skills without worrying about basic problems of material existence—at least for a short period of time (Kassam 2017).

UBI models similar to those in Finland and Canada are being considered in other countries such as the Netherlands, Germany, India, and Kenya. Germany, in particular, has had more and more requests for the introduction of UBI for all citizens. Götz Werner, the founder and co-owner of the German drugstore retail chain DM, the largest in Europe, is one of the most influential advocates of a UBI of one thousand euros for everyone in Germany (Werner 2013). Werner is credited with saying, "It is not shameful to get rich, but it is shameful to die rich."

The idea of UBI, however, is also being challenged in some economically and socially advanced environments. For example, on September 23, 2015, the Swiss parliament rejected a legislative initiative signed by 120,000 citizens to introduce the right to a guaranteed annual allowance in cash for all citizens ranging from 30,000 to 34,000 CHF, which is estimated to be the minimum amount for decent living in Switzerland. Opponents of the idea of a guaranteed annual income for all citizens believe that its adoption would demotivate many people to do anything and earn money, and that one's laziness should not be paid for. A public opinion poll conducted immediately after the decision to reject the initiative in the Swiss parliament showed, however, that as many as 49 percent of citizens support the initiative, while 43 percent are against, and the rest declared themselves undecided.

The left supports the idea of UBI. It sees the UBI "as a part of a broader program for poverty eradication, which also offers frameworks for reform and participation: more options for jobs, education, negotiations on wages and working conditions, activation at work and in the local community" (Ružica 2016). The UBI also has its admirers on the right, however. For example, Charles Murray, a respected conservative American scientist, supports this idea. He stated in 2016 that UBI is "our only hope to deal with a coming labor market unlike any in human history" and said it "represents our best hope to revitalize American civil society" (Varney 2018).

Additionally, "billionaire entrepreneurs in Silicon Valley have backed UBI" (Ibid.). A group of the seventeen richest American billionaires, led by George Soros, sent an open letter on June 24, 2019 to all 2020 U.S. presidential candidates seeking the additional taxation of the wealthiest Americans. They argue that

> The next dollar of new tax revenue should come from the most financially fortunate, not from middle-income and lower-income Americans.

> America has a moral, ethical and economic responsibility to tax our wealth more. A wealth tax could help address the climate crisis, improve the economy, improve health outcomes, fairly create opportunity, and strengthen our democratic freedoms. Instituting a wealth tax is in the interest of our republic (An Open Letter 2019).

The letter especially emphasizes that the funds collected by the taxation of the richest, estimated at over three billion dollars, could "substantially fund the cost of smart investments in our future, like clean energy innovation to mitigate climate change, universal child care, student loan debt relief, infrastructure modernization, tax credits for low-income families, public health solutions, and other vital needs" (Ibid.).

Further, the

billionaires Richard Branson, Elon Musk, and Bill Gates all believe the rise of artificial intelligence will mean the elimination of jobs and the necessity of a universal basic income. Some have argued it is 'a human right to have enough money to live on,' especially during a time of worsening wealth inequality. But others argue a universal income is nothing more than a pipe dream and citizens aren't entitled to cash handouts from the government (Barker 2019).

The radical right argue that UBI is nothing more than daydreaming, a utopia. "Asking a government to give cash handouts to its citizens is impractical, and the idea that humans are entitled to free money would hardly be considered a human right by many" (Ibid.).

Elon Musk, the founder of Tesla and SpaceX, explained why universal basic income will soon be a political necessity at the World Government Summit in Dubaiin 2017."

There will be fewer and fewer jobs that a robot cannot do better. I want to be clear. These are not things I wish will happen; these are things I think probably will happen. And if my assessment is correct and they probably will happen, then we have to think about what are we going to do about it? I think some kind of universal basic income is going to be necessary. The output of goods and services will be extremely high. With automation there will come abundance. Almost everything will get very cheap. I think we'll end up doing universal basic income. It's going to be necessary. The much harder challenge is, how are people going to have meaning? A lot of people derive their meaning from their employment. So if there's no need for your labor, what's your meaning? Do you feel useless? That's a much harder problem to deal with (Davis 2017).

At the core of introducing UBI is the decision that every state should find the means necessary to guarantee a basic income for socially vulnerable citizens. There are many countries in the world which, because of their economic underdevelopment and poverty, are unable to provide the funds needed for such a purpose, however. It is for this reason why the international community should come to the aid of those countries, primarily through the existing system of UN. The total resources of the UN, especially its economically most powerful member states, can objectively make it possible for all socially endangered human beings in the world to be guaranteed at least enough food so they do not die of starvation.

In the twenty first century, global solidarity is one of the key factors of maintaining world peace and stability and is needed today more than ever before.

The UN has constantly fought against global poverty and hunger ever since its founding, especially in the most economically backward countries. Faced with many negative social consequences that the rise and domination of neoliberalism brought, the UN has, especially after the disappearance of socialism, started to deal more intensively with burning global social issues. For example, the UN General Assembly declared October 17 as the International Day for the Eradication of Poverty in 1992, February 20 as the World Day of Social Justice in 2008, and unanimously adopted the 2030 Agenda for Sustainable Development in 2015. This agenda established the following strategic objectives: to fight against hunger and poverty in all forms and in all parts of the world, to promote full and productive employment and decent work for all, to reduce inequalities within and between countries, and to provide access to justice for all. The UIN has called and continues to call on rich countries to provide more help to poor and less developed countries.

Everything that the UN has done so far in terms of fighting poverty has been noble and important, but not enough. Its measures and activities have failed to stop the widening and deepening of the gap between the rich and the poor, which is why it is necessary to turn the page and establish an international fund for the socially endangered in the world. This should be done according to the same logic by which the IMF and the World Bank were established in the UN system, or the same way the World Trade Organization (WTO) was established, outside the UN system, but in close cooperation with the IMF and the World Bank.

An international fund for the care of the socially vulnerable in the world would be the fourth pillar of the world economic order—a new global economic and financial mechanism to ensure the economic and social security of every socially vulnerable person, and raise and develop funds for that purpose in an appropriate manner. This could be done, for example, through national funds established for the care of socially vulnerable persons.

The amount of universal income for all vulnerable citizens is a matter of social convention, and can be higher or lower, but should certainly be as high as possible relative to the poverty line. Perhaps it should be around 10 USD per day—about 300 USD per month and around 3,600 USD per year. This would make it possible for every inhabitant o our planet to have at least the basic conditions for a decent life because it is truly odd that in the twenty first century, with our achieved technological progress, people go to bed hungry or die of hunger.

Bearing in mind that there were 7.4 billion inhabitants on our planet in July 2017, and that the global GDP amounted to 127 thousand trillion USD that year, assuming that about 3.5 billion people on the planet are socially vulnerable and estimating the basic income per socially vulnerable citizen is 10 dollars per day, it would be necessary to allocate 12.6 trillion dollars—9.9 percent—of global GDP for this purpose (The World Factbook III 2019). Of course, if the total number of socially vulnerable people in the world is lower, a smaller portion of global GDP would be allocated for that purpose. That allocation would also be lower if the basic income per vulnerable resident is less than 10 dollars. These are undoubtedly extremely large funds, but they are only as big as the problem of poverty in the contemporary world. Eradicating poverty is expensive because this problem has not been addressed for centuries; it has constantly increased and is now intolerable, so it must be solved without delay, regardless of the price that needs to be paid. Nevertheless, humanity is able to pay that price because the achieved level of global social wealth and our current global GDP makes it possible.

The real problem, however, is on the other side. It is the unwillingness of the rich to accept more equitable and more responsible economic relationships in distributing global wealth and income. They are always more willing to allocate larger funds for purchasing weapons than for fighting against poverty, regardless that social inequalities and poverty are the greatest potential threat to world peace and stability. Peace cannot be preserved by keeping stockpiles of deadly nuclear weapons, but through reducing world poverty and increasing solidarity and economic equality in society.

The introduction of UBI for all citizens and the progressive taxation of the rich are important instruments in the fight against poverty, but are not sufficient. Victory over poverty can be achieved primarily by employing able-bodied members of society, especially the young and educated, through greater investments in creating new productive jobs in underdeveloped economies around the world, and not by arming – investing in killing people.

Therefore, the challenge with guaranteed UBI for socially vulnerable people and all inhabitants of the world is not a lack of global income and wealth, but primarily the way global wealth is distributed because of the proverbial selfishness of the rich and their refusal to give up part of their wealth to benefit poor, socially vulnerable people around the world.

47.

COVID – 19 PANDEMIC: GLOBAL SOLUTIONS TO THE GLOBAL PROBLEM

The COVID-19 pandemic, which has seriously threatened all countries and peoples around the world on every continent since the beginning of 2020, has already produced and still produces economic damage and social problems of unprecedented proportions. Practically, the global economy is on the verge of a great economic crisis, if not already in it. Millions of people are left without jobs, without livelihoods, with no ability to pay off housing and other loans. Many will be left homeless. The prospects for a faster economic recovery of the national economies of many countries and the global economy are not in the slightest encouraging.

The main issue is that very nature of the novel coronavirus is still an enigma for science because of its constant mutation. It is unknown when an effective vaccine or cure against this dangerous virus will be found or how long the pandemic will last. Some medical professionals have announced the arrival of the second wave, producing additional fear and panic among many people around the world who are worried about their existence and future. There seems to be no end in sight to this pandemic.

The COVID-19 pandemic is a global problem and is not only medical, but also economic and social. Its solution must be global, not national. An urgent search for specific answers and solutions to many other global problems have been put on the agenda by this pandemic, from reviving the global economy and providing necessary assistance to companies to solving the basic needs and issues of people affected by the pandemic.

The introduction of UBI into the global system would largely cover basic living expenses for those who are traditionally poor and those who left without the necessary means of subsistence because of job losses in the general economic crisis caused by the pandemic.

The outbreak of the COVID-19 pandemic particularly emphasized the necessity and importance of a well-functioning health care system for the population nationally and globally, and the timely provision of the food needed for people's survival.

Searching for answers to these two acute global problems, the Slovenian philosopher Slavoj Žižek says

> We should focus on what is crucial, which is, first, health care. The coronavirus epidemic is a universal crisis. In the long term, states cannot preserve themselves in a safe bubble while the epidemic rages all around. We need coordinated efforts, centralized at least in some sense, and we need to get ready for long periods of infection. We shouldn't think in terms of money when it comes to health. Materially, we have the means to organize some kind of global health care. If we don't, our global unity is liable to disappear, and it could be the end of globalization as we know it. People will continue to die in certain places, at the same time that others try to continue functioning as isolated bubbles.

> The international bodies need to be strengthened, among them the much maligned World Health Organization [WHO].

The next serious problem [Žižek sees] is a food shortage. WHO is constantly warning that the pandemic could lead to mass starvation, so we need to reorganize our agriculture and food distribution. The state should simply guarantee that nobody actually starves, and perhaps this even needs to be done on an international scale, because otherwise you will get refugees (Jacobson/Zizek 2020).

48.

PEACEFUL OR VIOLENT CHANGES

New needs give rise to new forces.

Petar II Petrović Njegoš

When injustice becomes law, resistance becomes duty.

Thomas Jefferson

Those who make peaceful revolution impossible will make violent revolution inevitable.

John F. Kennedy

If you fight you might lose, if you don't, you have already lost.

Berthold Brecht

The magnitude of social inequalities in the world and in individual states, measured by the income the rich and the poor have at their disposal, is so high, intolerable, and unsustainable, that the poor are ready to explode at any moment and trigger large-scale social unrest, endangering lasting peace and stability in the world.

Thanks to the capitalist order created in their own self-interest, the rich have almost managed to appropriate and privatize all social wealth created and accumulated over the centuries, along with social wealth created and accumulated by the current generation of workers and working people. Most of the available natural wealth is also in the possession of the rich or under their control. Such a situation cannot last indefinitely. It has to change at some point.

A new non-capitalist social order and a society of social justice and democratic socialism, a just society, can be reached in one of two ways: through peaceful, evolutionary means or violent revolution. The best way to bring about these changes would be the peaceful, non-violent, evolutionary way, guided by truth, justice, and fairness, and not by violent, armed revolution. Non-violently changing the current situation with the existing production relationships in society has its limitations. The evolutionary path is inherently complicated, slow, and takes too long, so its final outcome is usually nowhere in sight. After all, the commitment to evolutionary social change is what brought the world into the current economic, social, and political crisis—not a violent revolution.

Violent social uprisings and revolutions always erupt when the subjugation, oppression, and exploitation of certain social groups exceed the limits of economic, social, and political tolerance and endurance. The basic form violent revolutions manifest themselves in has always been the armed resistance of oppressed masses against the terror of cruel conquerors, oppressors, usurpers, and exploiters. That is why the historical judgments on any violent revolution should not be based on the number of victims and the devastation it caused, but also on the consideration of all the causes that led to the outbreak of the revolution. In fact, the whole truth about every revolution can only be learned through objective scientific analysis from a sufficient historical distance about its ultimate social reach and implications, and not solely focused on the number of victims, defeats, and failures. For example, if the French Revolution of 1789 never happened, humanity would look completely different today—the world would be more backward in every aspect, especially democratically. Or, if it were not for the Serbian Revolution of 1804, Serbia would have remained under Ottoman rule for much longer. It is still too early to make a final historical assessment of the October Revolution of 1917 and the other socialist revolutions that followed it, regardless of all the negative judgments made, especially those made after the fall of the Berlin Wall.

The existing neoliberal capitalist order could be changed by peaceful revolution in an evolutionary way only if the ruling capitalist class—especially its superclass representing the world of capital—was ready for a historical compromise with the representatives of the labor world—workers and all other working people—and willing to renounce a part of its power and monopoly of capital in favor of non-capitalist social strata. The political experience with captalists has hitherto unequivocally confirmed that capitalists and the capitalist class do not give anything to anyone voluntarily—not their capital acquired through exploitation, nor their power, won and maintained by force.

Current social conditions seem harmonious and ideal from the capitalist class viewpoint. They can not see a single objective reason why workers and working people should be dissatisfied with such a social order or why they should seek its change, peacefully or violently. Unlike the capitalist exploitative class, exploited social classes feel that the capitalist order and capitalist laws, institutionalized a system of exploitation that they must unconditionally obey. Any reminder and warning that the capitalist class is constantly getting rich by exploiting the labor of other people is considered heresy and a threat to the fundamental values of the capitalist order. In such a social relationship imposed by the capitalist class through its institutionalized dictatorship and maintained by force, oppressed working people are intimidated by the possible consequences of "endangering the rule of capitalist law" and are not ready to offer more organized resistance to the imposed state of affairs. This is because "no one who lives in poverty would not trade that life for a better one, but what most people probably want is the life they have. They fear losing that more than they wish for a different life, although they probably also want their children to be able to lead a different life if they choose" (Menand 2016).

Left leaning political parties in the state they are now—ideologically disoriented, organizationally fragmented, divided among themselves—cannot be the bearers of radical changes in modern neoliberal capitalism, neither peacefully nor violently. They do not objectively pose any threat to the system of neoliberal capitalism: they only have a theoretical chance to change the system by peaceful means by winning over right leaning parties in "free and democratic elections," through the competition of their political programs. On the other hand, leftist parties also have no chance of changing the order by violent revolutionary means by being the leaders of an organized rebellion of dissatisfied, exploited, and impoverished working masses against the capitalist class.

An outbreak of spontaneous, passive political resistance to the current capitalist system could occur, however—not only nationally, but globally. In the long run, the already drastic and growing economic and social inequalities between the rich and the poor and the enormous concentration of capital and power in the hands of a small number of the rich and the richest cannot continue without an adequate response from the poor and the poorest groups of society.

One possible form of such resistance is civil disobedience. During the struggle for Indian indepence from the British Empire, the Indian thinker and politician Mahatma Gandhi showed and proved in practice that civil disobedience through non-violent, passive, and civil mass protest—applying the philosophy of non-violence satyagraha, which he developed—can achieve revolutionary goals and implement desired political changes in society. Gandhi's philosophy of satyagraha was the inspiration for civil rights legends Nelson Mandela and Martin Luther King.

Anti-capitalist sentiment is widespread throughout the world. Dissatisfaction with the capitalist order is especially prevalent among younger generations who do not see the fulfillment of their dreams and happiness possible under capitalism. This is why spontaneous social and revolutionary uprisings and coups are not the spirits of an evil past, but an ominous reality or the near future. A main instigator of the possible outbreak of a revolution could be the "philosophy of empty stomach," and not a pre-defined ideological and political platform, similar to the outbreak of the 1789 French Revolution or the 1917 October Revolution. Great social disturbances always "occur when social classes lose their balance" (Matjez 1948: 20).

It is precisely the lack of balance between social classes that is an important determination for contemporary neoliberal capitalism. "Class struggle is not the struggle for socialism. It is a struggle for material security. The circumstance that the class tied to work has to struggle to make ends meet posits a devastating judgment about bourgeois society" (Bonefeld 2017).

Due to the constantly present fear of a possible outbreak of spontaneous revolutionary uprisings, the capitalist class is always on alert, ready at any moment to confront any attempt to change the capitalist system, using all available means, legal and illegal, and including the use of force if necessary.

Salvador Allende, the democratically elected president of Chile and prominent Latin American Marxist, was killed in a military coup on October 11, 1973. His presidential palace was bombed and Allende's body was found in his office.

It is no secret today that the responsible political services of some governments which, incidentally, emphasize their democracy, have done everything they could to overthrow the democratic rule of parliament in Chile and some other countries, and to establish the rule of military coups as soon as the people's democratic right to freely elect their parliament and democratic policies of that parliament no longer corresponded – as it is usually said – 'to our national interests,' that is, to the interests of certain external forces (Kardelj 1977: 44).

The capitalist class, mighty and powerful in all respects, is ready today, as it has always been, to defend its order with all available means in order to preserve its acquired vast wealth and untouchable power. They are ready to wage a civil or international war if doing so is in its self-interest. Among the exploited and dissatisfied social masses, the capitalist class has predominantly succeeded in extinguishing the belief in the possibility of revolution and hope that anything significant can be changed in contemporary neoliberal capitalism. Such a social situation, created by the capitalist class, is fatal to the democratic and civilizational progress of society.

Why are there no preconditions in today's capitalism for the outbreak of revolutions as seen in the past? Because the capitalist class has declared the exploitation of workers part of its business policy, its business, and considers any rebellion of the exploited working class and working masses against such a situation to be violence and a threat to proclaimed human rights and democratic freedoms. In fact, the idea of revolution was

> declared violence, and the procedure—pro-democratic...Today, the revolution is seen as a defeated idea, which certainly affects its active potential...There is no

revolution because the irreconcilable antagonism of labor and capital has been turned into solvable ecological, religious and sexual tensions…The mass temporarily employed precariat cannot block production, and that is the key counter-revolutionary circumstance. Nevertheless, we must grow accustomed to thinking about the end of capitalism, even though we do not know what will replace it and when. If true revolutions change the man and if they are on the other side of the existing, if they are what is not, and should be, then they do not recognize the existing as necessary. In that sense, Marx is the father of revolution, and Descartes is the grandfather (Kuljić 2016).

It is worth recalling the great Russian poet Vladimir Mayakovsky in the global economic and political domination of the capitalist class and the sovereignty of capital over labor present today. Mayakovsky

in 1909, threw the ten messages of revolution into his fellow citizens' face, for which he spent 10 months imprisoned. These messages are as follows: 1. Revolution begins—when people no longer accept dissatisfaction as a normal state, and you are silent, citizens! 2. Revolution begins—when the anger of the hungry cannot be bought with the money of the full, and you are hungry, citizens! 3. Revolution begins—when the workers refuse to be slaves and steal what belongs to them, and you are silent, citizens! 4. Revolution begins—when the moral law does not exist, and the written laws apply only to the poor, and you are poor, citizens! 5. Revolution begins—when the state humiliates the old, and arrests or expels the young, and you are silent, citizens! 6. Revolution begins—when the people serve the government, instead of the government serving the people, and you serve, citizens! 7. Revolution begins—when the artists stop being cowards and speak out loud, while you are silent, citizens! 8. Revolution begins—when free speech and free thought are forbidden, and you are forbidden, citizens! 9. Revolution begins—when there is work and bread only for those who glorify and praise the emperor, and you are silent, citizens! 10. Revolution begins—when the police, army and security services are not guardians of freedom, but occupiers of their own people, and you are occupied citizens! (Mayakovski 2017).

Mayakovsky's messages credibly reflect our reality: the intolerable social situation in which the exploited, impoverished, and disenfranchised working and popular masses around the world find themselves today.

It is true that "

capitalism has brought about great material advances. But though this way of organizing our affairs has had a long time to demonstrate that it is capable of satisfying human demands all round, it seems no closer to doing so than ever. How long are we prepared to wait for it to come up with the goods? Why do we continue to indulge the myth that the fabulous wealth generated by this mode of production will in the fullness of time become available to all? (Eagleton 2016: 10).

The options for revolt and revolution are always open and possible, and are unpredictable.

The neoclassical standard theory has created a monopoly for itself. As a result, the situation of the poor is likely to get worse before things start to change. We have to wait for the global version of the revolutions of 1848...The new classical economic theory, unable to explain economic inequalities, combined with Samuel Huntington's *Clash of Civilizations* creates a political bomb, just waiting to explode (Reinert 2006: 115 and 135).

Obviously, the crises and troubles of modern neoliberal capitalism have characteristics and dimensions that mean the causes of a revolution might come from a "new commotion from below" resulting in possible social changes (Nikolić N.: 2017). After all, various social formations have emerged and disappeared throughout history. Why would capitalism be excluded?

This, of course, does not mean the end of capitalism is "within reach." In fact, "'the final crisis of capitalism' may take all but a century" (Marcuse 1972: 134).

> The power of capitalism to make the forces of the opposition harmless, and not always by brutal force, is highly developed in highly developed capitalist countries today. It stands a better chance because the revolutionary change is not achieved the same way as hitting a target by shooting from a gun; it takes a long time to reach the final goal, and on that path is where the power of the existing conditions shows itself in numerous obstacles and detours, deceptions and traps (Lukić 1976: XXV).

49.

WHY MARX IS UNAVOIDABLE

Marx was an intellectual giant.

Jürgen Kocka

As an economic theorist, Marx was above all a very learned man.

Joseph Schumpeter

Marx was a humanist.

Louis Menand

Marx predicted our current crisis and pointed to the way out.

Yanis Varoufakis

In the absence of better and fresher ideas on how to exit the systemic crisis of contemporary capitalism—and also as the reaction to the cruelty that comes with uncontrolled neoliberalism— Marx has lately become increasingly popular in the broadest cultural circles of the world, especially in the West, the bastion of capitalism. His thoughts and messages are increasingly used in the analysis and critique of the contradictions of contemporary capitalism, and are increasingly less identified with the practice of statist socialism such as Stalinism.

Marx's scientific preoccupation was analyzing the capitalist mode of production in the nineteenth century, not dealing with the "rudimentary future," as he himself pointed out. "Marxism is a (critical) theory of capitalism, not a theory of socialism...Marx has rarely and reluctantly [written] about socialism—mostly only when he was pressed to do so. He considered it a utopia to write about a society that did not exist" (Horvat 1981: 110).

Marx was very cautious in his predictions of the future. He did, however, expect that socialist revolutions would first break out and win in industrially developed capitalist countries in Western Europe, such as Germany, England, France, as well as in the U.S. But quite the opposite happened. Contrary to Marx's expectations, socialist revolutions broke out in rural and industrially backwards regions: Russia, Yugoslavia, Albania, China, and Cuba. With the exception of Czechoslovakia, no other country where socialism was imposed by force after World War II (Poland, Hungary, Romania, Bulgaria, Mongolia, North Vietnam, and North Korea) was in a different economic position. The Czech Republic was the most developed part of the Habsburg Monarchy before the start of World War I in 1914. During the interwar period, Czechoslovakia was just behind Great Britain and France in its level of industrial development.

Marx's predictions about the solidarity and unification of the proletariat in all countries did not come true either. Since the end of the nineteenth century, workers in developed capitalist countries have had higher wages and live better than workers in poor and underdeveloped countries. The gap between those workers has constantly increased since then, so their solidarity began to systematically "fall off, only to eventually disappear" (Milanović 2012: 98).

Even during the wars fought in the nineteenth and twentieth centuries, workers were usually on opposite sides, shooting and killing each other, putting their personal interests and the interests of the nation and state they were fighting for before and above proletarian internationalism.

The communist elites of former socialist countries "appropriated" Marx and declared him their own. Due to Marx's harsh criticism of the capitalist mode of production, the West could hardly wait for this appropriation and gladly renounced Marx as their own, despite Marx being from Germany. Nowadays, however, the West considers him a *bourgeois intellectual* and a *great genius*, along with Adam Smith and David Ricardo, leading Western thinkers and classical economists.

Global interest in Marx's most important works, including the *Manifesto of the Communist Party*, commonly known as *The Communist Manifesto* (a joint work of Marx and Friedrich Engels, first published on February 24, 1848), particularly increased after the outbreak of the global economic crisis of 2007 and 2008 and the erosion of the global financial system. The "Capitalist system still dominates the world today—for the most part, in its extremely brutal, neoliberal form. It makes Marxism still relevant today. This can be seen, among other things, in the increased interest of Western countries in this theory, primarily in Marx's thought" (Vidojević 2015: 342).

There is a growing interest in American and European academic communities in Marx's scientific work and in Marxism. For example, the lectures of the renowned American professor David Harvey, a theorist of Marxism, are always attended by a significant number of New York City academics, but also ordinary New Yorkers, and especially members of the younger generation. Marx's works are now on the shelves of the most prestigious bookstores in the largest Western centers of business and culture, which are often luxuriously equipped. The demand for his works is growing everywhere because it is not possible to fully understand the depth of the social contradictions of contemporary capitalism without him. With the outbreak of the global economic and financial crisis of 200 and 2008, Marx's work *Capital* suddenly found itself on the desks of the directors of the world's leading corporations, especially in the U.S. and Europe, who were looking for possible answers to the causes of the crisis. Obviously, they felt the capitalist reality was better than the ideologues and apologists of the capitalist order—the sworn opponents of Karl Marx.

Marx's *Capital* (the first volume was first published in 1867 while Marx was still alive, and the second and third volumes posthumously)

> has survived and has been continuously printed in last century and a half…This is a book proclaimed to be dead or outdated…many times, but it keeps coming back. The last example of the revival of interest for this book and its good sale happened after the global financial crisis outbreak in 2008…Obviously, there has to be something going on to its advantage—it still really gives a useful frame for understanding important elements of capitalism, despite of difference in its contemporary manifestations…Naturally, there is so much more to say about capitalism which we cannot find in this book: the role of unpaid work, especially in socially-owned reproduction and domestic hard work; relation of economic system to its natural environment and so on. However, a strong contemporary resonance of many of these concepts means it cannot be surprising people still use this somewhat menacing book, for their insights and understanding (Ghosh 2017).

Marx's scientific work is not perfect; it has its flaws and shortcomings because it was created by a human, not a divine being. As it stands, however, it is very contemporary—it surpasses the time in which it was created, regardless of all the structural, economic, and technological changes that have happened in the meantime. No one before or after Marx has been able to better convey such a precise diagnosis of the disease capitalist society suffers from, and no one better than him has criticized the capitalist mode of production and the capitalist order as a whole, advocating for its radical change—that is, its destruction.

At the start of the global economic and financial crisis of 2007 and 2008, Marx's scientific works were so interesting and significant that in a widely conducted survey in Great Britain, Marx was proclaimed the most significant and influential creator in the history of civilization. He used scientific evidence to represent and defend the interests of workers, the working class, and all working strata of society. He was and remains the ideologue of all the exploited and disenfranchised, not only in the West, but in the entire world. This influence is exactly why Marx is still relevant, especially with much of today's younger generations, who are increasingly determined to seek a more certain future than the one offered by current neoliberal capitalism. Because, unfortunately, governments of almost all contemporary liberal-capitalist states do not represent the interests of all their citizens, but the interests of the richest.

Marx was misunderstood by many. They distorted the results of his theoretical generalizations, misinterpreted him, and changed his thoughts into their contradictions. "Hence there were so many 'Marxisms' that Marx had to claim that he was not a Marxist" (Lukić 1976: XI).

Marx always vigorously opposed any attempt to turn his teachings into dogma because he was a true anti-dogmatist. The dogmatic and authoritarian interpretation of Marx's theoretical views caused a great deal of damage to the concept of socialism and created numerous problems—not only theoretical and methodological, but also practical and political, especially in understanding the very meaning of socialism.

"'I am not a Marxist,' Marx is said to have said, and it's appropriate to distinguish what he intended from the uses other people made of his writings" (Menand 2016). In other words, Marx wanted to clearly and publicly oppose the dogmatic interpretation of his work and distance himself from self-proclaimed "Marxist dogmatists," who interpreted his theoretical thought differently from its original meaning. For example, despite the fact that "Marx did not, however, provide much guidance for how a society would operate without property or classes or a state," some "Marxists" declared his theoretical views to be "scientific socialism" (Ibid.). There are simply no similarities between Marx and self-proclaimed Marxists. "For most of the twentieth century, 40 percent of humanity suffered from hunger, gulags, censorship and other forms of repression carried out by self-proclaimed Marxists" (Bilt 2018).

French philosopher Jacques Attali, one of the most influential contemporary European thinkers, claims that Marx is wrongly associated with communism, i.e. "Sovietism," and that he was a true advocate of the global free market, and therefore an economic philosopher of the new world order (Živković 2012).

Marx is one of those thinkers who is probably the most respected, but also the most contested.

With good reason, he has been accused of having underestimated the civilizing impact of markets while overestimating labor as the only source of newly created value. Marx has also come [into] criticism for his lack of attention to the importance of knowledge and organization as sources of productivity, his mistaken predictions about the social repercussions of industrial capitalism, and his almost quaintly old-fashioned European mistrust of the market, exchange, and self-interest. Nevertheless, Marxist analysis remains an original, fascinating, and fundamental framework, a point of reference to this day for most subsequent interpreters of capitalism, no matter how much they may criticize Marx... (Kocka 2016:10–11).

Marx's scientific thought has managed to survive fierce criticism, disputes, and prominent critics such as Eugen Böhm-Bawerk, the most prominent representative of the Austrian school of psychology, along with many others. Marx's work will be relevant as long as capitalism exists as a social order. As the social contradictions of neoliberal capitalism grow more intense—which is quite probable—it is certain that interest in *Capital* and other works of Marx will also grow worldwide. The capitalist class is not ready to make any significant changes in the relationship between labor and capital, thereby keeping Marx relevant.

The biggest opponents of Marx's scientific thought have always been and will be mainly those whose material interests are, directly or indirectly, related to the power of capital, profit management, and living at the expense of someone else's unpaid work. As Marx said, since ideas always coincide with material interests, every opinion can be challenged or considered infallible.

The scientific method Marx applied throughout his scientific works and in his economic and other analyses of the capitalist mode of production is especially valuable. The Hungarian philosopher György Lukács was probably right when he said "that orthodoxy in Marxism refers exclusively to the method" (Lukács 1923: 13, and Sweezy 1959: 21). Lukács is also credited with answering the question "What is Marxism?" with "I don't know, but I feel that it is something very, very specific."

Marx's works have "retained their intellectual firepower over time. Even today, 'the Communist Manifesto' is like a bomb about to go off in your hands" (Menand 2016).

So why is *the Manifesto of the Communist Party* still relevant today? Because this work is

> "proof that there is nothing as practical as a good theory...It is a writing that is simultaneously a fragment and a whole, an unfinished compass for navigating the infinite material of history. A substantive note on the social dimension of history and a warning on the necessity of combining theory and practice... An enlightening project of a never final, unstoppable movement towards a more socially just society" (Kuljić/Manifest 2018).

The Manifesto of the Communist Party demystified capitalist so-called normalcy and the bourgeoisie, which "turned all dignified professions into their own paid wage workers" (Ibid.).

Marx's works establish a better understanding of the complexities and contradictions of capitalist social reality at the beginning of the twenty first century, not just the nineteenth and twentieth centuries. Marx's scientific study and theoretical generalization focuses on capital and labor in their complexity, especially the relationship between those two main factors of social production in capitalism, not merely describing nineteenth century working conditions. The unresolved relationship between capital and labor is where the main causes of all the troubles and hardships of the modern world are rooted.

Louis Althusser, a French Marxist philosopher, believes that Marx "advocated two revolutions: a scientific one, related to materialism and economics, and the contemplative one, philosophical. Such an approach is needed today" (Badiou 2014).

Understood in a non-dogmatic, creative way, "Marx's analyses along with his distinctive method of enquiry end his mode of [theorizing] are invaluable for our intellectual struggles to understand capitalism of our time. His insights deserve to be taken up and studied critically with all due seriousness" (Harvey 2018: xiv).

This kind of perspective on Marx and the entirety of his scientific work could be practically useful in the search for a new form of democratic socialism, a social order that would be more humane and socially just than neoliberal capitalism. In that sense, without exaggeration, it could be said that Marx is *ante portas*.[5]

The current leader of the People's Republic of China, President Xi Jinping, in his address at the two hundredth anniversary of Marx's birth (May 5, 1818) in the Great Hall of the People in Beijing, called Marx "the greatest thinker of modern times" and Marxism "a powerful ideological weapon for us to understand the world, grasp the law, seek the truth, and change the world," that would always be the leading theory of China and the Communist Party (Huang 2020).

Peter Singer, an Australian philosopher, says: "Marx's influence can be compared to that of major religious figures like Jesus or Muhammad" (Singer 2018: 1). In his book *Marx: A Very Short Introduction*, Singer "listed some of Marx's predictions: the income gap between workers and owners would increase, independent producers would be forced down into the ranks of the proletariat, wages would remain at subsistence levels, the rate of profit would fall, capitalism would collapse, and there would be revolutions in the advanced countries" (Menand 2016). Today "is harder to be dismissive" of most of Marx's predictions (Ibid.).

---

[5] Latin, meaning at the gates; at the door; knocking at the door.

Marx saw the basic contradiction of capitalist society in the separation of labor and capital; in the monopoly of capitalists (the capitalist class) have on the means of production (capital) created by the labor of workers; in the alienation of surplus labor from workers (alienated labor); in the exploitation of the working class by the capitalist class; in the supremacy of capital over labor and capitalists over workers; in the socially disadvantaged position of the working class, where workers are forced to sell their labor force on the market as a commodity.

Marx also built a dialectical-materialist understanding of history as a continuous process of harmonizing the development of productive forces and production relationships—in other words, the understanding of socioeconomic formation as a natural historic process. In the critique of capitalism's development, Marx showed the transience of conditions created by capitalism itself. He was convinced that the conflict between labor and capital was a "class conflict" that could only be resolved by revolution, violence, the "dictatorship of the proletariat," and the simultaneous victory of socialism in all or most capitalist countries.

All in all, and considering all known disputes of Marx's work, his critique of the capitalist mode of production must always be a fundamental theoretical and ideological starting point for the political and practical actions of the modern left. Marx's theoretical thought is indispensable to finding ways and means to transform our contemporary capitalist order into a just society of the new age and in practically shaping necessary revolutionary changes to our global character. This does not mean, however, that Marx's thought by itself is sufficient for the development of a theoretical platform for a new socialism. Some of the views it includes, especially on communism, fall into a naive utopia. Other problems could also be found. But that is not the main thing about his thought. The theory of exploitation, absolute and relative impoverishment, the cyclical crisis of capitalism, its transformation into a world system, civilizational and dehumanizing functions of capital, the theory of alienation, the importance of technology in the development of modern society, etc.—they are necessary (of course, innovated) for the construction of the [aforementioned] platform (Vidojević 2015: 242–243 and 395).

In order to construct a just or more just society, new creative ideas are needed. In this respect, Marx's scientific thought is unavoidable—especially his scientific method, which he applies in his analysis of the capitalist mode of production. Marx's scientific body of work is a reservoir of valuable ideas that can give rise to new critical theoretical thoughts and the search for possible ways out of the problems and contradictions of contemporary neoliberal capitalism. This is why Marx has his prominent and unavoidable place in the twenty first century.

CONCLUDING CONSIDERATIONS

I did not leave the field of socialism, but for me today,
it is what we would, conditionally, call social –
the desire for a fairer and freer world,
the pursuit of a fairer distribution of goods.

Milovan Djilas

The greatest threat to the world peace and security in the twenty first century is the neoliberal hegemony of the capitalist social order. Over the past five decades, a world of inappropriate and unsustainable social inequalities has been created and right-wing extremism and populist movements have been encouraged.

In its essence, capitalist society has always been a society of *social injustice*. All previous attempts to transform capitalist society into a society of social justice and equality or to introduce more elements of solidarity have failed, including the well-known concept of the welfare state, no matter how praised, desired, and supported it is by many actors of international politics and law. It was not possible to bring about social justice because it inherently denies the nature of relationships of capital that are the basis of the capitalist social order and its mode of production. Simply put, social justice and exploitation are mutually exclusive. It is the fate of the capitalist social order.

The global economic and social reality defies ruling neoliberal ideology, which is no longer as powerful, compelling, and influential as it when the Berlin Wall fell in 1989 and during the fall of socialism. The key postulates of neoliberalism—the monopoly of private property and the fetishism of the free market—are increasingly open to questioning. There is doubt about whether the capitalist system is able to offer consistent, long-term solutions to overcome its own contradictions and crises—which have lasted too long and have no end in sight—but also whether it is able to timely predict and prevent new possible crises. The capitalist order is increasingly distant from its desired state. In some cultural circles in the West, there are whispers about the possible "end of capitalism," which will happen sooner or later.

Perhaps the only real alternative to contemporary neoliberal capitalism and the failed socialism of the twentieth century—embodied in its "command economy," state intervention "from top to bottom" and "market negation"—is to build a new civil democratic society, that is non-capitalist and non-exploitative and more socially just, humane, and freer than our current neoliberal capitalist social order. This new society would be tailored to man; it would have a human face, and would offer equal opportunities for all, without the monopoly of private property, market fetishism, the exploitation of other people's labor, the economic dictates of capital, and without the political dictatorship of the capitalist class in society. The commitment to a new civil democratic society—a society of social justice, a just society—can also be understood as a search for a third path in the future development of society—the search for a kind of a liberal socialism.

1. In this new democratic civil society of social justice, a just society, there would be property pluralism. It would therefore include all historically known and possible forms of property: private property, state property, social property, personal property along with all other possible derivative forms of property: common (collective) property of associated workers, corporate, joint-stock, mixed, cooperative, endowment, and waqf property. Property monism (the monopoly of private

property) as it currently exists would be replaced by property pluralism and the systemic equality of all possible forms of property in society. The diversity of property forms is the most important characteristic of a truly free and democratic society.

2. The final judgment on the social justification and economic efficiency of the forms of ownership would be made by the market, not by the state with its subjectivist and voluntarist decisions and measures. No privately-owned enterprise is a priori successful, just as no state-owned or socially owned enterprise is a priori unsuccessful. The only objective measure of evaluation for everyone's work, business results be they positive or negative, and for every economic entity, regardless of ownership form, is the determination of the relationship between supply and demand on the market, regardless of its strengths and weaknesses. The market is the objective social category and is a product of the social organization of labor, not a product of social formation. The market is not the invention of capitalism, but of the heritage of a civilization that is over six thousand years old. Capitalism is an economically, socially, and politically unjust society, not because of the market, but because of the class separation of labor and capital and the permanent exploitation of workers inherent in capitalist relationships. Of course, the market is not an ideal mechanism for the social distribution of labor products. From time to time, the market experiences minor or major disruptions in supply and demand relations, which are then manifested in the form of an economic crisis. Society should protect itself against market disasters in the same way it protects itself against natural disasters, such as forest fires and floods. Instead of the neoliberal fetishization of the market,

367

objective and effective social control of the market is needed as much as possible.

3. Workers in private and state-owned enterprises would be guaranteed participation in the management and distribution of achieved profits. Systemic measures of the state would suppress the exploitation of people's labor and prevent the dominance of capital over living labor, as well as the dominance of living labor over capital. Socially owned enterprises and worker corporations would operate based on the principle of integrating labor and capital under the control of self-managed workers. In a new non-capitalist democratic society, there would be not be a dictatorship of the owners of capita—the capitalist class—nor a dictatorship of the proletariat—the working class—or the precariat, the occasional or temporary employees.

4. No state in the modern world can develop successfully by relying solely on the market or the state. Instead of overestimating or underestimating the roles of the market and the state, it is necessary to creatively harmonize their economic functions in a skillful and reasonable way, which can only be achieved by affirming the new role of planning in economically organizing society. Just as the market is not an invention of capitalism, economic planning is not an invention of socialism. Planning is a product of the civilizational development of society. At any point of social reproduction where the market is not always effective—for example, acts of public good or the constructing expensive infrastructure objects—the state must intervene in accordance with planned economic mechanisms, instruments, and measures. Without planning, it is not possible to prevent economic disruptions and the outbreak of

financial crises inherent in capitalism in a timely manner. Underestimating the importance and role of planning in social reproduction is one of the structural mistakes of the neoliberal social and economic system. Likewise, any overestimation and fetishization of the role planning plays in the development of society is as fatal as the overestimation and fetishization of the market.

5. In a just society, the competent management of available resources, increase in social wealth, and the maximization of companies' effects on income generated by their market operations, regardless of their form of ownership, would systematically expand the material capabilities of society and enable the achievement of strategic goals of social justice, equality, and solidarity. This would be accomplished through the introduction of UBI, free education, and health care for all citizens. The state and society would take special care of citizens who need social assistance and special kinds support.

6. The taxation of assets and income in society would be based on the principle that whoever has more contributes more to the prosperity of the state, society, and citizens—i.e, progressive taxation. The non-market transfer of an adequate share of income to benefit of the poor and the creation of a system where the poor become a key factor in improving their social position would allow for the progressive narrowing of economic and social disparities between the rich and the poor. The progressive taxation of assets and income would be conducted in a way that does not limit the creative and entrepreneurial spirit of economically influential entities in society.

7. On the other side of the monopoly of private property in contemporary capitalist society is a system dominated by right-oriented political parties, which do not have any significant ideological differences, therefore meaning that their competition is nothing but an imitation of a real multiparty system. The direct political product of the monopoly of private property is the domination of the one-party system—otherwise known as political monism in society. Property pluralism is the material basis of true political pluralism in society and is the most important condition for ensuring an equal relationship between the political parties of the right and left in free electoral competition. Property monism strongly favors the political parties of the right, which are intrinsically linked to private capital and the interests of the capitalist class and is why they constantly and convincingly win "free" elections. The political parties of the left are in a far less favorable position because they do not have a tangible material base and depend on the power of capital, so they are usually forced to side and make pacts with right-wing political parties. Property pluralism would open the door to the development of true democracy and freedom. Instead of the monopoly of capitalist class, especially its superclass—the factocracy, based on private property—new non-capitalist, non-exploitative political forces would appear. These forces would base their status and real power in society on non-private ownership of means of production: state, social, common, and personal property ownership. Without property pluralism and a better political position for left-wing parties, it is illusory to dream of the end of capitalism and the creation of a new democratic non-

capitalist social order, a society that would be economically just and socially responsible.

8. The civil society of social justice and equality that would replace neoliberal capitalism, whose future is in question, is not a utopia, but a vital need for the largest part of humanity. It can be achieved through a creative synthesis of everything confirmed through previous and current capitalist practices and former socialist practices—especially Yugoslav socialist self-management—as socially reasonable solutions, in addition to new thoughts and ideas suitable to a new, just era of economics and politics.

9. A just society cannot be achieved without new leaders with knowledge and fresh ideas who understand the times we live in and the necessity for comprehensive social change. There is almost no country in the world today where the broadest strata of people are satisfied with their "democratically" elected leaders. The leadership crisis has become a global problem. In some social environments, especially in some countries who moved from socialism to capitalism, electoral procedures are often manipulated. The same people have held top positions in governments and reman the leaders of political parties for too long. The most competent people in society, especially members of the younger and better educated generation, find it difficult to find their place in these conditions, which is why in there is an open or secret desire for rebellions, coups, "people's events," "colored revolutions," or a real revolution in many societies. Judging by historic experience, only those events help the most capable political personalities of future leaders come to light, instead of languishing in pariah political circles.

10. The UN, regardless of the fact that their dominant positions are held by the exponents of the interests of capital and neoliberal consciousness, should put the issue of building a new, more socially responsible and just non-capitalist democratic society on their agenda. Creating a new civil society of social justice, a just society, with the direct and active participation of authentic representatives of the poor and poorest people in the world is of the utmost importance. The UN needs to address economic and social inequality in the world and the separation of labor and capital in a more organized and intensive manner, similarly to how it justifiably handles climate change. These economic and social issues are currently an even greater threat to sustainable development than climate change. This is not just about promoting decent work—one of the binding goals of the 2030 Agenda for Sustainable Development—but the necessity for eliminating all forms of wage, precarious, and slave labor, thereby eliminating threats to peace, stability, and prosperity in the world.

REFERENCES

A

A Handbook of Yugoslav Socialist Self-management, STP (Socialist Thought and Practice), Belgrade 1980.

Adizes, Ichac & Elisabeth Mann Borgese (Ed.), *Self-management: New Dimensions to Democracy*, American Bibliographical Center-Clio Press, Santa Barbara/London 1975.

Ali, Tariq, *The Clash of Fundamentalisms: Crusades, Jihads and Modernity*, Verso, London/New York City 2011.

Alvaredo, Facundo, Lucas Chancel, Thomas Piketty, Emmanuel Saez, Gabriel Zucman, *World Inequality Report 2018*, World Inequality Lab, www.wir2018.wid.world, accessed July 29, 2019.

"America's New President: The Trump Era," *The Economist*, November 12–18, 2016.

"An Open Letter to the 2020 Presidential Candidates: It's Time to Tax Us More," June 24, 2019, www.medium.com, accessed November 11, 2019.

Andrić, Ivo, *Sveske/Notes*, Prosveta, Belgrade 1982.

Antonov-Ovsejenko, Anton, *Staljin: portret tiranina/Stalin: a portrait of a tyrant*, Naprijed, Zagreb 1986.

Aristotle, *O pravdi i pravičnosti/Aristoteles/ On Justice and Fairness*, August 9, 2014, accessed July 29, 2019.

Ashoff, Nicole M., "The Free-Market Fantasy," *Jacobin*, April 15, 2015, www.jacobinmag.com, accessed April 11, 2019.

Avdijev, V. I., *Istorija starog istoka/History of Ancient East*, Edicija, Belgrade 2009.

B

Bacevich, Andrew J., *American Empire: The Reality and Consequences of U. S. Diplomacy*, Harvard University Press, Cambridge/London 2002.

Badiou, Alain, *The alleged power of capitalism today is merely a reflection of the weakness of its opponent*, May 2017. *www.versobooks.com*, accessed September 14, 2020.

Badiou, Alain, *"Kapitalizam je bolest čovečanstva, ali su ljudi opčinjeni njime kao deca šljaštećim igračkama"*/"Capitalism Is a Sickness of Humankind, but People Are Fascinated by it as Children with Clattering Toys," *Nova srpska politička misao*, November 24, 2014, www.nspm.rs, accessed April 11, 2019.

Badju, Alen, *"Jugoslavija će se ponovo ujediniti, to je samo pitanje trenutka: ovo tvrdi najveći savremeni francuski filozof!"*/ "Yugoslavia Will Reunite, it is only a Matter of Time: this is Claimed by the Greatest Contemporary French Philosopher!," *Espreso*, September 5, 2019, www.espreso.rs, accessed January 21, 2020.

Barker, Savannah, "Is Universal Basic Income a Human Right?" www.thetylt.com, accessed July 31, 2019.

Bakić, Jovo, *Levičarsko-anarhistička kritika američkog imperijalizma i tumačenje nestanka Jugoslavije/Leftist-Anarchist Critique of American Imperialism and Interpretation of the Disappearance of Yugoslavia, u zborniku radova Društvo rizika: promene, nejednakosti i socijalni problemi u današnjoj Srbiji/Society of Risks: Changes, Inequalities and Societal Problems in Contemporary Serbia*, Institute of Sociogical Research, Faculty of Philosophy in Belgrade, Belgrade 2008.

Barber, Lionel, "EU chief Jean-Claude Juncker on the Brexit Bill and the Eroticism of Power," *Financial Times*, March 24, 2017.

Béja, Alice, "*Ljevica ne smije pristati na normalizaciju Trumpa*"/"The Left Cannot Permit the Normalization of Trump," *Novosti*, January 9, 2017, www.portalnovosti.com, accessed July 29, 2019.

Bienkov, Adam, "A major new report into rising inequality warned that the growing gap between rich and poor is now a threat to Western democracy," *Business Insider*, May 14, 2019, www.businessinsider.com, accessed July 29, 2019.

Bilandžić, Dušan, *Historija Socijalističke Federativne narodne Republike Jugoslavije—Glavni procesi/History of the Socialist Federal People's Republic of Yugoslavia—Main Processes*, Školska knjiga, Zagreb 1978.

Bilt, Karl, "*U čemu je Marks pogrešio*"/"What Marx Was Wrong About," *Danas*, May 11, 2018, www.danas.rs, accessed July 31, 2019.

Boffa, Guiseppe, *Povijest Sovjetskog Saveza/History of the Soviet Union*, Otokar Keršovani, Opatija 1985.

Bonefeld, Werner, "Ordoliberalism and the Death of Liberal Democracy," January 13, 2017, www.salvage.zon, accessed July 29, 2019.

Bukvić, Rajko, *Vašingtonski konsenzus i deindustrijalizacija istočne i jugoistočne Evrope/ The Washington Consensus and the Deindustrialization of Eastern and Southeastern Europe*, New Serbian Political Thought, Belgrade, January 7, 2011.

Butler, Phil, "How Yugoslavia was Syrianized 25 years ago," *Modern Diplomacy*, March 4, 2016, https://moderndiplomacy.eu, accessed March 3, 2020.

Bžežinski, Zbignjev, "*Otkrivanje Amerike: odlazak hegemona*"/"Discovering America: The Departure of the Hegemon," *Politika*, February 12, 2012.

C

Calic, Marie-Janine, *History of Yugoslavia*, Purdue University Press, West Lafayette 2019.

Chan, Melissa, "Joe Biden Is Warning About the Collapse of the 'World Order' as He Says Goodbye," *Time Magazine*, January 18, 2017, www.time.com, accessed November 7, 2019.

"Chomsky: Occupy Wall Street 'Has Created Something That Didn't Really Exist' in U.S. – Solidarity," May 14, 2012, www.democracynow.org, accessed July 31, 2019.

Chomsky, Noam and C. J. Polychroniou, *Optimism over Despair: on Capitalism, Empire, and Social Change*, Haymarket Books, Chicago 2017.

Cvjetičanin, Danijel, "*Kad je knjaz Miloš veći socijalista od današnjih levičara"/*"When Prince Miloš is a bigger socialist than today leftists," *Politika*, January 6–7, 2017.

Ć

Ćinmin, Čang, (Qingmin, Zhang), *Diplomatija savremene Kine/Contemporary China's Diplomacy*, Albatros Plus, Belgrade 2015.

D

Dalio, Ray, "How America's Capitalist System is 'Broken,'" interviewed by David A. Grogan, *CNBC News*November 8, 2019, www.cnbc.com, accessed August 11, 2019.

Dašić, David Đ, *Istorija diplomatije: evolucija diplomatskog metoda u političkoj istoriji/ The History of Diplomacy: The Evolution of the Diplomatic Method in Political History*, second edition, Institute of International Politics and Economics, Belgrade 2015.

Daugherty, Greg, "America's Slowly Disappearing Middle Class," www.investopedia.com, June 25, 2019, accessed December 15, 2019.

Davis, Kathleen, "Elon Musk Says Automation Will Make a Universal Basic Income Necessary soon," February 13, 2017, www.fastcompany.com, accessed January 17, 2020.

Dyker, David A., *Yugoslavia: Socialism, Development and Debt*, Routledge, New York   City 1990. According to G.W. Hoffman and F.W., *Yugoslavia and the New Communism, Twentieth-Century Fund,* New York City 1962.

Deneen, Patrick J., *Why Liberalism Failed*, Yale University Press, New Haven/London 2018.

Draut, Tamara, "Defining the Working Class," April 16, 2018, www.demos.org, accessed July 31, 2019.

Društvo rizika: promene, nejednakosti i socijalni problemi u današnjoj Srbiji/Society of risks: Changes, Inequalities and Societal Problems in Contemporary Serbia, Institute of Sociogical Research, Faculty of Philosophy in Belgrade, Belgrade 2008.

Dušanić, Jovan B, *Ekonomija postmoderne/Postmodern Economy*, Faculty of Economics, University of Banja Luka, Banja Luka 2016.

E

Eagleton, Terry, "Why Marx Was Right," Yale University Press, New Haven/London 2011, https://epdf.pub, accessed December 4, 2019.

Estrin, Saul and Milica Uvalic, "From Illyria towards Capitalism: Did Labour-Management Theory Teach Us Anything about Yugoslavia and Transition in Its Successor States?," *Comparative*

Economic Studies, 2008, www.palgrave-journals.com/ces, accessed December 10, 2029.

Eurostat, *Unemployment Statistics*, January 31, 2018, www.ec.europa.eu, accessed November 7, 2019.

F

Food and Agriculture Organization of the United Nations, "Global Hunger Continues to Rise," September 11, 2018, www.fao.org, accessed November 7, 2019.

Friedman, Milton, *Capitalism and Freedom: Fortieth Anniversary Edition*, University of Chicago Press, Chicago/London 2002.

Fuentes, Karlos, "*Obama razbija podelu na dobre i zle*"/"Obama Breaks the Division on Good and Evil Ones," *Politika*, May 12, 2009, www.politika.co.rs, accessed November 7, 2019.

Furman, Dmitrij, *Čovek koji je prestrojio ceo svet/A man who rearranged the whole world*, Nezavisna gazeta, 1. mart 2011, prilog u knjizi: Mihail Gorbačov, *Sam sa sobom*: (*uspomene i razmišljanja*)/*Alone with Myself*: (*Memories and Reflections*), Laguna, Belgrade 2014.

G

Gaddis, John Lewis, *We Now Know: Rethinking Cold War History*, Oxford University Press, New York City 1997.

Galbraith, James K., "The Future of the Left in Europe: Austerity is a disaster, so why is the left in disarray?" *The American Prospect*, August 17, 2016, www.prospect.org, accessed March 27, 2020.

Garton Ash, Timothy, "Were We Stupid? Reflections on the Hopes of 1989, 30 Years on," lecture for the endowment of Ilije M. Kolarca, Belgrade, February 13, 2019.

Ghosh, Jayati, "150 years of '*Das Capital*': How relevant is Marx today?," *Al Jazeera English*, August 22, 2017, www.aljazeera.com

Giddens, Anthony, *Treći put—obnova socijaldemokratije*/ *Third Way—Renewal of Social-Democracy*, Political kultura, Zagreb 1999.

Gnjatović, Dragana, *Foreign capital in Yugoslavia 1941–1991*, Srbija i komentari za 1990/91, Endowment of Miloš Crnjanski, Belgrade 1991.

"Goldprice," September 14, 2020, www.goldprice.org

Gorbačov/Gorbachev, Mihail/Mikhail, *Sam sa sobom*: (*uspomene i razmišljanja*)/*Alone with Myself*: (*Memories and Reflections*), Laguna, Belgrade 2014.

Gore, Al and David Blood, "Toward Sustainable Capitalism: Long-term Incentives Are the Antidote to the Short-term Greed that Caused Our Current Economic Woes," *Wall Street Journal*, June 24, 2010, www.wsj.com, accessed December 20, 2019,

"A Manifesto for Sustainable Capitalism: How Businesses Can Embrace Environmental, social and governance metrics," *Wall Street Journal*. December 14, 2011, www.wsj.com, accessed December 20, 2019.

Grečić, Vladimir, "*Demografska budućnost Srbije*"/"Demographic Future of Serbia," *Politika*, May 9, 2019.

Gow, Haven Bradford, "Defining the Just Society," March 30, 2014, www.kirkcenter.org, accessed August 1, 2019.

Guerin, Fred, "We Must End Neoliberalism, or Neoliberalism Will End Us," www.truthout.org, August 11, 2019, accessed August 14, 2019.

Guzina, Vojislav, "*Ekonomija po meri države*"/"The Economy Tailored by the State," *Politika*, January 17, 2018.

H

"*Habermas: Jugoslavija je bila divan projekat!*"/"Habermas: Yugoslavia Was a Wonderful Project!," *Espona*, November 11, 2018, www.espona.me, accessed July 29, 2019..

Huntington, Samuel P., *Clash of Civilizations and the Remaking of World Order*, Simon & Schuster, London 1997.

Harvey, David, *Seventeen Contradictions and the End of Capitalism*, Profile Books, London 2014.

Harvey, David, *Marx, Capital, and the Madness of Economic Reason*, Oxford University Press, New York City 2018.

Henley, Jon, "Finland Trials Basic Income for Unemployed," *The Guardian*. January 3, 2017, www.theguardian.com, accessed August 1, 2019.

"Hillary Clinton Speech at the American Legion Convention in Cincinnati," *Time Magazine*, August 31, 2016, https://time.com, accessed December 12, 2019.

Horvat, Branko, *Politička ekonomija socijalizma/Political economy of socialism*, Globus, Zagreb 1981.

Horvat, Branko, *Socijalistička privatizacija bolja od kapitalistsčke/Socialist Privatization is Better than Capitalist Privatisation*, 2002

"Statement after Joseph Stieglitz published *Controversies of Globalisation*," www.upss-nis.org, accessed July 29, 2019.

Huang, Zheping, "China's Huge Celebrations of Karl Marx are not Really about Marxism," *Quartz*, May 4, 2018, https://qz.com, accessed January 12, 2020.

Hubmann, Georg, "Unequal Europe—Collating the Data," *Social Europe*, May 9, 2019, www.socialeurope.eu, accessed July 29, 2019.

I

Ivanov, B. J., V. M. Kare, E. I. Kuksina, A. S. Orešnikov, and O. V. Suhareva, *Kratka istorija Rusije: od najstarijih vremena do XX veka/A brief history of Russia: from the earliest times to the 20th century*, Logos, Belgrade 2009.

International Labour Organization, *World Social Protection Report: Building economic recovery, inclusive development and social justice*, 2014/2015, www.ilo.org, accessed September 15, 2020.

Ivesic, Tomaz, *Between Critic and Dissent: The Transnational Entanglement of the Fall of Milovan Djilas*, Central European University, www.academia.edu, Budapest 2016, accessed January 3, 2020.

J

Jackson, Lucas, "We're in the Longest Economic Expansion ever—but it's the Rich who are Getting Richer," *NBC News*, July 2, 2019, www.nbcnews.com, accessed July 29, 2019.

Jacobson, Jonathan, "Slavoj Zizek's 'Brutal, Dark' Formula for Saving the World," *Haaretz*, June 4, 2020, www.haaretz.com, accessed June 21, 2010.

Jacques, Martin, "The Death of Neoliberalism and the Crisis in Western Politics," *The Observer* via www.martinjacques.com, August 21, 2016, accessed July 29, 2019.

Jenkins, Philip, *A History of the United States*, Red Glob Press, London 2017.

Josephs, Mary, "Fast Facts on ESOPs," *Forbes*, January 19, 2018, www.forbes.com

Jović, Radoman, *Japan iz diplomatske beležnice/Japan out of a Diplomat's Notebook*, Štampar Makarije/Ohtoih, Belgrade/Podgorica 2017.

Jugoprevoz Kruševac a.d., "*Donošenje odluke o raspodeli dobiti*"/"Making a Decision on the Distribution of Profit,"*Jugoprevoz Kruševac*, June 29, 2016, www.jugoprevozks.co.rs, accessed September 14, 2020.

K

Kaplan, Thomas, Kate Conger, and Reid J. Epstein, "Bloomberg campaign opens first attack on a Democratic rival: Bernie Sanders," *New York Times*, February 17, 2020.

Kardelj, Edvard, *The Integration of Labor and Social Capital under Workers' Control*, edited by Ichac Adizes & Elisabeth Mann Borgese, *Self-management: New Dimensions to Democracy*, American Bibliographical Center-Clio Press, Santa Barbara/London 1975,

Pravci razvoja političkog sistema socijalističkog samoupravljanja/Development Directions of the Political System of Socialist Self-management, Komunist, Belgrade 1977,

The System of Socialist Self-management in Yugoslavia, Socialist Self-management in Yugoslavia 1950–1980: Documents, selected and edited by Blagoje Bošković and David Dašić, Socialist Thought and Practice, Belgrade 1980,

Contradictions of Social Property in a Socialist Society, Socialist Thought and Practice, Belgrade 1981.

Kassam, Ashifa, "Ontario Plans to Launch Universal Basis Income Trial Run this Summer," *The Guardian*, April 24, 2017, www.theguardian.com, accessed August 1, 2019.

Kaufman, Joyce P., *A Concise History of U.S. Foreign Policy*, Rowman & Littlefield Publishers, Lanham 2010.

Kegley Jr., Charles W. and Eugene R. Wittkopf, *World Politics: Trend & Transformation, Ninth Edition*, Wadsworth/Thomson Learning, Belmont 2004.

Keucheyan, Razmig, *The Left Hemisphere: Mapping Contemporary Theory,* Verso, London/Brooklyn 2014.

Kidrič, Boris, *Izgradnja socijalističke ekonomike FNRJ/Socialist Economy Building of the Federal People's Republic of Yugoslavia Collected Works, Volume III*, Kultura, Belgrade 1960.

Kissinger, Henry, *Diplomacy*, Simon & Schuster, New York/London/Toronto/Sydney/Tokyo/ Singapore 1994

Kochhar, Rakesh, "The American Middle Class is Stable in Size, but Losing Ground Financially to Upper-Income Families," Pew Research Center, September 6, 2018, www.pewresearch.org, accessed July 29, 2019.

Kocka, Jürgen, *Capitalism: A Short History*, Princeton University Press, Princeton 2016.

Komazec, Slobodan, *Izgubljene bitke stabilizacije i razvoja na pogrešnoj strategiji/Lost Battles of Stabilisation and Development Based on the Wrong Strategy*, Science and Society, Belgrade 2008.

Kramer, Samuel Noah, *History Begins at Sumer*, University of Pennsylvania Press, Philadelphia 1981.

Krek, Maja, "*Šta znači 'prosečna zarada' ako je većina nema?*"/"What 'Average Income' Means if the Majority doesn't Have it?," *Peščanik*, January 4, 2018, www.pescanik.net, accessed July 29, 2019.

Krugman, Pol, *End This Depression Now!*, W. W. Norton & Company, New York 2012.

Kuljić, Todor, *Prevladavanje prošlosti: uzroci i pravci changes slike istorije krajem XX veka/Overcoming the past: causes and directions for the change of the view of history of the end of the 20th century,*

Helsinki Committee for Human Rights in Serbia, Belgrade 2002,

Sećanje na titoizam/*Remembering to Titoism*, Čigoja, Belgrade 2011,

"*Klasno društvo bez klasne borbe*"/"Class Society without Class Struggle," *Danas*, October 26, 2012,

"*Zašto nema revolucije*"/"Why There Is No Revolution," *Politika*, November 3, 2016,

"*Duge senke komunističkog Manifesta*"/"The Long Shadows of the Communist Manifesto," *Politika*, February 21, 2018.

L

Latour, Bruno, "*Više ne težimo globalizaciji*"/"We do not Strive for Globalization," *Politika*, September 24, 2017.

Lazarević, Branko, *Dnevnik jednog nikoga*: *drugi deo—1947*/*The Diary of a Nobody*: *Second Part—1947*, Volume VIII, Institute for Textbooks, Belgrade 2007.

Lincoln, Abraham, *First Annual Message*, December 3, 1861, www.presidency.ucsb.edu, accessed July 28, 2019.

Lippmann, Walter, *The Good Society*, Little, Brown and Company, Boston 1938, accessed via www.monoskop.org.

Lipsey, Richard G., Peter O. Steiner, and Douglas D. Purvis, *Economics, Eighth Edition*, Harper & Row, New York 1987.

Lopandić, Duško, *Europeana unija i Srbija*: *novo vreme i novo okruženje*/*The European Union and Serbia*: *New Times, New Circumstances*, European Movement in Serbia, Belgrade 2017.

Lukács, György, *Geschichte und Klassenbewustsein*, Malik-Verlag, Berlin 1923.

Lukić, Radomir D, *Predgovor, Privreda i society, prvi deo*/*Foreword* for Max Weber's *Economy and Society, Part I*, Prosveta, Belgrade 1976.

"*Lula relembra miséria e luta contra a fome no Piauí*" / "Lula Recalls Misery and the Fight against Hunger in Piauí," Instituto Lula, September 3, 2017, www.institutolula.org, accessed August 1, 2019.

M

Maire, Edmond, *Samoupravljanje—sutršnjica/Socialist Self-management—World of Tomorrow,* Workers' Press, Belgrade 1977.

Magris, Claudio, "*Nalazimo se u Četvrtom svetskom ratu*" / "We Are in Fact in World War IV," *Politika,* June 28, 2017, www.politika.rs, accessed July 28, 2019.

Mandelbaum, Michael, *The Case for Goliath: How America Acts as the World's Government in the 21st Century,* Public Affairs, New York 2005.

Mandić, Blažo, *Tito—Neispričano: ljudi događaji, autobiografski fragmenti – politika, književnost, slikarstvo, muzika, film... / Tito—Untold: people's events, autobiographical fragments – politics, literature, painting, music, film, etc., second edition,* Službeni glasnik, Belgrade 2017.

Manifest za novi socijalizam, tačka 2. i 3/*Manifesto for new socialism,* no. 2. and 3, Center for New Socialism. Belgrade 2013.

Marković, Milenko, "*Ima li capitalizam alternativu?*" / "Is there an Alternative to Capitalism?," *Republika,* no. 568–569, Belgrade, March 1–31, 2014.

Marcuse, Herbert, *Merila vremena/Measures of Time,* Grafos, Belgrade 1978,

Counterrevolution and Revolt, Beacon Press, Boston 1972.

Marx, Karl, *Das Capital, Volume I, Fourth Edition,* 1890, accessed via content.csbs.utah.edu,

Grundrisse: *Foundations of the Critique of Political Economy* (*Rough Draft*), Penguin Books in association with New Left Review, London 1973, accessed via www.marxists.org on November 22, 2019.

Marx, Karl and Frederick Engels, *Manifesto of the Communist Party*, 1848, www.marxists.org, accessed September 14, 2020.

Martelli, Roger, "*La gauche est vivante*"/"The Left Is Alive," April 23, 2017, www.regard.fr., accessed July 31, 2019. .

Matiege, Albert, *Francuska revolucija/The French Revolution*, Prosveta, Belgrade 1948.

Matrix World, "*Psihopatija društva: 386oliko bogatih protiv 386oliko siromašnih?*"/"Social Psychopathology: How Many Rich Against How Many Poor?," November 7, 2011, www.matrixworldhr.com, accessed July 29, 2019.

Matvejević, Predrag, "*Nacionalnost postaje važnijom od humanosti*"/"Nationality Becomes more important than humanity,"*Autograf.hr*, February 2, 2017, www.autograf.hr, accessed November 6, 2019.

Maurice, Eric, "Hollande: The EU will be multi-speed or will 'Explode.'" *EUobserver*, March 6, 2017, www.euobserver.com, accessed July 29, 2019.

"*Mayakovsky*: *Deset poruka o revoluciji*"/"Ten Messages on Revolution," *Narodni Front*, November 10, 2017, www.narodni-front.org.rs, accessed August 1, 2019. .

Mayer, Margit, "*Neophodna je solidarnost*"/"Solidarity is Required," *Mašina*, December 13, 2016 , www.masina.rs, accessed 29.07.2019.

Menand, Louis, "Karl Marx, Yesterday and Today," *New Yorker*, October 10, 2016, www.newyorker.com, accessed December 22, 2019.

Mesec, Luka, *"Ljevica se vraća u ofenzivu"*/"The Left is Back on the Offensive," *Novosti*, April 29, 2017, www.portalnovosti.com, accessed July 29, 2019.

Michell, Peter R. and John Schoeffel (eds.), *Understanding Power: The Indispensable Chomsky*, The New Press, New York 2002.

Miklaucic, Michael, "An Interview with Stanley McChrystal," *PRISM: A Journal of the Center for Complex Operations* 6, No 3, Washington, D.C., December 7, 2016, cco.ndu.edu, accessed July 28, 2019.

"Milovan Djilas 1989 godine: Kako je nastalo samoupravljanje i kako je nestao komunizam"/"Milovan Djilas 1989: How Socialist Self-management Was Established and How Communism Disappeared," *Nedeljnik*, April 2, 2016. www.nedeljnik.rs, accessed July 29, 2019.

Milanović, Branko, *Global Inequality: A New Approach for the Age of Globalization*, The Belknap Press of Harvard University Press, Cambridge/London 2016,

Bogati i siromašni: kratka i neobična istorija globalne nejednakosti/Rich and Poor: A Short and Unusual History of Global Inequality, Službeni glasnik, Belgrade 2012.

Milošević, Nenad, *"Lenjin i kotroverze Oktobarske revolucije"*/"Lenin and October Revolution controversies," *Polja* 507, Cultural Center of Novi Sad, November/December 2017.

Mimiko, N. Oluwafemi, *Globalization: The Politics of Global Economic Relations and International Business,* Carolina Academic Press, Durham 2012, according to *The North–South Divide*, https://ipfs.io, accessed July 29, 2019.

Mišić, Milan, *"Odlazak hegemona"*/"The Departure of the Hegemon," *Politika*, February 12, 2012, www.politika.rs, accessed November 21, 2019.

Morning Star Self-Management Institute, www.morningstarco.com, accessed December 6, 2019.

N

Nasr, Seyyed Hossein, *"Božanska i ljudska Pravda"*/"Divine and Human Justice,"August 29, 2014, dzemet-oberhauzen.de, accessed July 29, 2019..

Nad, Boris, *"Apsolutni kapitalizam i (ne)mogućnost pobune"*/"Absolute Capitalism and the (Im)possibility of Rebellion," August 3, 2019, www.iskra.com, accessed August 7, 2019.

National Center for Employee Ownership, "How an Employee Stock Ownership Plan (ESOP) Works," January 24, 2018, www.nceo.org, accessed November 6, 2019,

"The Economic Power of Employee Ownership," www.esopinfo.org, accessed January 27, 2020.

Nehru, Jawaharlal, *Selected Works of Jawaharlal Nehru, Vol. 7*, Orient Longman, New Delhi 1979.

Newport, Frank, "Looking Into What Americans Mean by 'Working Class,'" Gallup, August 3, 2018, https://news.gallup.com, accessed December 13, 2019.

Niemietz, Kristian, *Socialism: The Failed Idea that Never Dies*, The Institute of Economic Affairs/London Publishing Partnership, London 2019.

Nikolić, Nikola, *"Kako se potrošila revolucionarna suština"*/"How the Revolutionary Essence Got So Worn-Out," *Vijesti*, January 16, 2017, www.vijesti.me, accessed July 29, 2019.

Nikolić, Tomislav Ž., *Akcionarstvo i samoupravljanje radnika/Zbornik Radova Akcionarska Društva/Shareholding and*

Self-Management of Workers/Proceedings of Joint Stock Companies, Mladost, Belgrade 1989.

Nilaya, Josh, "The Re-Emergence of Socialism in America," *NPR*, November 18, 2015, www.wnpr.org, accessed November 19, 2019.

O

Ocić, Časlav, *Ka obali plovi/It Floats Towards the Shore*, Society for Economic History, Belgrade 2017.

Olsen, Niklas, "How Neoliberalism Reinvented Democracy, an interview led by Daniel Zamora," *Jacobin*, April 6, 2019. www.jacobinmag.com, accessed July 29, 2019.

"Orpheus: World's Foremost Chamber Orchestra Since 1972," www.orpheusnyc.org, accessed November 6, 2019.

Oxfam International, "Richest 1% Will Own More than All the Rest by 2016," January 19, 2015, www.oxfam.org, accessed December 4, 2019,

"Just 8 Men Own Same Wealth as Half the World," January 16, 2017, accessed December 4, 2019.

"Richest 1 Percent Bagged 82 percent of Wealth Created Last Year—Poorest Half of Humanity Got Nothing," January 22, 2018, accessed December 4, 2019,

"Fight Inequality, Beat Poverty," accessed December 4, 2019,

"World's Billionaires Have More Wealth than 4.6 Billion People," January 20, 2020, accessed January 21, 2020.

P

Pal, Amitabh, "Interview with Gene Sharp," *The Progressive*, February 28, 2007, www.progressive.org, accessed July 29, 2019.

Panović, Zoran, *"Kriza levice, ili kako danas i kardeljizam deluje ostvarljiv"/*"Crisis of the Left, or How Kardeljism Seems Possible Today," *Nedeljnik*, September 29, 2016.

Pantelić, Ana, *Suzbijanje siromaštva u countries u razvoju/Eradication of Poverty in Developing Countries,* Institute of International Politics and Economics, Belgrade 2017.

Pope Francis, *"Já não escravos, mas irmãos, Mensagem do para o 48º Dia Mundial da Paz"/*"No longer slaves, but brothers, Message of the 48th World Day of Peace," *Rádio Vaticano*, August 21, 2014, www.arqrio.org, accessed July 29, 2019.

"Pope Francis: Komunisti su ukrali glavnu ideju hrišćanstva"/"Pope Francis: Communists Stole the Core Idea of Christianity," *Analitika*, June 29, 2014, portalanalitika.me, accessed July 29, 2019.

"Papa liderima EU: Bez nove vizije, Uniji preti—smrt"/"Pope to the EU Leaders: Without a New Vision, Death Lurks over the Union," *Tanjug*, March 24, 2017, www.tanjug.rs, accessed July 29, 2019.

Peović Vuković, Katarina, *"Kraj kapitalizma—način postavljanja hipoteze"/*"The End of Capitalism—a Way of Making a Hypothesis," Worker's Front, April 3, 2017, www.radnickafronta.hr, accessed August 1, 2019.

Piketty, Thomas, *Capital in the Twenty-First Century*, the Belknap Press of Harvard University Press, Cambridge/London 2014.

Piketty, Thomas, *"Neznanje i nacionalizam izazivaju strah"/*"Ignorance and Nationalism Induce Fear," *Politika*, March 8, 2015.

Piper, Kelsey, "Bill Gates: I've Paid $10 Billion in Taxes. I Should Have Paid More," *Vox*, February 27, 2019, www.vox.com

"Putin Reveals Russia's 'Invincible Missile' in Pre-Poll Speech,"
BBC News, March 1, 2018, www.bbc.com, accessed July 29,
2019.

R

Rachman, Gideon, "America is Now a Dangerous Nation," *Financial
Times*, August 14, 2017, www.ft.com, accessed December 19,
2019.

Radičević, Nenad, *"Nemci gube veru u kapitalizam"/*"Germans Are
Losing Faith in Capitalism," *Politika*, September 3, 2017.

Radišić, Nikola, *"Profesor sa Oksforda: Od pada komunizma najviše
profitirala—Kina"/*"Oxford Professor: China Has Profited Most
from the Fall of Communism," *N1*, February 13, 2019,
www.rs.n1info.com, accessed July 29, 2019.

Rangelov, Nevenka, *"Da li u Serbia zaista ima 47.350
programera?"/*"Does Serbia Really Have 47.350 IT's?,"
December 6, 2017, www.startit.rs, according to *The State of
European Tech Report 2017*.

Rascoe, Ayesha & James Oliphant, "Obama Paints Trump as No
Friend of the Working Class," Reuters, September 13, 2016,
www.reuters.com, accessed July 29, 2019.

Reinert, Erik S., *Globalna ekonomija: kako su bogati postali
bogati i zašto siromašni postaju siromašniji/Global Economy:
How the Rich Got Rich and why the Poor Get Poorer*, Čigoja,
Belgrade 2006.

Roberts, Ivor, *Conversation with Milošević*, University of Georgia
Press, Athens 2016.

Robertson, James, "The Life and Death of Yugoslav Socialism,"
Jacobin, July 17, 2017, https://jacobinmag.com, accessed
January 12, 2020.

Rosenberg, Eli, "The GM Strike is One of the Largest in Decades. Other Unions Say it is Inspiring Them," *Washington Post*, October 18, 2019, www.washingtonpost.com, accessed December 1, 2019.

Ružica, Miroslav, "*Univerzalni bazični dohodak*: *utopija, planetarna inovacija ili samo trik*" / "Universal Basic Income: Utopia, Planetary Innovation or Just a Trick," *Danas*, February 8 and 15, 2016.

Ružica, Miroslav, *Bauk prekarizacije*/*The Monster of Precarization*, *Danas*, February 27–28, 2016.

S

Siddiqui, Sabina and Ben Jacobs, "Donald Trump: 'We Will Stop Racing to Topple Foreign Regimes,'" *The Guardian*, December 7, 2016, www.theguardian.com, accessed July 29, 2019.

Sachs, Jeffrey D., *The Age of Sustainable Development*, Columbia University Press, New York City/Chichester/West Sussex 2015.

Samuelson, Robert J., "The New World Order, 2017," *Washington Post*, January 1, 2017, www.washingtonpost.com, accessed July 31, 2019.

"Sanders Statement on Trump," November 9, 2016, www.sanders.senate.gov, accessed July 31, 2019.

Singer, Peter, *Marx: A Very Short Introduction, Second Edition*, Oxford University Press, Oxford 2018.

Sowell, Thomas, *Basic Economics: A Citizen's Guide to the Economy*, Basic Books, New York City 2000.

Stanojlović, Seška, "*Deset godina od studentskih demonstracija u Kini*: *Tjenanmenski kontrapunkt*" / "Ten Years since the Student Demonstrations in China: Tiananmen Counterpoint," *Vreme* 13, Belgrade, June 5, 1999.

Stević Gojkov and Zagorka N, "*Ekološka pravda—izazov savremenog doba*"/"Ecological Justice—The Challenge of Contemporary Times", *Nacionalni interes* 2, 2016.

Stiglitz, Joseph, "*Najgore je prošlo, ali svetska ekonomija ostaje i dalje slaba*"/"The Worst is Over, But the World Economy Still Remains Weak," *Politika*, July 5, 2009, www.politika.co.rs, accessed July 29, 2019.

Stiglitz, Joseph E., *The Great Divide: Unequal Societies and What We Can Do About Them*, W. W. Norton & Company, New York City 2015.

"Lessons from the Financial Crisis and Their Implications for Global Economic Policy," Columbia Business School 2018, www.gsb.columbia.edu, accessed December 21, 2019.

"After Neoliberalism," *Project Syndicate*, May 30, 2019, www.project-syndicate.org, accessed November 12, 2019.

"The End of Neoliberalism and the Rebirth of History," *Social Europe*, November 26, 2019, www.socialeurope.eu, accessed November 28, 2019.

Stojanović, M., "*SNS podržava 34 odsto građana, većina partija ispod cenzusa*"/"The Serbian Progressive Party is supported by 34 percent of citizens, most parties below the census," *Danas*, January 4, 2020, www.danas.rs, accessed Januaray 22, 2020.

Swaniker, Peter, "What Are the Pros and Cons of the Gig Economy?," *Forbes*, January 8, 2019, www.forbes.com, accessed July 31, 2019.

Sweezy, *Teorija capitalistsčkog razvitka/The Theory of Capitalist Development*, Naprijed, Zagreb 1959.

Š

Štrbac, Čedomir, *Koegzistencija i internacionalizam/Coexistence and internationalism*, Radnička štampa, Belgrade 1982.

T

Talbott, Strobe, *Foreword: Collision Course: NATO, Russia and Kosovo* by John Norris, Praeger, Westport 2005.

Taylor, Chloe, "IMF Chief Calls for Tax Hikes on the Wealthy to Reduce Inequality," *CNBC News*, January 8, 2020, www.cnbc.com, accessed January 11, 2020.

The Gore Story, www.gore.com, accessed January 4, 2020.

Traub, Amy and Heather C. McGhe, "State of the American Dream: Economic Policy and the Future of the Middle Class," June 6, 2013, www.demos.org, accessed July 29, 2019.

Touraine, Alain, *A New Paradigm for Understanding Today's World*, Polity Press, Cambridge/Malden 2007.

U

Unkovski–Korica, Vladimir, *"Da li je budućnost trampizam ili korbizam?"*/"Is the Future in Trumpism or Corbism?," *Politika*, November 12, 2016.

V

Varoufakis, Yanis, "Imagining a World without Capitalism," *Project Syndicate*, December 27, 2019, www.project-syndicate.org, accessed January 2, 2020.

Varney, James, "Universal Basic Income: Even conservative economist says it's 'our best hope,'" *Washington Times*, July 29, 2018, www.washingtontimes.com, accessed December 23, 2019.

Vasilijević, Vladan, *Demokratija na stranputicama: tri epistole i dvanaest eseja o upotrebi i zloupotrebi politike/Democracy in a Dead End—Three Epistles and Twelve Essays on the Use and Misuse of Politics,* Beogradski krug, Belgrade 1995.

Ventura, Christophe, *"Macron je alat neoliberalne obnove"/*"Macron is a Tool of Neoliberal Renewal," *Novosti,* May 21, 2017, www.portalnovosti.com, accessed November 7, 2019.

Vidojević, Zoran, *Porazi i alternative: pretnja pustoši ili etika otpora/Defeats and Alternatives: The Threat of Wasteland or the Ethics of Resistance,* Zavod za udžbenike, Belgrade 2015.

Vidojević, Zoran, *"Je li moguć spoj socialism i liberalizma"/*"Is the Joining of Socialism and Liberalism Possible?," *Danas,* February 27–28, 2016.

Vilets, H.T., *Sovjetska Rusija, Istorija Rusije/Soviet Russia, History of Russia,* Dimitrije Obolenski and Robert Oti, Clio, Belgrade 2003.

Vlaović, Gojko, *"Partija u kojoj je Jovo Bakić odložila osnivanje"/* "The party Jovo Bakić is in has postponed its establishment," *Danas,* December 17, 2019, www.danas.rs, accessed December 20, 2019.

Vučetić, Radina, *"O čemu govorimo kad pričamo o Jugoslaviji"/*"What Are We Talking About When We Talk About Yugoslavia", *Vreme.* 1408/09, Belgrade, December 28, 2017.

Vujačić, Danilo, *"Značaj učešća zaposlenih u raspodeli dobiti"/*"The importance of employee participation in profit sharing," *Politika,* December 12, 2019.

Vujović, Sreten, *Umesto predgovora ili u traganju za trećim putem/*predgovor zbornika radova: *Društvo rizika: izazovi, nejednakosti i socijalni problemi u današnjoj Serbia/Instead of an Introduction, or Searching for the Third Way, Foreword of Society of risks: changes, inequalities and social issues in contemporary*

Serbia, Institute for Sociological Research, Faculty of Philosophy in Belgrade, Belgrade 2008.

W

Wartzman, Rick, "If Self-Management Is Such a Great Idea, Why Aren't More Companies Doing It?," *Forbes*, September 25, 2012, www.forbes.com, accessed November 11, 2019.

Weller, Chris, "Obama just warned Congress about robots taking over jobs that pay less than $20 an hour," *Business Insider*, March 10, 2016, www.businessinsider.com, accessed January 17, 2020.

Werner, Götz, "The Idea of Unconditional Basic Income: a Copernican Tur," January 5, 2013, www.youtube.com, accessed August 1, 2019.

West, Cornel, "Pity the Sad Legacy of Barack Obama," *The Guardian*, January 9, 2017, www.theguardian.com, accessed July 29, 2019.

Williamson, John, "The Washington Consensus as Policy Prescription for Development," Institute for International Economics, www.pii.e.com, January 13, 2004, accessed August 1, 2019.

Wolff, Richard D., "*Nazire se novi socijalizam*"/"New Socialism is Looming," PCNEN, August 9, 2016, www.pcnen.com, accessed July 29, 2019.

"Trump, Capitalism's Crisis, and a New Way Forward," Occidental College, April 23, 2018, www.oxy.edu, accessed August 1, 2019.

World Bank, "Jobs Data," March 20, 2018, www.worsldbank.org, accessed September 15, 2020.

"Understanding Poverty," PovcalNet and Poverty & Equity Data Portal, March 21, 2019, accessed September 15, 2020.

World Factbook I, "Country Comparison: GDP/Purchasing Power Parity–PPP," U.S. Central Intelligence Agency, 2019, www.cia.gov, accessed September 15 2020.

World Factbook II, "Country Comparison: GDP—Per capita PPP," U.S. Central Intelligence Agency, 2019, www.cia.gov, accessed September 15 2020.

World Factbook III, "World," U.S. Central Intelligence Agency, 2019, www.cia.gov, accessed September 15, 2020.

World Counts, "How Many People Die From Hunger Each Year?," April 5, 2019, www.theworldcounts.com, accessed September 15, 2020.

Y

Yokoyama, Keiko, "A Real Alternative to Neoliberalism," *Social Europe*, October 19, 2017, ww.socialeurope.eu, accessed July 28, 2019.

Z

Zakaria, Fareed, *The Post-American World*, W. W. Norton & Company, New York/London 2009.

Zweig, Michael (ed.), *What's Class Got To Do With It?: American Society in the Twenty-First Century*, Cornell University ILR School, Ithaca, https://digitalcommons.ilr.cornell.edu, January 2004, accessed December 13, 2019.

Ž

Ždanov, A. A., *O međunarodnoj situaciji/About the International Situation*, Kultura, Belgrade/Zagreb 1947.

Živković, Ivona, "Prikaz knjige Žaka Atalija: *Kratka storija budućnosti*"/"Jacques Attali book review: *A Short History of the*

Future," *Vizionarski*, March 22, 2012,
www.vizionarski.wordpress.com, accessed November 7, 2019.

Župánić, Sergej, *"EU posrće pod siromaštvom, iznenadit će vas gdje je Hrvatska"/*"EU Struggles Under Poverty, It Will Surprise You where Croatia Stands," *Express*, November 14, 2016,
www.express.hr, accessed November 7, 2019.

LITERATURE

A

Aristotle, *Nikomach Ethics*, Izdavačka knjižarnica Zorana Stojanovića, Novi Sad 2013.

Atkinson, Anthony B., *Inequality: What Can Be Done?*, Harvard University Press, Cambridge *2015*.

Attali, Jacques, *Kratka istorija budućnosti/A Short History of the Future*, Arhipelag, Belgrade 2010.

B

Bakić, Jovo, *Yugoslavia—devastations and their Elucidators,* Filozofski fakultet Univerziteta u Beogradu, Belgrade 2012.

"Bagehot: Corbyn and the bourgeois dream: Labour's leader will badly disappoint his young supporters," *The Economist*, London, July 8, 2017.

Bauman, Zygmunt, "How Neoliberalism Prepared the Way for Donald Trump," *Social Europe*, November 16, 2016, www.socialeurope.eu, accessed September 15, 2020..

Béja, Alice, *"La radicalisation du parti républicain aux Etats-Unis: comprendre le monde qui vient,"* *Espirit*, June 2010, www.esprit.presse.fr, accessed September 15, 2020.

Bell, Daniel, *The End of Ideology: On the Exhaustion of Political Ideas in the Fifties, with The Resumption of History in the New Century*, Harvard University Press, Boston 1962.

Bjeloš, Maja, *Who Are the Protesters in Serbia, and What Do They Really Want?*, London School of Economics and Political

Science and European Politics and Policy, April 2017, blogs.lse.ac.uk, accessed September 14, 2020.

Blackburn, Robin, *An Unfinished Revolution*: *Karl Marx and Abraham Lincoln*, Verso, New York City/London 2011.

Borchardt, Klaus-Dieter, *European Union Rights Alphabet*, European Union, Luxemburg 2010.

Brincat, Shannon (ed.), *Communism in the 21st Century, Volumes I-III,* Praeger, Santa Barbara/Denver/Oxford 2014.

Burnham, James, *The Managerial Revolution*: *What is Happening in the World*, John Day Co, New York City 1941.

D

Dašić, David, *Društveno-ekonomski sistem Jugoslavije*: *razvoj i aktuelni problemi/The Socio-economic system of Yugoslavia*: *development and current problems,* Jugoslovenski zavod za produktivnost rada, Belgrade 1985.

Dašić, David Đ, *Diplomatija*: *savremena i ekonomska/Diplomacy*: *contemporary and economic*, Altera, Belgrade 2013.

"Democrats Pile Pressure on Bush as Glitches Hit US Poll," *Word News*, November 8, 2006.

Drucker, Peter, *Post-Capitalist Society*, HarperCollins, New York City 1993.

E

Erceg, Filip, *O socijalizmu i komunizmu/On socialism and communism*, Čemu: časopis studenata filozofije 11, vol V, Zagreb 2003.

F

Faulkner, Neil, *Povijest Oktobarske revolucije/The History of October Revolution,* Fraktura, Zagreb 2017.

Favretto, Ilaria & Xabier Itcaina (eds.), *Protest, Popular Culture and Tradition in Modern and Contemporary Western Europe,* Palgrave Macmillan, London 2020.

Fukuyama, Francis, *The End of History and the Last Man,* Free Press, New York, NY 1992.

G

Galbraith, John Kenneth, *The Affluent Society,* Houghton Mifflin Harcourt, Boston, 1958.

Galbraith, James, "The Future of the Left in Europe," *The American Prophet,* August 17, 2016, www.prospect.org

Gasmi, Gordana, *Quo Vadis EU?: Relevantni pravni i institucionalni faktori/Quo Vadis EU?: Relevant legal and institutional factors,* IUP, Belgrade 2016.

Gligorov, Vladimir, John Stuart Mill, Max Weber, Friedrich August von Hayek, and Karl Popper, *The Critique of Collectivism,* Filip Višnjić, Belgrade 1988.

Got, Ričard, *Hugo Chavez and Bolivar revolution,* МИР Publishing: Ambasada Bolivarske republike Venecuele, Belgrade 2015.

H

Hamza, Agon, "Marx's Dyslexia," *Los Angeles Review of Books,* March 16, 2018, www. lareviewofbooks.org, accessed July 28, 2019.

Höffe, Otfried, *Is democracy ready for the future?: On modern politics,* Novi 2017.

Horvat, Branko, *Political ekonomija socializml The Political Economy of Socialism,* Globus, Zagreb 1981.

Hosfeld, Rolf, *Karl Marx—Biography*, Krug Commerce, Belgrade 2017.

Humphreys, Joe, "Karl Marx at 200: What did he get right?," *The Irish Times*, May 1, 2018.

I

Ikenberry, G. John, Thomas Knock, andAnne-Marie Slaughter, *The Crisis of American Foreign Policy: Wilsonianism in the Twenty-First Century*, Princeton University Press, Princeton 2011.

J

Jeffries, Stuart, "Marx, Capital and the Madness of Economic Reason review—a devastating indictment of how we live today," *The Guardian*, November 1, 2017, www.theguardian.com, accessed September 15, 2020.

Jugoprevoz Kruševac, "Decision on profit distribution," *Jugoprevoz Kruševac*, June 25, 2020, www.jugoprevozks.rs, accessed September 16, 2020.

K

Karl, Rebecca E., *Mao Zedong and China in the Twentieth-Century World: A Concise History (Asia-Pacific: Culture, Politics, and Society)*, Duke University Press, Durham 2010.

Klaus, Vaclav, *Evropa i EU/Europe and EU*, Službeni glasnik, Belgrade 2010.

Klaus, Václav, *Europe: The Shattering of Illusions*, Bloomsbury Continuum, London 2013.

Kovačević, Živorad, *Amerika i raspad Jugoslavije/America and the Demise of Yugoslavia,* Filip Višnjić/Fakultet political nauka, Belgrade 2007.

Kuttner, Robert, "The Man from Red Vienna," *New York Review of Books,* December 21, 2017, www.nybooks.com, accessed September 14, 2020.

L

Levi, Bernar Anri, *"Revolucija jedini spas za Evropu"/*"Revolution is the only Salvation for Europe," *Vijesti,* May 7, 2017.

Lippmann, Walter, *The Good Society,* Little, Brown and Company, Boston 1938.

M

Mao Tse-Tung (Mao Zedong), *Quotations from Chairman Mao Tse-Tung: The Little Red Book,* Peking Foreign Languages Press, Beijing 1966.

Kineska revolucija/The Chinese Revolution, Vuk Karadžić, Belgrade 1968.

Marcuse, Herbert, *Reason and Revolution: Hegel and the Rise of Social Theoiry,* Routledge & Kegan Paul, London 1973.

Marcuse, Herbert, *One-dimensional Man: Studies of the Ideology of Advanced Industrial Society,* Beacon Press, Boston 1964.

Masarik, Tomaš Garik, *O boljševizmu (1920–1921)/On Bolshevism (1920–1921),* Zavod za udžbenike, Belgrade 2014.

Milutinović, Vladimir, *Neoliberalna bajka: kritika neoliberalne ideologije/Neoliberal Fairytale: Critique of Neoliberal Ideology,* Dosije, Belgrade 2014.

Milutinović, Vladmir, *Kraj "kraja istorije,"* Škola kritičkog mišljenja: kritičko mišljnje na delu/ *The end of "the end of history,"* School of Critical Thinking: Critical Thinking in Action, December 22, 2016, www.tacno.net, accessed September 14, 2020.

Mises, Ludwig von, *Human Action: a Treatise on Economics*, Mises Institute 1998, www.mises.org.

Monbiot, George, "The Zombie Doctrine," April 15, 2016, www.monbiot.com, accessed September 15, 2020.

Mulaj, Isa, "Self-management Socialism Compared to Social Market Economy in Transition: Are there Convergent Paths?," www.academia.edu, 2009, accessed September 14, 2020.

N

Norris, John, *Collision Course: NATO, Russia and Kosovo*, Praeger Publishing, Westport 2005.

Nove, Alec, *The Economics of Feasible Socialism, Revisited*, Routledge, Abingdon 2010.

O

"*Oland: Evropa kaska za svijetom*"/"Holland: Europe is late for the world," *PCNEN*, March 6, 2017, www.pcnen.com, accessed September 14, 2020.

Oxfam International, "Richest 1 percent bagged 82 percent of wealth created in 2018, and poorest half of humanity got nothing," January 22, 2018, www.oxfam.org, accessed September 15, 2020.

P

Pettinger, Tejvan, "Washington consensus–definition and criticism," *Economics Help*, April 15, 2017, www.economicshelp.org/blog, accessed November 6, 2019.

Polanyi, Karl, *The Great Transformation: The Political and Economic Origins of Our Time, Second Edition*, Beacon Press, Boston 2000.

Polanyi, Karl, *A Life on the Left*, Columbia University Press, New York 2017.

R

Radičević, Nenad, "*Nemci objašnjavaju Trampu šta je u interesu SAD*"/"Germans explain to Trump what is in US interest," *Politika*, June 22, 2017.

Rawls, John, *A Theory of Justice, Revised Edition*, The Belknap Press of Harvard University Press, Cambridge 1972.

S

"*Sanders: Spreman sam da sarađujem sa Klintonovom da bismo pobedili Trumpa*"/ "Sanders: I am ready to cooperate with Mrs. Clinton in order to defeat Trump," *Novi magazin*, June 9, 2016.

Schmidt, Alfred & Gian Enrico Rusconi, *Frankfurtska škola, Predgovor*/*Frankfurt School, Preface, Vol III, Book II*, IC Komunist, Belgrade 1974.

"*Si Đinping: Marksizam sredstvo da Kina osvoji budućnost*"/ "Xi Jinping: Marxism is a means for China to conquer the future," *N1*, May 4, 2018, www.rs.n1info.com, accessed July 29, 2019.

Streeck, Wolfgang, "How Will Capitalism End?" *New Left Review* 87, May/June 2014, www.newleftreview.org, accessed September 14, 2020.

T

"The Rome Declaration (Declaration of the leaders of 27 member states and of the European Council, the European Parliament and the European Commission)," March 25, 2017, www.consilium.europa.eu, accessed September 15, 2020.

Tito–viđenja i tumačenja/Tito–Opinions and Annotations, Institut za noviju istoriju Srbije/Arhiv Jugoslavije, Belgrade 2011.

"Thousands of Serbians Join Anti-government Protest in Belgrade," *Al Jazeera English,* Jul 12, 2020, www.aljazeera.com, accessed September 14, 2020.

"Transforming Our World: the 2030 Agenda for Sustainable Development, Resolution of the General Assembly adopted on September 25, 2015," United Nations, A/RES/70/1, October 21, 2015, www.archive.ipu.org, accessed September 15, 2020.

U

Unkovski-Korica, Vladimir, *The Economic Struggle for Power in Tito's Yugoslavia, From World War II to Non-Alignment. I.B.* Tauris, London 2016.

V

Vanek, Jaroslav, *The General Theory of Labor-Managed Market Economies*, Cornell University Press, Ithaca/London 1970.

Vidojević, Zoran, Demokratija na zalasku/Democracy in Decline, Službeni glasnik/Institut društvenih nauka, Belgrade 2010.

"Vratimo socijalizam u igru: elementi za promišljanje socijalističke alternative"/"Let us bring socialism back in the game: consideration elements for a socialist alternative," *Book of Proceedings*, Centar za politike emancipacije, Belgrade 2015.

W

Weber, Max, *Privreda i society/Economy and Society Part I*, Prosveta, Belgrade 1976.

Werner, Götz W. and Adrienne Goehler, *1.000 Euro für jeden: Freiheit. Gleichheit. Grundeinkommen*, Econ Verlag, Berlin 2010.

Werner, Götz, "Guaranteed Basic Income," www.globalinfluence.world, accessed November 7, 2019.

Williamson, John, *What Washington Means by Policy Reform*, Peterson Institute for International Economics, Washington D.C. 1990.

Williamson, John, "The Washington Consensus as Policy Prescription for Development," lecture delivered at the World Bank Institute for International Economics, Washington D.C., January 13, 2004.

Wolff, Richard D., *Capitalism Hits the Fan: The Global Economic Meltdown and What to Do about It*, Interlink Publishing Group, Northampton June 3, 2013.

Wolfgang, Ben, "Ex-Czech president calls for revolution to save sovereignty of European countries from EU," *The Washington Times*, Washington D.C., September 25, 2018.

World Bank Group, "The Changing Nature of Work," 2019 *World Development Report*, Washington D.C., http://documents1.worldbank.org, pdf, accessed September 14, 2020.

Z

Zizek, Slavoj, *Pandemic!: COVID-19 Shakes the World*, OR Books, New York 2020.

INDEX OF PERSONAL NAMES

A

Abram, Abraham or Ibrahim, Old testament Biblical personality, assumed to have lived between 2000 and 1500. BCE; according to Bible, he changed his name. Abrahamiin Hebrew means "Father of Many Nations"; members of Abraham's faith or Sons of Abraham: Christians, Hebrews, and Muslims

Alexander the Great or Alexander III of Macedonia (Greek: Αλέξανδρος Γъ ὁ Μακεδών, 356–323 BCE), king of ancient Macedonia, created an empire from Greece to northwestern India, one of the most significant figures in the history of the world.

Ali, Tariq (1943), British–Pakistani historian.

Allende, Salvador Guillermo Gossens (1908–1973), psychiatrist by profession, politician and statesman from Chile, president of Chile from November 3, 1970 to September 11, 1973, when he was murdered.

Althusser, Louis Pierre (1918–1990), French Marxist philosopher.

Andropov, Yuri (Ю́рий Влади́мирович Андро́пов, 1914–1984), politician and statesman, a general of the USSR Army, hero of socialist labor, USSR ambassador to Hungary, chief of the KGB from 1967–1982, general secretary of the Central Committee of the CPSU from 1982–1984. and president of the Supreme Council of the USSR (head of state) from 1983–1984.

Aristotle (Ἀριστοτέλης, 384–322. B.C), Greek philosopher and orator, Plato's pupil, one of most influential personalities in the history of European philosophy.

Attali, Jacques (1943), French economist, political philosopher and theorist.

B

Badiou, Alain (1937), French philosopher, one of the most popular contemporary theorists.

Bakarić, (alias Kuperstein) Vladimir, 1912–1983, law PhD, Croatian and Yugoslav politician, participated in People Liberation Fight.

Bakić, Jovo (1970), a Serbian sociologist and professor in the philosophy department of Belgrade University.

Bakunin, Mikhail Alexandrovich (*Михаил Александрович Бакунин*, 1814–1876), influential Russian revolutionary and founder of modern anarchism.

Bartels, Larry Martin (1956), an American scientist and professor of public policy and international relations at Vanderbilt University in Nashville, Tennessee.

Bazdulj, Muharem (1977), Bosnia–Herzegovina publicist, interpreter, and author.

Bell, Daniel (1919–2011), an American sociologist, professor at Harvard University, and writer, best known for his contributions to the study of post-inustrialism.

Bezos, Jeffrey "Jeff" (1964), an American businessman.

Biden, Joseph "Joe" Jr. (1942) an American politician, law professor, former vice-president of Barack Obama (2009–2017).

Blair, Tony (1953), British politician, prime minister (1997–2007) and leader of Labour Party (1994–2007).

Blood. David (1959), financial management expert.

Bloomberg, Michael (1942), American businessman and politician.

Böhm-Bawerk, Eugen. (*Eugen Böhm Ritter von Bawerk*, 1851–1914), Austrian economist, a minister of finance (1895–1904).

Branson, Sir Richard Charles Nicholas (1950), English business magnate, investor and philanthropist, and founder of the Virgin Group, which controls more than 400 companies.

Brecht, Bertolt (Eugen Berthold Friedrich "Bertolt" Brecht, 1898–1956), German theatre theoretician, playwright, and poet.

Brezhnev, Leonid (**Леони́д Ильи́ч Бре́жнев**, 1906–1982), Soviet politician, secretary general of the CPSU from 1964–1982, president of the Presidium of the Supreme Soviet 1960–1964 and 1977–1982.

Brzezinski, Zbigniew (Brzeziński Kazimierz Zbigniew, 1928–2017), American geostrategist and former advisor of national security to U.S. President Jimmy Carter (1977–1981).

Buffett, Warren (1930), American businessman.

Bukharin ,Nikolai Ivanovich (**Буха́рин Никола́й Ива́нович**, 1888–1938), Russian Marxist and revolutionary, creator of the New Economic Policy (NEP, НЭП – *Новая экономическая политика*) proposed by Vladimir Lenin in 1921.

Bukowski, Henry Charles (*Heinrich Karl Bukowski*, 1920–1994), German American poet, novelist, and short story writer.

Bush, George Walker (1946), American politician, member of the Republican Party, and U.S. president (2001–2009).

C

Cardoso, Fernando Henrique (1931), Brazilian politician, sociologist, and professor. Served as the president of Brazil (1995–2002).

Carter, James Earl "Jimmy" Jr. (1924), American politician, member of the Democratic Party, and U.S. President (1977–1981), and winner of the 2002 Nobel Peace Prize.

Castro, Fidel Alejandro Ruz (1926–2016), Cuban communist revolutionary and statesman.

Chalic, (Čalić) Marin Žanin (1962), German historian and professor at LMU University, in the East and South-East European history department in Münich.

Chaushesku, Nicolae (Nicolae Ceauşescu, 1918–1989), Romanian communist politician and leader, general secretary of the Romanian Communist Party party (1965-1989), president of the State Council (1967-1989), and president of the Republic of Romania from 1974 to December 25, 1989, when he was overthrown and executed.

Christ, Jesus, according to the *New Testament,* was born a year or two before 4 BCE and executed around 35 B.C.

Churchill, Winston (Sir Winston Leonard Spencer Churchill, First Duke of Marlborough, 1874–1965), was a British politician, prime minister of Great Britain (1940–1945 and 1951–1955), and the winner of the 1953 Nobel Prize for Literature.

Chernenko, Konstantin (Константи́н Усти́нович Черне́нко, 1911–1985), Soviet politician, the second secretary of the KPSS (1982–1984), the general secretary of the CPSU, and president of the Presidium of the Supreme Soviet of the USSR (1984–1985).

Chomsky, Avram Noam, (1928), American linguist, philosopher, and left-wing intellectual.

Chou, En-lai or Zhou Enlai (1898–1976), Chinese communist revolutionary, politician, statesman, and diplomat. Prime minister of the People's Republic of China (1954–1976) and minister of foreign affairs (1949–1958).

Clinton, Hillary (1947), American politician, diplomat, and lawyer. Clinton was the U.S. secretary of state (2009-2013), New York senator (2001-2009), First Lady (1993-2001), and the Democratic Party's 2016 presidential candidate.

Confucius (Kung Fu Tze, 551–479. B.C), Chinese teacher, editor, politician, and philosopher.

Constant, Benjamin (1767–1830), Swiss-French author of politics and religion.

Constantine I (circa 272–337), Roman emperor (324–337).

Corbyn, Jeremy Bernard (1949), British politician serving as the leader of the Labour Party since 2015.

Cutileiro, José Pires (1934), Portuguese diplomat, anthropologist, and writer.

D

De Gaulle, Charles André Joseph Marie (1890–1970), French army officer and statesman who led the French Resistance against Nazi Germany in World War II, and president of France (1965–1969).

Descartes, René (1596–1650), French philosopher, mathematician, and scientist.

Djilas, Milovan–Djido (1911–1995), Yugoslav communist, writer, and dissident, president of the Yugoslav Federal Assembly (25 December 1953 to 16 January 1954).

Djilas, Dragan (1967), Serbian politician and businessman, president of the Democratic Party (November 2012-May 2014), and Mayor of Belgrade (2008 to 2013). One of the founders and leaders of the opposition movement Alliance for Serbia

Djukanović, Milo (1962), Montenegrin politician, former prime minister of Montenegro (1991–1998, 2003–2006, 2008–2010, 2012–2016), and president of Montenegro (1998–2002 and April 2018 to the time of this writing).

Dumas, Roland (1922), lawyer and French socialist politician. Minister of foreign affairs for France (1986–1988 and 1988–1993), and president of the Constitutional Council (1995–2000).

E

Eagleton, Terence Francis "Terry" (1943), British literary critic, theorist, and distinguished professor of English literature at the University of Lancaster.

Ellison, Lawrence (1944), American businessman.

Engels, Friedrich (1812–1895), German philosopher, socialist thought theorist, historian, communist, political scientist, sociologist, journalist, and businessman

Erdoğan, Recep Tayyip (1954), Turkish politician, president of Turkey (2014-to the time of this writing), and former Prime Minister (2003–2014).

F

Ferguson, Niall Campbell (1964), Scottish historian, senior fellow at the Hoover Institute. Previously taught at Harvard University and New York University.

Franco, Francisco Bahamonde (1892–1975), Spanish general and politician who ruled Spain as dictator (1939 to 1975).

Friedman, Milton (1912–2006), American economist-monetarist and 1976 Nobel Prize Laureate in economics.

Fromm, Erich Seligmann (1900–1980), German social psychologist, psychoanalyst, and humanistic philosopher.

Fukuyama ,Yoshihiro Francis (1952), American political economist.

Furman, Dmitry (Дми́трий Ефи́мович Фу́рманruski, 1943–2011), a Soviet and Russian historian, a religious sociologist, political scientist, social philosopher, professor, and chief academic researcher for the Institute for Europe of the Russian Academy of Science.

G

Galbraith, John Kenneth "Ken" (1908–2006), Canadian-American post-keynesian economist and one of leading proponents of twentieth century American liberalism.

Gamarnik, Jakov (Я́ков Цу́дикович Гама́рник, 1894–1937), Soviet politician of Jewish descent, head of the political department of the Red Army (1930–1937), deputy commissioner of defense (1930–1934) and high commissioner of Belarus (1928–1929).

Gandhi, Mohandas Karamchand (1869–1948), founder of contemporary India and influential advocate of satyagraha (revolution by non-violent protests).

Gates, William Henry "Bill" III (1955), American businessman, founder of Microsoft and, for many years, the richest man in the world.

Genscher, Hans-Dietrich (1927–2016), German politician, former minister of foreign affairs for West Germany (1969–1974) and former vice-chancellor of West Germany and united Germany (1974–1992).

Georgieva, Kristalina (*Кристалина Иванова Георгиева-Кинова*, 1953), Bulgarian economist, current managing director of the IMF (from October 1, 2019 to the time of this writing), and chief executive of the World Bank (January 2017 to October 1, 2019).

Gerasimov, Gennady (**Генна́дий Ива́нович Гера́симов**, 1930–2010), Soviet diplomat and journalist, MFA spokesman, press secretary, and ambassador to Portugal.

Gore, Albert Arnold "Al" Jr. (1948), American politician, former vice-president to Bill Clinton (1993–2001).

Gore, Wilbert Lee "Bill" (1912–1986), American businessman and entrepreneur who co-founded W. L. Gore and Associates with his wife, Genevieve (Vieve).

Gorbachev, Mikhail (**Михаи́л Серге́евич Горбачёв**, 1931), a Russian and former Soviet politician, secretary general of the CPSU (March 11, 1985 to August 24, 1991), and the first and last president of the USSR (March 15, 1990 to December 25, 1991).

Guterres, Antonio (António Guterres, 1949), Portuguese politician and diplomat, UN secretary-general since January 1 2017, high commissioner for refugees (2005–2015), president of the Socialist International (1999–2005), prime minister of Portugal (1995–2002) and secretary general of the Socialist Party of Portugal (1992–2002).

György, Lukács (also Georg Lukács, 1885–1971), Hungarian Hegelian and Marxist philosopher, one of the founders of Western Marxism.

H

Habermas, Jürgen (1929), the most important representative of the second generation of the Frankfurt School of critique theory

Havel, Václav (1936–2011), Czech writer, dissident, and politician, last president of Czechoslovakia (1989–1992) and first president of the Czech Republic (1993—2003).

Harvey, David (1935), professor of anthropology and geography at New York University, Marxist theoretician and popularisator.

Hazlitt, William (1778–1830), British writer.

Hegel, Georg Wilhelm Friedrich (1770–1831), German philosopher.

Hobsbawm, Eric John Ernest (1917–2012), British Marxist historian.

Hollande, François (1954), French politician and former President of France (2012–2017).

Horvat, Branko (1928–2003), Yugoslav and Croatian economist and politician, the only candidate from the Balkans nominated for the 1983 Nobel Prize in Economics, founder and former director of the prestigious Yugoslav Institute for Economic Research (now the Institute of Economic Sciences) in Belgrade.

Hoxha, Enver (1908–1985), an Albanian communist leader and statesman.

Huntington, Samuel (1927–2008), American political scientist.

I

Iglesias, Pablo (*Pablo Manuel Iglésias Turrión*, 1978), Spanish politician, secretary-general of PODEMOS since 2014.

J

Jacques, Martin (1945), British journalist, academic, political commentator and author.

Jefferson, Thomas (1743–1826), one of founders of the U.S., the principal author of the Declaration of Independence, and the third U.S. president (1801–1809).

Jìnpíng, Xí (1953), Chinese statesman, president of the People's Republic of China, secretary-general of the Communist Party of China's Central Committee, president of the Central Military Commission since 2012, and president of China since 2013.

Jüncker, Jean-Claude (1954), Luxemburg politician, president of EU Commission since 2014, and the former Prime Minister of Luxemburg (1989–2009).

K

Kamenev, Lev (Ка́менев Лев Бори́сович, 1883–1936), Bolshevik revolutionary and Soviet politician, one of the first victims of Stalin's executions.

Kant, Immanuel (1724–1804), German philosopher and central figure of modern philosophy.

Kaplan, Fanya Yefimovna (Капла́н Фа́нни Ефи́мовна, 1890–1918), Russian revolutionary and terrorist.

Kardelj, Edvard–Bevc (1910–1979), Yugoslav politician from Slovenia, participated in national-liberation fight in World War II, leading ideologist and theoretician of socialist self-management, minister of foreign affairs for Yugoslavia (1948–1953), and president of the Yugoslav Federal Assembly (1963–1967).

DAVID DJ. DASIC

Kennedy, John F. (1917-1963), American politician, U.S. president from January 20, 1961 until his assassination on November 22, 1963, Massachusetts senator (1953-1960), and member of the House of Representatives of Massachusetts (1947–1953).

Kidrič, Boris (1912–1953), Yugoslav and Slovenian politician, one of most prominent leaders of the Yugoslav revolutionary movement, participated in the national-liberation fight in World War II.

King, Martin Luther Jr. (1929–1968), American Baptist clergyman, leader of the Black civil rights movement, famous for his protest methods of nonviolence and civil disobedience, winner of the 1964 Nobel Peace Prize, assassinated on April 4, 1968 in Memphis, Tennessee.

Kissinger, Henry (Heinz Alfred Kissinger, 1923), Jewish refugee who fled Nazi Germany in 1938, American statesman, political scientist, diplomat, and geopolitical consultant. Served as U.S. national security advisor (1969–1975) and secretary of state (1973–1977) under Richard Nixon and Gerald Ford's administrations. Kissinger was awarded the Nobel Peace Prize in1973, and is a professor in the department of international diplomacy at Georgetown University in Washington D.C.

Khrushchev, Nikita (Никита Сергеевич Хрущёв, 1894–1971), Soviet politician and statesman, the first secretary of the CPSU (1953–1964), and prime minister of the USSR (1958–1964), political commissar during World War II in the Battle of Stalingrad, participated in the Battle of Kursk and the defeat of Ukrainian nationalists in Stepan Bandera, a hero of the USSR and three times a hero of socialist labor.

Klaus, Václav (1941), Czechoslovakian economist, politician, and the former president of Czech Republic (2003-2013).

Kocka, Jürgen (1941), German historian, a major figure in the new social history.

Kojève, Alexandre (Алекса́ндр Влади́мирович Коже́вников, 1902–1968), Russian-born French philosopher and statesman.

Kuljić, Todor (1949), Yugoslav and Serbian sociologist and professor in the philosophy department of Belgrade University.

L

Latour, Bruno (1947), French anthropologist, sociologist, and philosopher,

Lenin, Vladimir Ilyich (Влади́мир Ильи́ч Улья́нов Ле́нин, 1870–1924), Russian communist revolutionary, statesman, philosopher, and theorist. Leader of the 1917 October Revolution in Russia, founder of the First Communist Party and Comintern, founder of the Russian Soviet Federal Socialist Republic and the USSR, and introduced New Economic Policy in 1921.

Lǐ Péng (1928), prime minister of China (1988–1998).

Lincoln, Abraham (1809–1865), American statesman and lawyer, U.S. president from 1861 until his assassination in 1865, member of the U.S. House of Representatives (1847–1849).

Lord Carington Peter Alexander Rupert (1919–2018), British politician, defense secretary (1970-1974), foreign secretary (1979-1982), and secretary general of NATO (1984-1988).

Lord Owen David Anthony Llewellyn (1938), British politician, physician, and foreign secretary (1977-1979).

Lula da Silva, Luiz Inácio (1945), politician, former president of Brazil (2003–2011), one of the founders of the Labour Party, imprisoned for corruption in April 2018 and released after 580 days in November 2019 because the court ruled his incarceration unlawful until his appeals are exhausted.

M

Maire, Edmond, 1931–2017, French sindical leader.

Magris, Claudio (1939), Italian writer, literary critic, and translator, one of the greatest scholars of history and culture of Central Europe.

Mandela, Nelson Rolihlahla (1918–2013), South-African revolutionary leader who fought against apartheid and former president of South Africa (1994–1999),

Mao Zedong (Mao Tse-tung, 1893–1976), Chinese politician, communist, and revolutionary. Leader of the Communist Party of China and victor over the Kuomintang in the Chinese Civil War. Secretary of the Communist Party of Chinia (1945-1976), president of the People's Republic of China (1954-1959), and leader of the People's Republic of China since its founding in 1949 until his death in 1976.

Mario, Vargas Llosa (*Jorge Mario Pedro Vargas Llosa*, 1936), Peruvian writer and politician, 2010 Nobel Prize winner in literature.

Markovic, Svetozar (1846–1875), influential Serbian socialist, political activist, literary critic, philosopher, and publicist.

Marx, Karl (1818–1883), German philosopher and theorist of socialist thought. Economist, historian, sociologist, political theorist, journalist, socialist revolutionary, and leading figure of the International Workers' Association, often called the First International (1864–1876).

Marcuse, Herbert (1898–1979), German American philosopher and sociologist, one of the luminaries of the Frankfurt school of critical theory. Marcuse escaped from Nazi Germany in 1934 and immigrated to the U.S.

Marshall, Alfred (1842–1924), British scientist, one of the most influential economists of his time.

Marshall, George Catlett Jr. (1880–1959), American officer and statesman, former chief of staff of the U.S. army (1939–1940), secretary of state (1947–1949), and minister of defense (1950–1951).

Mayakovsky, Vladimir (Vladimirovich (Маяко́вский Влади́мир Влади́мирович, 1893–1930), Soviet and Russian poet, playwright, artist, and actor.

McCain, John Sidney (1936–2018), U.S. politician and naval officer, Arizona senator (1987–2018), and chairman of several Senate committees (armed services 2015–2018, Indian affairs 2005–2007, and trade 1995–1997), member of the U.S. House of Representatives (1983–1987), and 2008 Republican presidential nominee. McCain participated in the Vietnam War and spent six years in captivity.

McChrystal, Stanley A. (1954), former commander of interational aid forces and commander of U.S. forces in Afghanistan.

McKinley Jr., William (1843–1901), American politician, U.S. president (1897–1901), assassinated September 14, 1901.

Mélenchon, Jean-Luc Antoine Pierre (1951), French politician and member of the national assembly.

Menand, Louis (1952), American critic, essayist, and professor at Harvard University.

Mesec, Luka (1987), Slovenian politician and member of Parliament.

Milanović, Branko (1953), Serbian-American economist, poverty, inequality, and social policy expert.

Miliband, Edward Samuel (1969), former leader of the British Labour Party (2010–2015).

Milošević, Slobodan (1941–2006), Serbian and Yugoslav politician, law graduate, leader of Serbian communists (1986–1989), and the former president of Serbia (1989–1997) and the Federal Republic of Yugoslavia (1997–2000).

Mitsotakis, Kyriakos (1968), Greek politician, president of the New Democracy party (greek: Νέα Δημοκρατία) since 2016. Prime minister of Greece since July 8, 2019.

Mobutu, Sese Seko (*Joseph-Désiré Mobutu*, 1930–1997), Congolese politician and military dictator, president of Zaire (Democratic Republic of the Congo) from 1965 to 1997.

Moses (Hebrew as Moshe, Arabian as Mussa), lived between 1391. BCE and 1271 BCE, although Christian tradition marks his year of birth as 1592or 1571 BCE. Prophet in Abraham's religion and founder of Judaism

Moša, Pijade–Čiča Janko (1890–1957), painter, publicist, art critic, revolutionary, Serbian and Yugoslav communist. Close collaborator of Tito, and president of the Yugoslav Federal Assembly (1954–1957).

Muhammad (570–632), messenger of God, prophet, and creator of Islam.

Murray, Charles Alan (1943), American political scientist, sociologist, and writer.

Musk, Elon Reeve (1971), South African-American businessman, technology entrepreneur, investor and engineer. Founder, CEO, and chief engineer/designer of SpaceX, CEO and product architect of Tesla. Was named the fifty-fourth most powerful man in 2018 on the Forbes list of the most powerful people in the world

N

Nehru, Jawaharlal (1889–1964), Indian statesman and politician, first prime minster of India from 1947 until his death in 1964.

Nikolic, Tomislav-Thomas (1952), construction technician, Serbian politician, president of the Republic of Serbia (2012–2017), presdietn of the Serbian Progressive Party (2008–2012), member of the Serbian Radical Party (1991–2008), the prominent party in Serbai since February 2003.

Njegoš, Petar II Petrović (1813–1851), spiritual and secular leader of Montenegro, secular ruler of Montenegro (1833–1851).

O

Obama II, Barack Hussein (1961), American politician and lawyer, U.S. president (2009-2017) and Illinois senator (2005–2008).

Orbán, Viktor (1963,) Hungarian politician, prime minster of Hungary (1998-2002, 2010-present).

Ortega, Amancio (1936), Spanish business tycoon.

P

Pareto, Vilfredo Federico Damaso (1848–1923), Italian engineer, sociologist, economist, political scientist, and philosopher.

Pence, Michael (1959), American politician and jurist, U,S. vice-president under Donald Trump, (2017-present).

Pinochet, Augusto José Ramón Pinochet Ugarte (1915–2006), Chilean general and dictator of Chile (1973 to 1990).

Planinc, Milka (1924–2010), Croatian and Yugoslav politician, president of the Communist Alliance Central Committee of Croatia (1971–1982) and prime minister of the Socialist Federal Republic of Yugoslavia (1982–1986),

Plato (Πλάτων, 424/423–348/347. B.C), Greek philosopher and orator, pupil of Socrates, teacher of Aristotle, founder of the Athens Academy.

Plenković, Andrej (1970), Croatian politician, diplomat, prime minister of Croatia (2016-present).

Pope Francis (*Jorge Mario Bergoglio*, 1936), elected pope on March 13, 2013.

Putin, Vladimir (**Влади́мир Влади́мирович Пу́тин**, 1952,) Russian politician, president of Russian Federation (2000-2008, 2012-present) and former prime minister of the Russian Federation (1999–2000 and 2008–2012).

R

Rawls, John Bordley (1921–2002), American moral and political philosopher in the liberal tradition, taught political philosophy at Harvard.

Reagan, Ronald Wilson (1911–2004), American film actor and U.S. president (1981–1989).

Ricardo, David (1772–1823), British economist.

Rousseff, Dilma Vana (1947), Brazilian politician, economist, and former president of Brazil (2011–2016, when overthrown); at a young age she led a group of Marxist city guerilla fighters against military dictatorship. She was arrested, tortured, and spent two years in jail between 1970 and 1972.

Roosevelt, Franklin Delano (1882–1945), U.S. president from 1933 until his death in 1945.

Roosevelt, Theodore (1858–1919), American statesman, politician, conservator, naturalist, and writer. U.S. president (1901–1909), U.S. vice-president from March 4, 1901 to September 14, 1901, and gobevernor of New York (1899–1900).

S

Saez, Emmanuel (1972), French and American economist, professor of economics at the University of California, Berkeley.

Sachs, Jeffrey David (1954), American economist, academic, professor at Columbia University, known as one of the world's leading experts on economic development and the fight against poverty.

Sanders, Bernie (1941), Vermont senator (2007-present) and member of the U.S. House of Representatives (1991–2007).

Schäuble, Wolfgang (1942), German politician who belongs to the Christian-Democratic union.

Schröder, Gerhard (1944), German politician, former president of the social-democratic party in Germany, and former chancellor of Germany (1998–2005).

Shakespeare, William (1564–1616), English poet, playwright, and actor, widely regarded as the greatest writer in the English language and the world's greatest dramatist.

Sharp, Gene (1928–2018), American political scientist, founder of the Albert Einstein Institution, a non-profit organization dedicated to advancing the study of nonviolent action, and professor of political science.

Singer, Peter (1946), Australian philosopher.

Slim, Karlos Helú (1940), Spanish business magnate.

Smith, Adam (1723–1790), Scottish economist and philosopher.

Socrates (grč. Σωκράτης, 470–399) BCE Athenian philosopher and symbol of the Western philosophical tradition.

Soros, George (Schwartz György, 1930), Hungarian-American investor, politician, and philanthropist.

Sowell, Thomas (1930), American right-wing economist, one of the most famous Black critics of Marxism.

Stalin, Joseph Vissarionovich–Jugashvili (Иосиф Виссарионович Сталин–Джугашвили, 1878–1953), Georgian revolutionary and Soviet leader, general secretary of the Communist Party of the USSR (1922–1952) and premier (1941–1953).

Stefanović, Borko-Borislav (1974), founder of the Serbian Left (Serbian: Levica Srbije).

Stenmark, Jan Ingemar (1956), former World Cup alpine ski racer from Sweden.

Stiglitz, Joseph E. (1943), American economist, professor at Columbia University, recipient of the Nobel Memorial Prize in Economic Sciences (2001).

Stoltenberg, Thorvald (1931–2018), Norwegian politician, minister of defense (1979–1981), and minister of foreign affairs (1987–1989 and 1990–1993),

Strache, Heinz-Christian (1969), Austrian politician, Austrian nationalist leader, and president of the Freedom Party of Austria since 2005.

T

Tadic, Boris (1958), psychologist, Serbian politician, president of the Republic of Serbia (2004–2012), former president and honory president of the Democratic Party, and the current president of the Social Democratic Party.

Talbott, Strobe (1946), former U.S.secretary of state deputy (1994–2001).

Thatcher, Margaret Hilda (1925–2013), Baronesse, former prime minister of Great Britain (1979–1990).

Taylor, Frederick Winslow (1856–1915), American mechanical engineer who sought to improve industrial efficiency, considered the father of scientific management.

Temer, Michel (Michel Miguel Elias Temer Lulia, 1940), Brazilian politician and jurist, vice-president of Brazil (2011-2016), president since August 31, 2016, when Dilma Rousseff was overthrown.

Tillerson, Rex (1952), former president and CEO of the American oil corporation ExxonMobil (2006–2016) and U.S. secretary of state (February 2017-March 2018).

Timothy, Garton Ash (1955), British historian, author, and commentator, professor of European studies at Oxford; much of his work is concerned with the late modern and contemporary history of Central and Eastern Europe.

Tito, Josip Broz (1893–1980), president of socialist Yugoslavia (1945-1980).

Tony, Blair (*Blair Anthony Charles Lynton*, 1953), British politician, prime minister (1997–2007) and leader of Labour Party (1994–2007).

Touraine, Alain (1925), French sociologist and originator of the term "post-industrial society."

Trump, Donald J. (1946), American businessman and U.S. president (2017-present).

Trotsky, Leo (Лев Давидович Троцкий, first name Лейба Давидович Бронштейн, 1879–1940), Jewish Bolshevik revolutionary of Ukrianian and Russian descent, Soviet politician, and Marxist theorist. One of the leaders of the 1917 October Revolution, the People's Commissar for Foreign Affairs of the RSFSR (1917–1918) and the People's Commissar for War and Naval Affairs for the USSR (1918–1925), liquidated during Stalin's Great Purge of 1940.

Tsipras, Alexis (*Αλέξης Τσίπρας*, 1974), Greek politician and president of Radical Left Coalition.

Tukhachevsky, Mikhail (Михаил Николаевич Тухачевский, 1893–1937), marshal of the USSR and leading Soviet military leader and theorist from 1918 until his death in the Great Purge.

Tudjman, Franjo (1922–1999), participated in the Yugoslav liberation war and WWII. Brigadier-general, historian, academician, statesman, and the first president of sovereign Croatia (1990–1999).

V

Valens, Lech (Lech Wałęsa, 1943), president of Poland (1990—1995), leader of the Independent Self-Governing Trade Union Movement Solidarity, and winner of the 1983 Nobel Peace Prize.

Vardi, Moshe Ya'akov (1954), Israeli mathematician, computer scientist, and professor in the U.S. and Israel.

Varoufakis, Ianis (1961), Greek economist, former member of the Hellenic Parliament in 2015, representative of the ruling Radical Left coalition, and former minister of finance (2015).

Vance, Cyrus Roberts (1917–2002), American lawyer and U.S. secretary of state from (1977–1980).

Vučić, Aleksandar (1970), graduate of the University of Belgrade Faculty of Law, president of Serbia (2017-present), former prime minister of Serbia (2014–2017), and president of Serbian Progressive Party.

W

Weber, Maximilian "Max" (1864–1920), German sociologist and philosopher.

Williamson, John (1937), English economist, professor of economic sciences at MIT in Boston, leading economist for the World Bank for South Asia, and advisor for the IMF.

Wolff, Richard David (1942), American Marxian economist, Professor emeritus of economics at the University of Massachusetts Amherst.

Woodrow Wilson, Thomas (1856–192), American politician, lawyer, and academic. U.S. president (1913-1921), governor of New Jersey (1911-1913), and president of Princeton University (1902-1910).

Wright, Erik Olin (1947), American sociologist and representative of analytical Marxism.

X

Xiaoping, Deng, (1904–1997), a Chinese revolutionary, statesman, reformer, and diplomat. The architect of modern China, Xioping was president of the Central Advisory Council Commission (1982–1987), the president of the Central War Commission (1981–1989), and the supreme leader of the People's Republic of China State Commission (1978–1989).

Y

Yaobang, Hu (1915–1989), Chinese politician, secretary general of the Central Committee of the Communist Party (1980–1987), president of the CPC Central Committee (1981–1982), and secretary general of the Secretariat of the Central Committee of the Communist Party of China (1980–1982).

Z

Zakaria, Fareed Rafiq (1964), American Indian journalist, political scientist, and author.

Zoroaster (second half of the seventh to the first half of the sixth century BCE), Persian philosopher, prophet, and priest, founder of Mazdaism, a cult of wisdom, and central figure of Zoroastrianism.

Zinoviev, Grigory (**Григо́рий Евсе́евич Зино́вьев**, 1883–1936), a Jewish Bolshevik revolutionary and Soviet politician, one of the most powerful politicians in the early years of the Soviet state, the first president of the Comintern (1919–1926), and victim of Stalin's Great Purge.

Ziyang, Zhao (1920–2005), secretary-general of the Communist Party of China (1987–1989)

Zizek, Slavoj (Slavoj Žižek 1949), Slovenian philosopher, cultural critic, theoretical psychoanalyst, and post-structuralist philosopher among those inspired by Marxism.

Zuckerberg, Mark (1984), American businessman and computer programmer.

Zweig, Michael (1944), Professor emeritus of economics at the State University of New York at Stony Brook, and where he founded and formerly directed the Center for Study of Working Class Life.

Ž

Živkov, Todor (*Тодор Христов Живков*, 1911–1998), Bulgarian communist leader (1954–1989).

ABOUT THE AUTHOR

David Đ. Dašić was born in Montenegro (Brezojevice, Plav, 1941) and graduated from the Faculty of Economics. Dašić obtained his MA and PhD degrees from the University of Belgrade law school, where he was elected to all teaching titles, earned the title of Professor Emeritus, and became a member of the Serbian Scientific Society.

Dašić held multiple public roles in the SFRY and Montenegro. Dašić was an adviser to the SFRY Presidency, functionary in the leadership of Montenegro, deputy federal minister for energy and industry, chairman of the Yugoslav portion of the Permanent Commission on the Peaceful Uses of Nuclear Energy at the Council for Mutual Economic Assistance (COMECON) in Moscow, special adviser to the federal government, ambassador within the Federal Ministry of Foreign Affairs, and the deputy head of the Foreign Economic Relations Division (1987–1989). Dašić was also the consul general of SFRY in New York City and adviser to the UN Economic and Social Council (1989–1992), foreign policy special advisor to the

Yugoslav Prime Minister, ambassador extraordinary and plenipotentiary of the FRY in Brazil (1994–1999), and was the head of Montenegro's trade mission in Washington D.C. (1999–2001).

He completed his diplomatic career in 2004 and has since continued his academic studies. Dašić is currently a full professor at the Law Faculty of Union University and the European Center for Peace and Development at the United Nations University in Belgrade, as well as a visiting professor at the Diplomatic Academy of the Ministry of Foreign Affairs of the Republic of Serbia.

He has published over 250 bibliographic units (books, monographs, articles, brochures, translations, presentations, press releases, reviews, etc.) in macroeconomy, microeconomy, international economy, international relations, and diplomacy. Among other published books: *History of Diplomacy–Evolution of Diplomatic Method in Political History, Diplomacy- Contemporary and Economic, Principles of International Economy, Principles of Economics, Market Economy – Micro and Macro Considerations,* and *System and Price Policy.*

Eight of his books can be found in the U.S. Library of Congress and he has been the reviewer and editor of ten books and quoted in numerous texts.

He speaks fluent English and Portuguese and is familiar with French and Russian.

Dašić was awarded with the Medal of Labour with a golden wreath.

He can be contacted via email at david@daviddasic.com

Printed in Great Britain
by Amazon

86271240R00251